Aghor Medicine

Aghor Medicine

Pollution, Death, and Healing in Northern India

Ron Barrett

Foreword by Jonathan P. Parry

UNIVERSITY OF CALIFORNIA PRESS
Berkeley · Los Angeles · London

University of California Press, one of the most distinguished university presses in the United States, enriches
lives around the world by advancing scholarship in the
humanities, social sciences, and natural sciences. Its
activities are supported by the UC Press Foundation
and by philanthropic contributions from individuals
and institutions. For more information, visit
www.ucpress.edu.

Unless otherwise noted, all photographs are by the
author.

Chapter 5 was previously published in different form
as Ronald L. Barrett, "Self-Mortification and the
Stigma of Leprosy in Northern India," *Medical
Anthropology Quarterly* 19, 2 (June 2005): 216–30.
Copyright © 2005 by the American Anthropological
Association.

University of California Press
Berkeley and Los Angeles, California

University of California Press, Ltd.
London, England

Library of Congress Cataloging-in-Publication Data
Barrett, Ron.
    Aghor medicine : pollution, death, and healing in
northern India / Ron Barrett ; foreword by Jonathan P.
Parry.
        p.   cm.
    Includes bibliographical references and index.
    ISBN 978-0-520-25218-9 (cloth : alk. paper)
    ISBN 978-0-520-25219-6 (pbk. : alk. paper)
    1. Medical anthropology—India—Varanasi (Uttar
Pradesh).   2. Aghoris—Rituals.   3. Healing—
Religious aspects—Aghoris.   4. Leprosy—Treatment—
India—Varanasi (Uttar Pradesh).   I. Title.
GN296.5.I4B37   2008
306.4'6109542—dc22   2007007627

Manufactured in the United States of America

17 16 15 14 13 12 11 10 09 08
10 9 8 7 6 5 4 3 2 1

For Baliram Pandey

Contents

Illustrations

TABLES

Foreword

Jonathan P. Parry

Ron Barrett's lucidly written and totally absorbing account of Aghor medicine is a landmark addition to the already considerable anthropological and Indological literature on the sacred north Indian pilgrimage city of Banaras. But it is also a major contribution to the sociology of Indian renunciatory traditions, describing the way in which these practices qualify and relativize the values of hierarchy and their place in a pluralistic system of healing practices. Thus, this book also has real significance for the field of medical anthropology.

Barrett's study is based on more than two years of field research in Banaras; before this period, he had worked there for some months as a trained nurse in a street clinic for leprosy patients and their families sponsored by a nongovernmental organization. That experience crucially informs his text, and many of his most valuable and original insights are about the relationship between Aghori ascetics and leprosy patients. Also important is the fact that by the end of his fieldwork, he had become a disciple of the lineage. Participant observation is a difficult balancing act, and the dangers of toppling one way or another are serious. Barrett remains beautifully poised, writing with the insight and sympathy of an insider while maintaining the analytical detachment of an outside observer. His account is sufficiently reflexive to allow us to locate its author in relation to his subject, yet it scrupulously avoids the self-indulgent autobiographical parading that in some recent writings threatens to drown out the rather more interesting voices of the anthropologists' informants. One of its great merits is that it shows how Aghori philosophy, and the practices it informs, constitutes a profound reflection not only on existential conundrums common to humanity at large but also on some of the most central questions of social science. What, for example, are the roots of social inequality? Why are some people stigmatized? Barrett manages to de-exoticize that philosophy and practice without diminishing their intrinsic interest and distinctiveness. Strategically, he does not discuss the antinomian practices with which the Aghori ascetic is most closely associated in the popular imagination until the end of the book.

Aghori practices, one has to admit, are eye-catching—at least given a bald account of them. They supposedly include coprophagy and necrophagy and the consumption of other highly polluting substances, the use of skulls as food bowls, the offering of menstrual fluids to the sacred fire, the practice of meditation while seated on a corpse, prolonged periods of ascetic austerities at the cremation ground, and the dispensation of blessings to lay householders by means of a beating. The logic behind them is the fundamental unity of divine creation and the need to deeply internalize an understanding of that unity to attain salvation. Aghori practice calls for devotees to realize their identity with the rest of the cosmos and to confront their mortality. The adept must aim to achieve a mental state of nondiscrimination that recognizes the divine as all-pervasive and omnipresent. In the ultimate scheme of things, the opposition between the pure and the impure, and hence between the Brahman and the Untouchable, is illusory. Caste, and other forms of social hierarchy, is thus radically relativized. Consistent with that fact— as Barrett informs us in chapter 1—the Aghor tradition developed as "an ideology of resistance to the pervasive social inequalities and power dynamics of Banaras during the British Raj." The immediate end is a particular state of mind. The antinomian practices are a specific—but not exclusive—means to it. Though they provide a faster route to attaining that state than others, they make for a more dangerous path to travel, and madness and death threaten the adept whose ascetic discipline proves inadequate. In the exemplary case, however, they yield extraordinary and miraculous powers. By virtue of these powers, the Aghori is capable of acting in the world as a worker of wonders and as a healer of the most recalcitrant of human illnesses.

In recent decades, however, the association between the Aghori ascetic and these extreme practices—of which my own earlier account (Parry 1982) had attempted to make some sense—has been deliberately downplayed. The sect has undergone significant reform, and today the dominant strand in its ideology focuses on social service to the truly disadvantaged over the quest for individual salvation—or, perhaps better, stresses the first as a means of achieving the second. Barrett vividly brings the story up to date.[1] Under the initial inspiration of the late Awadhut Bhagwan Ram, lay Aghori disciples now run schools for street children and leprosy clinics; and some one hundred Aghori ashrams exist in various parts of northern India as well as one in California. In the popular imagination, the sect's treatment of leprosy wounds has progressively displaced the perception that the Aghori's preeminent ascetic austerity is the contemplation of corpses and the consumption of human flesh. Gone are the days when the now-eased-out boatmen and "untouchable" Dom funeral attendants from the ghats were the most regular visitors to the Kina Ram Ashram. These groups have been replaced by a much larger number of mainly middle-class and high-caste devotees. Indeed, the disciples of the lineage now include millionaires, nationally important dignitaries (including three state governors), and senior politicians (including one ex–prime minister of India). Clearly, the sect has progressively found its way into mainstream society.

The paradoxical consequences of this evolution are predictable, though nonetheless interesting. The world renouncer has been drawn back into the world—for he must now increasingly rely on trusted lay followers to implement his worldly objectives (which, in practice, is apt to mean that he relies on members of his family). Moreover, Aghori social-service projects require material resources that only well-to-do devotees can furnish. This situation is a far cry from the old ideal of the Aghori who scavenges what nobody else wants and can therefore exist in complete independence from material entanglements with the householder. The emphasis on *sevā* (selfless service) has begun to subvert the renunciate's asceticism. His disciples meanwhile must remain in society and must at least compromise with its expectations—by participating, for example, in the orthoprax rituals of the wider kinship group and by not too flagrantly flouting the rules of caste interaction. Moreover, disciples now have a distinct propensity to unconsciously order themselves according to the old rules of precedence—a propensity that their preceptor himself may condone with equanimity. Though his followers may, as if by conditioned reflex, queue up for their food in strict order of worldly standing, they now at least dine together. A small increment in equality is better than none. Some accommodation to the world may be necessary to change it and is unquestionably called for in the immediate interests of the Aghori's new social mission.

As the disciples represent reform, it has been more a matter of style than of substance. The fundamental philosophy that marks their path remains unchanged. Though all but a few old-style ascetics are now reluctant to own, or explicitly associate themselves with, the more extreme practices with which their sect is linked, all are equally reluctant to repudiate these rituals and to deny that they ever participated in them. Indeed, Barrett suggests that the ideas that these practices embody remain central to Aghori identity and that the Aghori's cremation-ground austerities are the "bedrock" of their spiritual quest. If, as I see it, they dissociate themselves too radically from these practices, they are likely to lose not only their distinctiveness but also their reputation for the extraordinary supernatural powers that are the basis of their appeal to the laity. Reform, seemingly, cannot go too far without either producing a more anodyne and conventional style of religiosity that is almost indistinguishable from that of numerous other sects or provoking a backlash reassertion of "traditional" sectarian practices. Which of these two theoretical possibilities is more likely to win out is not yet clear.

Ordinary householders tap the miraculous powers that the Aghori attain through austerities for all kinds of purposes, from pursuing bureaucratic advancement and examination success to seeking cures for psychiatric disorders. The commonest afflictions for which ashram visitors seek relief, however, are infertility and a group of dermatological disorders that are classified as *kushth rog*. These disorders include leprosy and leukoderma, which people see as subspecies of the same sickness (though they are biomedically unrelated). As Barrett brings out, both barrenness and *kushth* entail a kind of social death. Reproductive failure jeopardizes the continuity of the descent line and thus represents an egregious dereliction of duty to the ancestors. A barren wife is the epitome of inauspiciousness. Leprosy is the epitome of pollution and untouchability. The leprosy patient is the virtual prototype of the outcast and—*socially* speaking—the disease infects the patient's family, which by extension suffers a "courtesy stigma" that can ruin the marriage prospects of all of its children. Cremation is symbolically constructed as a sacrificial offering of the self to the gods (Parry 1994). The corpse of a leper is, however, unfit for the sacrificial fire of the cremation ground (which is otherwise a great leveler and destroyer of sin) and must therefore be immersed in the Ganga River. By dressing the sores of the "leper," the Aghori demonstrates that he is even less discriminating than fire and even more capable of absorbing sin and pollution.

Thus, the treatment of leprosy patients provides a plausible surrogate for the Aghori's austerities on the cremation ground. It has done more, suggests Barrett—in what I see as one of his most important insights—to legitimize the Aghori and confer on them a new respectability than the Aghori have done to legitimize and destigmatize those who suffer the disease. The ascetic who embraces the leprosy patient exemplifies the Aghori ideal of nondiscrimination. The experience that is the consequence of "fate" or karma for the victim is for the Aghori an opportunity to perform *tapasyā* (austerity) and thus to enhance his powers. But in the meantime, the stigma from which the patient suffers has not significantly receded. In the ashram founded by Awadhut Bhagwan Ram in Parao, the leprosy patients remain largely segregated from other devotees' comings and goings, and their self-image seems no better than that of those who must cope in other—often much harsher and less forgiving—conditions. They have often been more or less dumped there by families eager to conceal their illness. Before the condition's onset, they were probably thoroughly socialized into the prejudices that the general population has about leprosy, and they are generally prone to believe that their social exclusion stems from their blemished natures rather than from society. When they talk, they avoid all gestures for fear of drawing attention to their afflicted limbs, and they avoid the use of possessive pronouns in discussing body parts—as though their hands and feet do not belong to them. These attitudes characteristically result in a bodily neglect that increases the danger of injury to their extremities, which have been anesthetized by infection.

Most people who bring their afflictions to the Kina Ram Ashram do so out of desperation and as a last resort when all else has failed. Once at the ashram, they bathe in its tank and ingest ash from its perpetually smoldering sacred fire. The tank is symbolically equated with the Ganga, which absorbs the filth and pollution of the city without losing its purity. The fire is symbolically equated with the cremation pyre, which consumes the sins of the deceased and affects his or her rebirth as an ancestor. Thus, the river and the pyre provide the prototypes or templates on which the efficacy of Aghor healing is symbolically founded. Similarly, Barrett argues, patients believe that the curative power of the actual medicines the Aghori dispense derive from completely conventional Hindu assumptions about the world. Thus, as in the model of food transactions, in which the status of the cook is the most important element, patients focus on the personal qualities of the doctor. So, for example, the really active ingredient of the medicine is the divine essence of the Aghori, which has entered the medicine through the healer's blessing, on the model of *prasād* (the consecrated leavings of the deity) in Hindu worship.

The ascetic, moreover, is himself in a sense the Ganga and the cremation pyre—a sink for the sins and pollution his patients dump on him. Most patients, their problems hopefully solved, leave the matter there, grateful that the Aghori will "digest" their impurities as best he can. Barrett calls this phenomenon the "transportive" model of pollution, whereby patients externalize and slough off problems onto somebody else. There is, however, another model available—one that supposes that impurity may be eliminated or even converted into a positive force. Most people operate with both understandings, but Barrett argues that the patients most likely to join the circle of long-standing disciples are those who emphasize the second "transformative" model, focusing on the Aghori's capacity to convert impurity into purity and pollution into power.

These disciples do not learn solely about "Aghor medicine," but more radically about "Aghor *as* medicine." They learn, that is, that the real problems lie not with the victims of discrimination but with those who perpetrate it; not with the "Untouchable" and the leprosy patients but with the high castes who oppress them and with the healthy who are unwilling to contemplate their own possible susceptibility to disfiguring disease and to death. As Barrett brilliantly brings out, that message is basically right. The social stigma of leprosy is much worse than the disease itself, which is only mildly contagious and is in most cases treatable with antibiotics. Multi-drug therapy can render the patient noninfectious in thirty days and cured in six to nine months, and simple precautions can prevent the onset of disabilities. The fact that so many of its victims in India suffer so much is almost entirely due to the social stigma that surrounds it, and that leads to systematic concealment and neglect. What the Aghori prescribe is not just medicine for the afflicted, but medicine for society.

Note on Transliteration, Abbreviations, and Names

Most of the Sanskrit and Hindi words in this text were transliterated according to conventions set forth by the U.S. Library of Congress. These words are italicized, except for proper names, with adjacent translations at their first usage and glossary entries for repeated words. Diacritical marks were removed from proper names of deities, people, and places.

Whenever possible, words are spelled according to their most common usage. Therefore, many of the -*a* endings in Sanskrit were dropped in favor of their standard Hindi forms, except for common terms such as *karma*. In addition, diacritical marks and italicization were left out of common terms such as *ashram*. For the sake of consistency within English sentences, I end plural Sanskrit and Hindi words with an *s* instead of a nasalized vowel. All ṣ and ś consonants were transliterated into *sh*

Abbreviations of sacred texts:

CS   Caraka Saṃhitā

KKh   Kāśī Kanda

RV   Ṛg Veda Saṃhitā

SP   Skanda Purāṇa

For the sake of informant confidentiality, I altered the names and identifying information of patients, ashram residents, and other interview participants. Although the Mishra family did not object to having their real names in this book—which they have previewed and approved—I nevertheless altered their names as a matter of convention. I use the real names of public figures such as the Aghori babas and the medical officers of ashram clinics.

Acknowledgments

This research was funded by grants from the American Institute for Indian Studies, the Wenner Gren Foundation for Anthropological Research, and the Mellon Foundation. Special thanks to the National Center for the Study of Human Culture for providing institutional affiliation, and for the generous support of the Emory University Graduate Fellowship Program. I am very fortunate to have been trained as a medical anthropologist at Emory, a place with unparalleled public health resources, a commitment to interdisciplinary research, and faculty who actually got along with one another most of the time.

I am very grateful to Baba Harihar Ramji (Hari Baba) for opening doors and providing wise counsel at every step of the research and writing process. I have learned more from him than words can express. I am also deeply indebted to Hari Baba's guru, Awadhut Baghwan Ramji, whose influence can be found throughout this ethnography. Thanks to the current head of the Kina Ram Aghor Sampradaya, Baba Siddhartha Gautama Ram, for his many blessings and quiet hand. Baba Pryadarshi taught me the value of listening. Baba Sambav Ramji generously granted access and support for the research at the Kusth Seva Ashram. Thanks also to Baba Anil Ramji, Baba Savak Ramji, Lal Baba, Pagala Baba, and the young Naga at Manikarnika.

The large majority of Aghori in this lineage are householders: men, women, and children who strive for nondiscrimination while living in the mainstream of Indian society. I have endeavored to represent their lives and voices throughout this book, which would have captured little of the Aghor tradition without their inspiration and information. Thanks to V. N. P. S. Asthanaji, Kamleshwarji, Raimasterji, Ram Naresh Tripatiji, Dr. H. N. Uppadhaya, Dr. Oja, Dr. Vaidhyaji (of Banora), Dr. Vindeshwari Singh, Dr. K. P. Singh, Dr. Umesh, Sagar Singh, Udaybhan Singh, Lalit Makhijani, Padma Kanoria, B. B. Singh, Shailaja Koirala, Sangita Singh, Dhananjay, Kanta, Nama, Shekar, Sant, and Virendra. Thanks to Bhairav, the human, for providing me with a window to the past, a door to the future, and a different perspective on Aghor. Thanks as well to Bhairav, the ashram dog—and the meanest, nastiest Great Dane I ever encountered—for keeping me on my toes.

Banaras has had an "internet" for thousands of years, networks of communication and connection that existed long before computers were invented. In producing this book, I relied heavily on this ancient internet, and I have many people to thank as a consequence. Arjuna (Bantu) Mishra has been my interpreter, key informant, close friend, and *guru bhāī*. Aghori through and through, the Mishra family provided my wife and me with unqualified love and support. The Mishras include Shanti, Tara, Dollie, Indu, and Narayan as well. Virendra Singh and his family provided language instruction and generous hospitality. Sujata Singh provided field translations and helped bridged the gender gap in challenging circumstances. Muhammed Yousef provided additional language instruction and extensive translations. Thanks as well to Vimal Moitra, Brijesh Singh, Professor Rana P. B. Singh, Ramu Pandit, Ratnesh Pathak, Robert Svoboda, and Dharamnidi.

Dr. Shiva Kumar Shastri was an exemplar of traditional Ayurveda in Banaras. Dr. V. B. Mishra and the Sankat Mochan Foundation provided important background on pollution in the Ganga. Just next door, Kalu Pahlwan, Siya Ram Yadav and the wrestlers of the Tulsi Das Akhara served me many generous meals of sand. I have to say, however, that Shanti's meals at Amar Bhavan were significantly tastier, and I miss the camaraderie of my fellow residents during the time that Bruce, Richard, and I managed the place. I am also very grateful for Srikant's music, Ambar's internet, Neval's connections, and Rakesh's ready supply of texts at Harmony Books. Thanks to the people who did so much with so little at Back to Life, especially Dale Mather and Tim Stemper for their leadership and compassion through good times and bad. I believe the program did more for the kids on the ghats than we will ever know.

On the American side, Peter Brown was the ideal graduate advisor. He read many drafts, listened to many rants, and provided me with just the right mix of structure and space to complete this rite of passage. George Armelagos has mentored me since I was an undergraduate. A father to many anthropologists, he has had an impressive career that proves that humanity and scholarship need not be exclusive of one another. Melvin Konner provided constructive advice at critical periods and showed me some of the ways that an anthropologist can make the world a better place. Joyce Flueckiger helped me make connections between religion and medicine while I swirled around in the masala that is India. She was Shakti Ma as teacher, giving time and nurturance above and beyond the call of duty.

Additional thanks go to my unofficial committee members, Carol Worthman, Charles Nuckolls, Bradd Shore, Dan Sellen, Paul Courtright, Laurie Patton, and Tara Doyle. Edoardo Beato, Krishna Shukla, Annika Bakman, and Lorilai Biernacki helped me resolve scholastic pursuits with spiritual ones. Special thanks to Victor Balaban for his intrepid photography and companionship in the field. Jishnu Shankar carefully read and commented on earlier drafts. Jonathan Parry provided important insights into the Aghori and into larger questions of ritual and social structure in India. Anne Sieck made extensive copyedits, as did Ravi Garg, Alica Riley, Ashni Mohnot, and Sudarsana Srinivasan. Thanks to the editorial staff at the University of California Press for all their support—Reed Malcolm, Kalicia Pivirotto, and Laura Harger—and to copyeditor Adrienne Harris. Thanks to my fellow hominids Chris Kuzawa, Thomas McDade, and Seamus Decker for the mutual grooming and regurgitated blood meals. Keith McNeal, Vinay Kamat, Daniel Lende, Mark Padilla, and Mary (Tassie) Crabbe also offered critical reflections. Thanks to my colleagues here at Stanford (and Stanford West) especially Jamie Jones, Libra Hilde, Bill Durham, Nancy Lonhart, Jen Kidwell, Daniel Dohan, Jim Fox, John Rick, Joanna Mountain, Doug and Rebecca Bird, and Ian Robertson.

Thanks to the folks at the Sonoma Yoga Ashram, including Shivani, Tom, Linda, Melissa, Penny, Howie, Victor, Ramdeo, Giulia, Pam, Rob, John, and Robin. Thanks to David Woolsey and Mariko Kawaguchi for their reflections. Thanks to the folks from my Colorado days: Paul Shankman, Dennis McGilvray, Darna Dufour, Dave Green, Lynn Sibley, Clay Dillingham, and Nicki Tuffel, for getting me into all this trouble in the first place.

I am deeply grateful to my wife, Katharine Barrett. She has been my friend and colleague throughout this process. A fellow anthropologist, Katharine spent many months in India engaged in participant observation and social work while writing up her own research. She read and wrote detailed comments for nearly every draft of every chapter of this book, and she provided emotional and spiritual support while simultaneously teaching and raising our children. Speaking of whom, I am very grateful for the abundance of Shakti in my life: Tara, Maya, Tiffany, and Avena. I would like to express my love and gratitude to my parents, Ron and Janet, for instilling the virtues of critical reasoning and compassion and for giving me the confidence to try anything once. Thanks to my ever-extending family: Diane, Jenny, Lawrence, Vivienne, Victor, Clara, Michael, Kim, Lee, Brandon, Julie, Jack, Bill Sr., Mary Pat, Bill Jr., Jieney, Jamie, Lisa, Steve, Anne, Sharon, Mark, Kimberly, Elizabeth, and all their children.

Finally, I thank all the patients of Aghor medicine. For the sake of confidentiality, I can only credit them collectively for sharing their lives and challenges during the most difficult of times. Aside from clinical work, my time in the field did not provide any direct benefits for their suffering, but I hope that its lessons will support further efforts to prevent and mitigate their discrimination. These people's contributions should count for more than the furtherance of theoretical discourse. Anthropology should always aspire for more.

Introduction

Early one Sunday morning in Banaras, India, people gathered to wash their hopes and afflictions in Krim Kund, an algae-covered pool that the gods had sunk into the south side of the city. Six mothers came to cure their children of *sukhāndī* (dehydration); their babies were like tiny wet skeletons crying and thrashing in the water. A retired jeweler with vitiligo bathed there in hopes of restoring his original skin color, along with his good standing in a divided family. A pair of brothers from one family escorted a pair of sisters from another to receive blessings for their joint marriages. An elderly woman struggled with a ghost on the veranda. Beside me, an ascetic chewed tobacco while distributing sacred ash to the bathers. Somehow, everything remained peaceful and calm.

This scene would have been typical for Banaras. As one of India's largest and most sacred pilgrimage centers, Banaras has been revered for centuries by Hindus, Muslims, Buddhists, and Jains, millions of whom come to visit its innumerable temples and shrines and to bathe along a three-mile stretch of steps (ghats) leading to the Holy Ganga (Ganges) River (figure 1). Whether coming for salvation, prosperity, or healing, most of these pilgrims have sought some form of ritual purification—a means of unloading their troubles and sins upon temple altars and holy men, the river Ganga, and the many sacred tanks fed by her springs and tributaries. Krim Kund is one such tank, and its Sunday bathers are little different than thousands of others throughout this holy city.

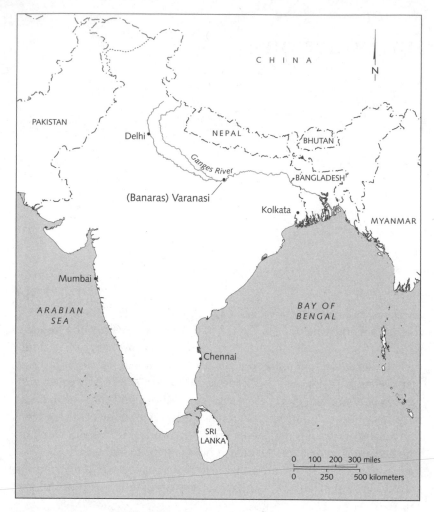

Figure 1. Map of Banaras (Varanasi) in India.

Yet Krim Kund is no ordinary tank. It nests within an ashram that has concrete skulls grinning down from either side of the front entrance. Inside, two more skulls sit like decapitated Buddhas beneath a peepal tree (figure 2). Beside the tank, a fire burns wood left over from nearby cremation pyres. These ashes, highly inauspicious in any other context, are sought by even the most orthodox of Brahmins, who swallow them and smear them on their foreheads and throats after bathing. The bathers treat the ashes like a medicinal powder, rubbing them over afflicted areas and saving the rest in small packets of folded newspaper. Krim Kund is

Figure 2. Concrete skull and signboard
beneath a peepal tree in Kina Ram Ashram,
2000. Photograph by Victor Balaban.

a kind of cremation ground as well as a bathing tank. It is the site of an
unorthodox but very popular religious healing rite established by a notorious, yet powerful, sect known as the Aghori.

The man who tended the fire and distributed the ashes to the bathers
on that Sunday was an Aghori renunciate. Defying the purity restrictions
of most Indian religious traditions, the Aghori actively embrace pollution and death in order to achieve a spiritual state of nondiscrimination.
Such associations have brought the Aghori a great deal of notoriety in
India. Popular stories describe them as wild-eyed, dreadlocked ascetics
who wander naked in the cremation grounds and carry human skulls as
begging bowls. The Aghori have been known to consume a wide variety
of ritually polluting substances, ranging from human flesh to human feces,

cannabis to country liquor. They are supposedly fierce and powerful, capable of bestowing both terrible curses and great blessings through the media of verbal and physical abuse. Yet this Aghori seemed to contradict all these images. Distinguishable only by a white prayer shawl, he was mild mannered and even a bit friendly. He seemed to be a calming presence, bringing a sense of stability to the anarchy around him. The tobacco was his only apparent vice.

Over the past few decades, members of this Aghor sect, the Kina Ram Aghori, have reformed most of their unorthodox practices. Where they once embraced untouchable substances on the cremation grounds, they have more recently come to embrace untouchable people through social service, providing education for street children and medical care to people with leprosy, vitiligo, and other stigmatized diseases. In the process, they have extended their membership into mainstream communities, becoming highly respected even among the more orthodox members of northern Indian society. Within a decade of these reforms, the Kina Ram Aghori expanded into more than a hundred and fifty ashrams throughout northern India, with a membership that includes three former state governors and a former prime minister of India. The Aghori have become not only socially legitimate but politically powerful as well.

Despite these changes, the postreform Aghori maintain their symbolic association with the cremation ground. Patients still connect the healing power of Aghor to ritual pollution and death. Such connections are especially evident at the ashram surrounding Krim Kund, the birthplace and headquarters of the Kina Ram lineage. Here, Krim Kund and the Ganga are connected by more than an underground spring, for the healing power of both stems from their ability to assimilate the qualities, both pure and impure, of the patients who visit them. One can say the same of the healers at the Kina Ram Ashram, some of whom are renunciates, but others of whom are devotee-physicians who prescribe herbal medicines manufactured on-site. These medicines, like the sacred ash, serve as media for the exchange of ritually polluting diseases and the healing power of Aghor.

This book examines the cultural dynamics of pollution, death, and healing through a medico-religious system that I define as Aghor medicine. Although this label was not in use locally at the time of my research,[1] I argue that Aghor medicine has two interrelated features that make it a distinctive healing system nevertheless. The first is the medicines of Aghor, an eclectic collection of practices ranging from religious rites of self-purification to modified Ayurvedic and biomedical treatments, all conducted with the blessing and guidance of Aghori ascetics. The second is "Aghor as medicine," a philosophy of nondiscrimination that challenges people to overcome their prejudices by confronting core fears and aversions, particularly those concerning death and disorder.

Combining Aghori medicines with a philosophy of nondiscrimination sets a unique stage for the dynamics of healing and purification. The Aghori willingly associate themselves with the ritual pollution of death and disease as an exercise for overcoming their aversions. In the process, they acquire a certain symbolic power by dwelling in places where few Indians dare to tread. The Aghori transform and transmit this power to patients through specific medicines and rituals. In exchange, patients dump their afflictions and impurities upon the Aghori according to well-known models of ritual purification, and these impurities provide further power to their healers.

Notably, more people are interested in the healing power of Aghor than in its philosophy of nondiscrimination. Most seek the Aghori as an option of last resort; they would readily unload their problems without having to confront the symbols of death that pervade the medicines of Aghor. Yet among those who find relief with Aghor medicine, some return to engage in the metaphysics underlying their cure. For this latter group, Aghor becomes more than a means of exchanging pollution and power; it becomes an opportunity to overcome core fears and aversions, especially those regarding their own mortality. It is therefore not surprising that most Aghor disciples were once patients themselves.

ISSUES OF DEFINITION

Despite the notoriety of the Aghori, one cannot easily find accurate information about this sect outside of its own ashrams. Many popular misconceptions about Aghor have been reinforced by exaggerations in the popular media. Unfortunately, the scholarship to date has made little headway in sorting out the confusion. This problem is largely because of difficulties defining who is an Aghori and what constitutes Aghor philosophy and practice. One of the goals of this book is to clarify some of these misconceptions and orient the reader to the major definitional issues, even if my own (operational) definitions are not sufficient to cover the entire scope of this topic.

The term *A ghor* literally means "nonterrible." The Aghori of the Kina Ram lineage emphatically state that the term does not refer to a particular group or religion. Instead, they assert that Aghor is a spiritual state of nondiscrimination that is free of hatred, fear, and aversion to anyone or anything. Nevertheless, the Aghori of the Kina Ram lineage have a clearly defined ethos and worldview that is consonant with Geertz's (1973) notion of a culture in the bounded sense of the word. They also fulfill the Durkheimian definition of religion as a "unified set of beliefs and practices relative to sacred things" (1965/1915: 62). However, depending on how you look at it, either everything or nothing is sacred in Aghor.

By extending this emic definition from the sacred to the social, one confronts several challenges in defining an Aghori and Aghor.[2] One challenge is to determine the historical origins of nomadic ascetics who had little if any artifacts or written records of their own. In an impressive survey of historical sources for cremation-ground asceticism, Lorenzen (1991) presents the ancient northern Indian *kāpālikas* as likely predecessors to the Aghori and similar sects. Lorenzen suggests that the *kāpālikas,* whose name derives from the word *kāpālin,* "one who carries a skull," were part of a general movement of *vamamarg,* a "left-hand path" of tantric tradition that emerged in India between the seventh and twelfth centuries C.E.

Owning little more than skulls for begging bowls, the *kāpālikas* were known for their extreme asceticism, unusual practices, and close association with the cremation grounds. Such asceticism, however, precluded the *kāpālikas* from forming monastic organizations, because their highly unorthodox practices mandated social isolation. Lorenzen is unsure whether the *kāpālikas* represented organized lineages at all or whether they were merely a broad category of similar-minded ascetics. Moreover, in the absence of the *kāpālikas'* own words, the only available history of these people consists of the etic interpretations of outsiders, who often did not approve of their practices. Thus, despite an extensive review of texts, including several puranas that depict the *kāpālikas* as ghouls, sadists, and sexual hedonists, Lorenzen admits that these accounts may well have been shaped by the orthodox agendas of their Brahmin authors.

With the evidence scattered in the cremation ground, one could choose to accept that Aghor is whatever a self-identified Aghori says it is. Svoboda (1986) takes this approach in a popular biography of a self-styled Aghori who eventually became his spiritual teacher. In the book, Svoboda describes Vimalananda as a cosmopolitan Bombayite who freely indulges in alcohol, sex, and gambling under the auspices of spiritual practice. He is a colorful character, a man with the gift of gab who presents his teaching with numerous allegories—all told with hyperbole in a cloud of cigarette smoke. Vimalananda's stories relate common folklore about Aghor practices, such as the *shav sādhana* (sitting meditation upon a corpse), a terrifying first meeting with the Goddess, the use of a skull bowl, and rites involving menstrual fluids, excrement, and human flesh.

Overall, Vimalananda's explanation of these rites is similar to that of the Kina Ram Aghori: that these are difficult and sometimes dangerous spiritual exercises conducted under the guidance of a guru to help one achieve a state of fearless nonattachment and nondiscrimination. Yet Svoboda also depicts Vimalananda as quite attached and possibly even addicted to his worldly vices. The guru's narratives emphasize explicit ritual sexual practices that run counter to the abstinence usually associated with Aghori asceticism. Furthermore, the overall tone of Vimalananda's narratives is far more egocentric than that of any of the Aghoracharyas (spiritual teachers of Aghor) that I knew. The latter spoke only of the supernatural abilities *(siddhis)* of their gurus, never of themselves.

Unfortunately, we have no way to cross-check Vimalananda's version of Aghor. Vimalananda died before the publication of his biography and designated Svoboda as his spiritual successor and sole public representative.[3] Svoboda also recounts that his guru never belonged to an organized lineage (1998). So in comparing Vimalananda with the multitude of Indian father figures who eagerly assume the role of expert mentor in a given topic of interest, the only feature that distinguishes the former is his biographer. Nevertheless, if most Aghori are like the *kāpālikas* before them, insofar as they have never shared a common corpus or organization, then who is to say that Vimalananda was not an Aghori?

The Kina Ram lineage is the only known Aghori sect to have a monastic base and internal historical records. Parry (1994, 1982) includes the sect in his ethnography of the rituals and business of death in Banaras. Although this part of his field research was brief, Parry nevertheless contributes some insightful analyses for future inquiry into Aghor philosophy and practices. He argues that even the most unorthodox Aghor practices have a basis in mainstream Indian liberation theology. If the point of worldly renunciation is to detach oneself from all desires and aversions, then the Aghori have taken this detachment to its logical extreme by embracing the most desired, and most reviled, with neither attachment nor disgust.

> The theological line that the Aghori put at the forefront, however, is the notion that everything in creation partakes of *Parmatma,* the Supreme Being, and that therefore all category distinctions belong merely to the

world of superficial appearances; no essential difference exists between the divine and the human, or between the pure and the polluted. As Lal Baba represented his own spiritual quest to me, he seeks to become "like that ideal Aghori, the sun, whose rays illuminate everything indiscriminately and yet remain undefiled by the excrement they touch" (Parry 1994: 261–62).

Lal Baba's solar simile encapsulates a concept of nondiscrimination that compares with the spiritual detachment of the prevalent nondualistic *(Advaita)* philosophy in popular Indian religious traditions today (Flood 1998). Indeed, several of my key informants cite the roots of Aghor in *Advaita.* They also refer to the *Tripurā Rahasya* in which Lord Datta-treya, the founding deity of Aghor, teaches nondualism in the worship of Shakti (see Rigopoulos 1998). So although some of the outward practices of the Aghori may be highly unorthodox, the underlying philosophy of these practices rests on mainstream religious ideals. Later in the book, I address the rare instances in which the postreform Aghori engage in old-style unorthodox practices. In these cases, "the practices" are nothing more than temporary spiritual exercises for overcoming the fears and aversions particular to the disciple's own upbringing and enculturation.

Parry also observes that, by living as scavengers, Aghori ascetics have solved the dilemma of how to maintain worldly independence while simultaneously relying on the alms of householders for their sustenance. Scavengers have no benefactors. Yet at the symbolic level, the ideal of worldly independence is relevant only when "gifts" received by religious authorities are considered to carry with them the sins of their clients and devotees (Raheja 1988; Parry 1986). Whereas the Aghori themselves have ostensibly moved beyond such distinctions, Aghor medicine presents a more complex dynamic of ritual pollution and purification, one in which healers readily wield the power that nondevotees attribute to them for having taken on the pollution of others and then direct this power toward therapeutic interventions.

Parry has been criticized for taking the more exotic practices of the Aghori out of context and giving them "excessively theological interpretations" (Gupta 1993: 13). Yet Parry uses these very interpretations effectively to de-exoticize such practices by positioning them within the framework of mainstream Indian religious ideologies. Moreover, none of the data that Parry uses to support his interpretations are inaccurate by themselves. Yet Parry's argument would have been better served if he had clearly delineated the kinds of information used to represent the

Aghori, and he could have more clearly distinguished contemporary from historical accounts as well as the testimony of nondevotee observers from those of practicing disciples. Among the latter, one should also distinguish between disciples who still actively engage in "old-style" practices and the large majority of postreform disciples who are more likely to confront their aversions in the arenas of social servicer than in the cremation grounds. Otherwise, readers could easily conflate these accounts into a single representation of Aghor.

In a broad survey of the Kina Rami and other northern Indian Aghori, Gupta (1993) argues that Aghor represents an extreme form of heterodoxy that she calls the "antidox." This antidoxy is designed to be a tool of resistance against the dichotomy of orthodox and heterodox but instead winds up reinforcing this division by serving as its negative example. Gupta further argues (1995, 1993) that the Kina Ram lineage has been a martial order since its inception, led by warrior caste Rajputs who have used Aghor ideology in struggles against their more orthodox Brahmin rivals in Banaras.

I concur that the Kina Rami have used, and continue to use, Aghor as an ideological weapon against the hegemony of some orthodox groups in Banaras, although not against Brahmins per se. I also agree that the more extreme forms of Aghor may actually reinforce social hierarchy by representing unusual exceptions to the status quo. Indeed, some scholars have made similar arguments for the reinforcement of social structure through carefully bounded exceptions more generally (Turner 1969), and for India's *varṇa* and *jāti* systems of caste more specifically (Srinivas 1996; Dumont 1966).

I disagree, however, with the argument that Aghor has been used as an ideological weapon in the struggle between competing upper castes. This argument harkens back to Dumont's theory that Indian systems of caste are perpetuated by struggles between the temporal authority of Kshatriya kings and the ritual authority of Brahmin priests (Dumont 1966). In contrast, the most famous conflicts of Baba Kina Ram, the founder and namesake of this Aghor lineage, were not with the Brahmins per se but rather with the kingly power of a Mughal prince and the maharaja of Banaras. Furthermore, Gupta's premise that the Kina Rami have historically been a martial order dominated by Rajputs is highly questionable. Gupta cites the extensive landholdings of the original Kina Ram centers, the organization of the lineage along Indian notions of kingship, and the use of Kshatriya terms and iconography as evidence that the Kina Rami constituted a martial order. Yet these features are common among many popular religious groups in Banaras, in which military, economic, and priestly authority have long been closely inter-twined (Dalmia 1996; Freitag 1989). Although a strong Rajput presence certainly is evident among the Kina Rami today, Brahmins have headed the lineage on two past occasions, and only a generation ago, the ranks of the Kina Rami were filled with fishing communities and the cremation attendants of the Dom sweeper caste.

The shortcomings of Gupta's argument result from several method-ological problems. With no supporting historical documents, Gupta relies heavily on interviews and oral histories for her thesis, drawing on a wide variety of informants both within and without the Kina Ram lineage. Though she is careful to distinguish between pre- and postreform Kina Rami, Gupta does not establish criteria for sorting all the other inform-ants who call themselves Aghori. As a result, the reader is unable to posi-tion these latter testimonies or to sort out the various agendas that underlie them. Among the Kina Rami themselves, Gupta relies solely upon interviews with male religious authorities, all mediated by high-status male research assistants. The Kina Ram Aghori, however, com-prise a much broader range of Indian social categories. Gupta's study would have been better served by including the voices of nonascetic families, women included, who constitute the majority of Kina Ram Aghor disciples. Their lives and voices would have generated new ques-tions and a richer ethnographic picture.

Scholarly debates notwithstanding, some of the most problematic issues of definition for the Aghori themselves concern their relationships to the ubiquitous yet highly contested categories of Hinduism and Tan-trism. The term *Hindu* originally described a broad range of ethnicities and localities: those northern Indian communities that have geographic or cultural associations with the Indus Valley (von Stietencron 1997). The term was institutionalized during the Mughal Empire to describe non-Muslim subjects whose beliefs did not fit into any other clearly labeled religious category. Hindus were thus defined by what they were not; they were non-Christian, non-Parsi, non-Jain, and so on.

During the latter half of the nineteenth century, Hinduism consoli-dated into a rallying point for national identity within emerging inde-pendence movements. It was strongly linked to pan-Indian (but still non-Muslim) religious revivals and reforms. It also satisfied Western ori-entalists' desire for a neatly delineated topic of study. These agendas informed the reification of Hinduism as a single world religion, despite its myriad beliefs and traditions. They also informed the revision and syndication of Hindu histories through the lenses of more recently popular ideologies (Thapar 1997; Inden 1990).

Nonetheless, Hinduism per se is not a problem for most Indian Aghori. Most insist that Aghor is not a religion but a psychospiritual state of nondiscrimination that can be achieved in any tradition. Hence, some Aghori self-identify as Hindus, and some Aghori do not. For those who do, difficulties arise when they must decide whether to observe ostensibly Hindu practices that run counter to the egalitarian and minimalist ethos of Aghor, such as those involving caste restrictions or expensive weddings and funerals. Though no one is likely to invoke the Hindu label publicly under these circumstances, it nevertheless looms large as an implicit question of identity. In this context, we can best see Hinduism as a "polythetic" category—that is, one that has no universal criteria for definition but rather a family of features (such as primacy of the Vedas, belief in karma and rebirth, and worship of certain deities) that are differentially shared by people who identify themselves as Hindu (see Ferro-Luzzi 1989). In deciding among these features, Hindu-Aghori signify their relationships to many other Hindu communities at local and national levels. As we will see, such decisions are often fraught with conflict and compromise.

The Aghori are more explicit about their ambivalence to Tantra. They are acutely aware of Tantra's popular associations with sexuality and sorcery and its distorted representations in the Indian and Western media. Having struggled enough with public representations of their own practices, Aghori leaders are reticent to take on a term that could lead to additional misunderstandings. This reticence is especially evident in the case for sorcery, for which the Aghori may be wrongly considered a potential cause as much as a potential cure, a common dilemma among many other shamanistic healing traditions (see Farmer 1992; Brown 1988; Levi Strauss 1963). Nevertheless, the Aghori have been pragmatic in adapting the term to suit particular circumstances. One senior renunciate eschewed the term when discussing Aghor with visitors from central India but reversed his position when speaking with Bengalis in Calcutta, where Tantra has more positive cultural connotations.

I am sensitive to these concerns of representation and thus have made sparse use of the Tantra label in this book. At the same time, I see a need to acknowledge areas of intersection between certain features of Aghor and those that contribute to operational definitions of Tantra in South

Asian religious studies. The task is nevertheless problematic; indeed, several of these definitions in the literature are prefaced with the famous quotation that Tantrism is "probably one of the haziest notions and misconceptions the Western mind has evolved" (Guenther 1971: 103).

The etymology of Tantra is based upon a metaphor of weaving; the Sanskrit root *tan* signifies the extension of threads in a warp. Tantra can thus be defined as an interweaving of traditions and teachings as "threads" in a text, a scriptural genre that can be dated from the eighth century C.E. (Smith 2005; Padoux 1989). These texts have been interpreted by many different traditions and "rewoven" by some into *Tantrashāstras,* specialized treatises on Tantra. Tantrism itself, however, originated as a largely Western construction, a colonial reference to the less orthodox Hindu religious traditions. Like Hinduism, Tantrism has since been reinterpreted and reified by Western orientalists (see Avalon 1960) as well as the upper strata of Indian societies (White 2003). Because of these processes, Tantra has come to resemble a tangled skein more than an organized collection of fabrics.

Despite (or perhaps because of) these problems, Tantra continues be a significant domain of religious studies. While operationally defined, Tantra has almost as many meanings as authors to discuss them. Urban (2003) argues for a dialectical approach to the term, accounting for interactions between the Western, Indian, scholarly, popular, and commercial interests that make up the many pluralistic constructions of Tantra. While recognizing this pluralism, White (2003) emphasizes particular antinomian features, such as ritual sexual exchanges and the use of intoxicants, "hard-core" practices that are uniquely associated with certain tantric schools. Other scholars provide lists of defining features with the disclaimer that these elements are incompletely shared by all tantric texts and traditions (Flood 1998; Brooks 1990).

Once again, the best course is to take a polythetic approach to the subject: one in which Aghor may share enough features with certain tantric traditions to claim some family resemblance but in which no single feature defines all of them as necessarily tantric.[4] In this manner, I will explore major features of Aghori beliefs and practices that are commonly associated with Tantra, such as antinomianism, the dynamics of male and female principles, mantra initiation, and self-deification within the guru-disciple relationship. As with other issues of definition surrounding Aghor, I will situate these features within the relationships and events of their surrounding ethnographic contexts.

POSITION AND METHODOLOGY

This book is based on twenty-two months of ethnographic field research in the northern Indian city of Banaras between 1999 and 2000, bracketed by additional shorter visits in 1996–97 and 2001–03. Conducting fieldwork in Banaras can be problematic. The city has been accommodating visitors for so many centuries that tourism has become an ancient tradition, and the boundaries between pilgrim, scholar, and sightseer are often difficult to ascertain. As a man in a society with significant gender inequalities and marked separation between male and female domains, I faced many trade-offs and challenges. Compounding these problems was my role as an American "research scholar," an unavoidable class title within a dominant yet ritually polluted caste group that evokes all that is ambivalent about "the West," mythical and otherwise. For better and worse, all these challenges shaped my ethnographic experience.

Fredrick Barth teaches that human relationships lie at the heart of the ethnographic method.[5] Just as issues of ethnicity, gender, and class positioned my informants and me within a particular configuration of relationships, they also shaped the research process and its representation. Reflexivity is inseparable from methodology; both are needed for the anthropologist to account for his or her reconstruction of a given ethnographic experience. And both are necessary for the reader to make an informed evaluation of the text.

Although I conducted more than one hundred fifty interviews in the course of my research, this study is grounded primarily in the method of participant observation. Such has been the tradition among anthropologists ever since Malinowski called upon the ethnographer "to put aside camera, notebook and pencil, and to join in himself in what is going on" (1984/1922: 21). Although Malinowski's basic definition of observation during "personal participation in native life" sufficed to distinguish early twentieth-century ethnographers from their armchair predecessors, more recent claims to participant observation have led to challenges of definition not unlike those of Aghor (cf. McCall and Simmons 1969). We cannot ascribe the term *participation* to all ethnographic observations. How, then, should we distinguish participant observation from the more general case of reactive observation, or from just plain "hanging out"?

Such distinctions and definitions can never be assigned an absolute truth value. Instead, we must determine their validity by their utility: the degree to which they help or hinder in the achievement of certain research objectives. Two major kinds of participant observation helped me approach an emic perspective on my subject matter, even if only to peel back a layer or two of a much larger hermeneutic onion. The first is the classic form of "active participation" in which the ethnographer increasingly engages in the distinctive behaviors of his or her informants in order to better understand those behaviors in their appropriate cultural context (Spradley 1980) and to gain certain insights that he or she can test later with other methods (Agar 1996). In Banaras, my participant observations reflected my transitioning role from guest to fictive member of a joint Indian family who were Brahmins by birth and Aghori by choice. This transition was largely driven by another, ascribed role as an American disciple of Hari Baba, the only Aghori ascetic living outside of India. These roles and relationships strongly shaped my ethnographic experience.

My relationship with the Mishra family began two years before I began the major segment of my field research. During a preliminary field visit to Banaras in the winter of 1996–97, I volunteered as a nurse at a street clinic for leprosy patients and their families that was sponsored by a nongovernmental organization (NGO). This NGO arranged for the children of these families to attend a school for indigent children. Tara Mishra was the founder and head teacher of this school. I later discovered that Tara's work was part of her social-service obligation as an Aghor disciple and that the school was cosponsored by an Aghor ashram in the United States. Only after I had made initial contact with the heads of the lineage in Banaras did I learn of the ashram in Sonoma, California—the only ashram led by a lineage-recognized Aghori ascetic outside of India. Hoping to gain some information and contacts, I visited the Sonoma Ashram just before embarking on my major field research. There I met Baba Harihar Ram, better known as Hari Baba, the founder and *mahant* of the Sonoma Ashram, disciple of Awadhut Bagwan Ram (Sarkar Baba), and paternal uncle of Tara Mishra.

Vigne (1997) states that one can never arrange a first meeting with the guru; the encounter just happens. I arranged to meet with Hari Baba as a potential informant, but as things turned out, he eventually became my spiritual teacher as well. Our first meeting was not dramatic, but I did feel a sense of peace and power in his gaze, which I found to be an unusual combination of feelings. I would again experience these feelings during my first visit to the Kina Ram *dhuni* in Banaras. Perhaps more objectively, I was impressed by Hari Baba's subdued and natural manner, his tolerance for difficult people, and his modest standard of living.

He lived in a single-wide trailer on rented property while a large proportion of the ashram's income went to the school in Banaras.

Coincidentally, Hari Baba was scheduled to leave for his annual visit to India at the same time that I was to begin my fieldwork. He invited my fiancée (and fellow anthropologist), Katharine, and me to join him and a few of his disciples on a monthlong visit of Aghor-related sites in Banaras and several northern Indian villages. During our travels, Hari Baba opened doors for me that would have otherwise been closed. He also connected me with his extended family, with whom Katharine and I became very close. I found, however, that these close relationships had costs as well as benefits. Although I did not decide to undergo spiritual initiation until the last months of my major fieldwork, the Kina Rami nevertheless considered me Hari Baba's disciple from the beginning. Being an American disciple connected with the Mishra family entailed a set of allegiances that sometimes impeded my access to certain domains of the Aghori lineage. Although these relationships helped me achieve a more emic perspective on my subject area, they also left me beholden to my informants in a way that could not help but influence the writing of this ethnography. Indeed, Hari Baba provided editorial guidance in the writing of this book.

I experienced a kind of culture shock just after Hari Baba's return to the United States. Until that time, I had made most of my contacts while riding the coattails of a holy man. Upon his departure, those initial relationships changed to some degree, reminding me that access is not the same as rapport. The latter took more time and effort. My attributed status as a member of the Sonoma Ashram evoked ambivalent feelings about the West that were common among many Indians. Although the Aghori describe their tradition as universal and nondiscriminatory—so much so that even Americans can become full-fledged disciples—many were distrustful of Americans because of our reputation for decadent living and our fickleness in relationships, qualities they considered incompatible with spiritual commitment. Despite the egalitarian ideology of the Kina Rami, their social relations were quite structured. Many of the adult male disciples found creative ways to test me in order to determine my place in their pecking order. More difficult still was my role as a "research scholar," for the Kina Rami felt that previous scholars had unfairly represented them. Consequently, they had legitimate concerns about whether I might also present an inaccurate picture of their tradition, or whether I would unduly focus upon the more exotic aspects of their spiritual practices.

I took my time, reminding myself of Barth's (1994) proscription against accommodating my research to my informants' agendas. A popular saying holds that IST stands for "Indian stretchable time." However, I eventually came to believe that everything in India happens exactly on time; the catch is that one simply cannot know what that time is in advance. With this notion in mind, I weaned myself from my wristwatch and did not break out my tape recorder until the tenth month of fieldwork. In the interim, I participated in the daily lives of the Aghori and worked on improving my language skills. I also used this time to learn more about the lives of leprosy patients in several colonies and treatment centers in Banaras.

During this clinic-based research, I relied on another kind of participant observation: one that built upon my previous experiences as a registered nurse generally and as a volunteer at a Banarsi street clinic more specifically. In contrast to the simultaneous actions and observations of active participation, I drew upon previous experiences in domains that partially intersected with those I was observing. Participation and observation became a tandem arrangement, not unlike Alter's (1992) in his study of Indian wrestling years after he practiced it as a child, or the role-switching that Wade (1984) describes in her work as a school administrator and ethnographer of African American student experiences. Alter, however, had actually been a wrestler, and Wade shared an African American identity with her student-informants. I could hardly expect to achieve the same degree of connection with Indian leprosy patients, having been neither an Indian nor a leprosy patient.

Cultural distance notwithstanding, my background as a registered nurse helped me assess clinical decision making from the healers' perspective. I could follow the biomedical process and trace its relative influence in the pluralistic mixtures of "masala medicines" that are often found in India. Nursing also gave me a framework for tracing therapeutic interventions across different healing systems. Bearing in mind the shortcomings of cross-cultural interpretation, I could use these assessments to help me identify whether, and to what degree, a physician's bedside manner was well practiced or merely performed for my benefit, as was sometimes the case.

Any anthropologist who has spent time in a developing country knows that a small amount of medical experience, and sometimes even the mere status of being a Westerner, can turn the ethnographer into a de facto doctor for communities with little access to adequate health-care resources. Such was the case for my being a nurse in Banaras, despite the fact that my American clinical experience left me ill prepared for the so-called tropical diseases that I encountered, not to mention the scant resources with which I treated them. Nevertheless, the time I spent working at the street clinic before starting my research, and the numerous times that I accompanied patients, both Indian and Euro-American, through the labyrinth of Banaras's unfriendly and often dangerous medical establishments, helped me make some sense of healer-patient interactions during my research. These experiences, as well as my visits to a variety of clinics and hospitals in other parts of northern and southern India, helped me approach an Indian frame of reference for evaluating the quality of care that I observed according to standards of access, rapport, communication, and holism that some observers characterize as "medicine answering" in parts of South Asia (Nichter and Nordstrom 1989).

On the downside, I had difficulty separating my roles as ethnographer and medical professional. My dual status sometimes created false expectations for the research. After being introduced to one informant as an "American doctor" and "[someone] who can help you," I had to explain in strong terms that I was neither and that my research would not directly benefit the person with whom I was talking. My fieldwork presented even more difficult dilemmas for my role as a nurse. Although I never let data collection take precedence over the welfare of a patient, I often had difficulty determining whether "help" was really helpful—if a hundred subtle suggestions were worth more than a single outright confrontation; if a bandage might enable a drug addict, or if a criticism would only fan the flames of the identified problem.

Language was a significant challenge during my first year of fieldwork. I had only recently changed my research site from South to North India. Consequently, I had only a year and a half of standard Hindi before I departed for the field. I continued my formal studies during the first ten months of fieldwork while immersing myself in the language in situ. Even when I became nominally proficient, I often grasped only the gist of complex conversations. Moreover, like most researchers in Banaras, I had picked up very little of the Bhojpuri that constituted a large portion of the Banarsi Boli spoken by most of my informants from eastern Uttar Pradesh and western Bihar (Simon 1993).

Because of these limitations, I relied upon research assistants for most of my interviews. Banaras has developed a very well established network of professional research assistants, but many can be as indistinguishable from tour guides as ethnographers can be from sightseers. One of these professional research assistants described this situation as "tour bus scholarship," whereby the only thing that distinguishes fieldwork from ordinary tourism is the researcher's all-too-precious theory (Pathak 1996). For this reason, many professional assistants attempt to determine the researcher's theory up front so that they can stage and interpret events to meet scholarly expectations. The most adept at this practice usually gain the most business and charge the highest fees.

I sought to minimize these pitfalls by hiring people whom I knew and trusted outside of professional networks and by training them myself. I also was careful not to reveal my theoretical agenda until the latter stages of fieldwork. I worked primarily with two assistants. Arjuna (Bantu) Mishra was an unmarried Brahmin male in his late twenties. He was a long-time Aghor disciple and nephew of Hari Baba. Sujata Singh was a college student in her early twenties. She was the youngest daughter and designated successor of my Hindi teacher, Virendra Singh. Bantu and Sujata contributed their own talents and chemistry to the ethnographic experience. With Bantu, I had both the advantage and disadvantage of having a key informant whose childhood friends included both Dom cremation attendants and the current head of the Aghor lineage, Baba Siddhartha Gautama Ramji (also known as Gautam Baba). Bantu introduced me to many people and provided me with invaluable insights on Aghor. Yet his motives and attitudes as an Aghor disciple sometimes hindered his ability to conduct research with sufficient detachment. In several instances, he contributed his own opinions and disagreed with informants during interviews. We eventually found a happy medium: Bantu learned to feign a bit of neutrality, and I learned to observe the play of interactions when the façade broke down. Bantu also helped test my methods in preliminary interviews of leprosy patients, and he accompanied me to many places and in situations where few people would have dared to venture, prompting him to tell me, "You always work with Sujata on all these nice things, but then you call on me when you want to visit hell." I responded that if I had to visit hell, I could think of no better friend to come with me.

I began working with Sujata in my tenth month of fieldwork, building upon the foundation that Bantu and I had previously established. By then, I had established some rapport with the residents and healers at the Kina Ram Ashram, and I had developed an interview schedule attuned to pilot projects in other areas. Even so, Sujata and I needed several months to establish effective working relationships with the physician and residents of the ashram, and to arrive at a common understanding about the kind of data that we could realistically obtain. We had some tricky moments during this second phase of research, especially in obtaining informed consent from and confidentiality for our patient-informants without offending the clinicians. We eventually settled upon an ethical and effective protocol.

Sujata proved to be the ideal complement to Bantu. As a non-Aghori, she was able to discuss controversial topics from a position of relative innocence and detachment. As a woman, she could bridge the gender barrier that often segregated me from female informants. Like Bantu, however, Sujata could not help but shape the events around us. As an unmarried woman from a respectable Rajput family, she also found herself in the role of key informant, especially on matters of gender and social hierarchy, offering her reflections on the situations around us.

All these roles and relationships conspired to shape this ethnography for better and worse. At the risk of sounding clichéd, however, I take sole responsibility for the shortcomings of this text. Gone is the myth of the lone anthropologist, but gone as well are the days when ethnography was practiced "there" and published "here." The boundaries between scholarly and informant communities have largely collapsed. Just as the living subject shapes the written object, so too the printed word may return to influence the communities from which it emerged. Published ethnography is thus a form of applied anthropology, a cultural intervention for which the writer must assume full responsibility.

POLLUTION, DEATH, AND HEALING

This book begins with the dynamics of ritual pollution and purification as prototypes for the ways that people approach Aghor medicine when they do not necessarily subscribe to its underlying philosophy. From here, I trace the cultural dynamics of pollution and death leading up to the initiation of some patients as Aghor disciples and potential healers themselves. Along the way, I try to answer two important questions. First, how are patients and healers with different belief systems able to interact productively within the same medico-religious context? This question holds the key to understanding the more general phenomenon of medical pluralism in India. Nichter (1992) uses the term *masala medicine* to describe India's diverse range of healing systems and the many combinations in which patients seek them and healers practice them. *Masala* originally described an eclectic mixture of spices, but in recent years, it has become a metaphor for India's multigenre Bollywood films (Mishra 2001) and its many creative mixtures of music and languages

(Natarajan 2001). One could argue that "masala pluralism" is the most pan-Indian characteristic of the nation's many communities, given their propensity to assimilate and amalgamate each other's beliefs and practices in every conceivable combination. Medicine is no exception in this regard.

In addition to recognizing degrees in biomedicine (also known as allopathic or English medicine), the government of India officially acknowledges four-year degrees in Ayurveda, Unani, Tibetan, and homeopathic medicine. These systems often borrow from one another. Cultural diffusion has blended elements of Ayurveda and Unani for centuries (Leslie 1992), and Tibetan healers openly acknowledge the Ayurvedic roots of their tradition (Janes 1995). Many practitioners outside of biomedicine prescribe "English" antibiotics under certain circumstances. Moreover, most distributing pharmacists are all too willing to sell their stock to the public without requiring written prescriptions (Kamat and Nichter 1998). In addition to its professional healers, India has an even larger number of unlicensed healers, religious healers, and astrologers, all of whom serve as key referral sources for the licensed professionals when they are not diagnosing and treating problems themselves (Glucklich 1997).

No matter how chaotic the situation may seem, the pluralism of Indian medical and religious systems does not exclude acceptance of certain common rules for their adoption and use. This study uses a framework of cultural models to elucidate these rules. Emerging from investigations of category formation in cognitive psychology and anthropology, this framework approaches culture as a large and heterogeneous collection of schemas and models that influence shared patterns of thought and behavior (Shore 1996; D'Andrade 1995; Quinn and Holland1987). Cognitive anthropologists sometimes debate the distinctions between cultural models and schemas (cf. Shore 1996; D'Andrade 1995; Casson 1993). For the purposes of this study, I use cultural models in two ways: in reference to the theory as a whole; and in reference to smaller and more explicit frameworks nested within cultural schemas. I then use these schemas to describe broader and more implicit patterns of thought and behavior within a given community of people.

Cultural models complement and expand upon a well-established framework of explanatory models (EMs) in medical anthropology. Closely tied to the human experience of illness and healing, EMs are "the notions about an episode of sickness and treatment that are employed by all those engaged in the clinical process" (Kleinman 1980: 105). Based upon the participant's own narratives, they describe beliefs about the etiology, pathophysiology, onset, course, and treatment of a given condition. With this information, the anthropologist can examine the interactions between the EMs of patients and healers and the way in which these relationships shape the therapeutic process.

A cultural-models framework relates these EMs and their interactions to cultural schemas that may extend beyond the healing process to other domains, such as religion, geography, and social hierarchy. For instance, I argue later that therapeutic interactions between healers and patients of Aghor medicine are informed by cultural models of purification that are commonly practiced in sacred sites of pilgrimage throughout India. Purification rituals within these sacred spaces are ideal examples of, or prototypes for, healing interactions between participants of different belief systems. Likewise, these sacred spaces are prototypes for the settings in which therapeutic interactions occur.

In chapter 1, I situate the Kina Ram Ashram within the history, sacred geography, and ritual activities of Banaras. Beginning with the hagiography of Baba Kina Ram, I discuss how Aghor emerged as an ideology of resistance against the ritual power of Brahmin priests and the economic and coercive power of local politicians and the merchant elite. Baba Kina Ram used his antinomian practices and healing powers to challenge maharajas, landlords, and priests. The Aghori were fond of telling how the Baba's very public breach of pollution taboos was a challenge both to local authorities and to the taxes that they levied for such transgressions. Rather than single out a particular person or group, Baba Kina Ram's activism brought public attention to complex exchanges of military, economic, and symbolic power between elite factions, a play that continues in present-day Banaras. At the same time, he established important precedents for some of the more recent developments in Aghor medicine.

Placing these dynamics within the sacred geography of Banaras, I show how the city's main cremation grounds and the river Ganga serve as prototypes for the sacred fire and waters of the ashram. These features are strongly connected to each other, not only by shared substances (cremation wood and river water) but also by a common principle of nondiscrimination, insofar as they are seen as limitless repositories for ritual pollution, including all forms of human sickness. For those who seek out the Aghori to cure their sicknesses, the ritual activities within the cremation ground (shmashān) and Ganga inform therapeutic interactions in Aghor medicine. These interactions are shaped by two cultural schemata of purification. One is transportive, in which pollution is externalized

and dumped onto someone or something else. The other is transformative, in which the pollution is converted or eliminated by an internalized
agent. These schemas exist in a variety of combinations: in temple ceremonies, food customs, and personal hygiene practices. The degree to
which they are present in Aghor medicine is reflected in common patterns of health seeking and treatment adherence, regardless of people's
specific explanatory models.

Chapter 2 sets the sacred geography of the Kina Ram Ashram into
motion by examining its central healing rite, a five-part sequence of ritual baths in Krim Kund, worship at the cremation fire of the *akhand
dhuni*, and the ingestion and application of its ashes. I focus on the most
prevalent illness categories for which people seek Aghor medicine: infertility, child health, and a collection of skin conditions known as *kushṭh*.
I present evidence to suggest that infertility and *kushṭh* share an astro-
logical connection to the Aghori by way of Krim Kund, which was probably once a solar tank. More important still, infertility and *kushṭh* are
highly stigmatized diseases. They are considered to be the most ritually
polluting of human conditions, punishments for previous transgressions
or curses passed from one person to another by way of ritual intermedi-
aries. In my research, these models were especially relevant for patients
who sought to dump their afflictions upon the *kund, dhuni,* and the
Aghori themselves by way of transportive purification. In this way, these
patients were able to seek the healing power of Aghor medicine while
avoiding the confrontations with mortality and pollution prescribed by
Aghor philosophy.

As with ritual purification more generally, the transportive and transformative approaches to Aghor medicine are not exclusive of one another.
Almost every therapeutic interaction involves a combination of the two;
with their relative emphasis depending upon the participant's agenda and
the healing modalities employed. Although non-Aghori patients tend to
use a transportive approach to ritual bathing at Krim Kund, the interactions with devotee-physicians that I observed and use of the ashram-
dispensed medications were strongly influenced by a more transformative
schema. This schema will prove key in later chapters, when we examine
the process of conversion from patient to disciple and the participant's
engagement in Aghori spiritual practices.

Chapter 3 brings the history and hagiography of the Kina Ram Aghor
lineage to the present day. It focuses chiefly on the reformation period
from the 1960s to the 1980s, in which the old-style Aghor practices gave
way to more socially accepted forms of activism and nondiscrimination.

This reformation took place during a leadership transition from Baba Rajeshwar Ram (Burhau Baba) to Awadhut Bhagwan Ram (Sarkar Baba). Burhau Baba was the last of the "old-style" Aghori. He was a large and imposing figure who wielded a heavy wooden staff and rarely wore anything but sandals. Burhau Baba railed against the increasing materialism of Indian society, preferring to spend time with his devotees at the *dhuni* or *shmashān,* where he was reputed to consume large quantities of cannabis and alcohol. He was greatly feared by the public, but many were willing to risk his insults and his staff to partake of his miraculous healing powers.

Sarkar Baba presented a marked contrast to his ferocious guru. Although he engaged in antinomian practices during the early years of his discipleship, Sarkar Baba was troubled by the endemic alcoholism among his disciples and the isolation of the Aghori amid so many social problems. He therefore reformed many traditional practices, banned intoxicants from the ashrams, and challenged his devotees to embrace polluted people instead of polluted substances. He founded a leprosy treatment clinic and a school for poor children, and soon, the lineage began to resemble a Gandhian social movement. Within less than a decade, the Kina Ram Aghori had branched out from the cremation grounds to the homes of mainstream Indian families and the highest seats of government. Yet for all their reforms and newfound legitimacy, the Aghori continued to foster their associations with ritual pollution and human mortality. In many cases, however, they channeled these activities into more socially productive projects. Because leprosy was considered to be one of the most untouchable of human conditions, the Aghori's efforts to treat the disease bridged their longstanding pursuit of nondiscrimination and their new emphasis on social service. Building upon the healing precedents set by Baba Kina Ram, Sarkar Baba made leprosy treatment the new form of *shmashān sādhanā* (cremation-ground practices) and a central prototype for Aghori engagement in worldly affairs.

Chapter 4 examines the healing dynamics of the Aghori's main leprosy treatment center, the Kusht Seva Ashram and clinic, with an emphasis on the lived experiences of its resident patients. Based on ashram patients' illness narratives and treatment experiences, I trace the interdependent relationships between the social and physical stigmata of this disease. Unlike the many outpatients who came through the clinic every day, these residents used the ashram as a leprosy colony, a sacred shelter for an easily treated but socially discredited disease. Although they were

well treated within the ashram walls, these patients clearly did more
to legitimize the Aghori than the other way around. Nevertheless, the
Aghori used their increased legitimacy to provide treatment to thousands of outpatients for no more than the (relatively modest) cost of their
medications. In this manner, Aghor medicine served as a medium for the
exchange of pollution and power between healers and patients.

The dynamics of medicine as medium were present for patients at
both the Kina Ram and Kusht Seva Ashrams; they commonly referred
to the efficacy of Aghori medicines in terms of *dawā aur duwā* ("medicine and blessing"), with special emphasis on the latter. The *duwā* of
Aghor medicine lay in the waters of Krim Kund, the ash of the *dhuni,*
the herbal medications, and the people who provided them. Religious
preferences notwithstanding, patients readily embraced and internalized
this *duwā* as a means of transforming their afflictions.

In chapter 5, I describe the ways in which the *duwā* becomes part of
the *duwā* of Aghor medicines and the more general implications of this
model for medical pluralism in India. Patients and healers believe that
the blessings of Aghor affect their medications on several levels. One is
by improving the overall quality of the drugs themselves. Indian manufacturers of herbal and biomedical pharmaceuticals have long had quality-
control problems (Kamat and Nichter 1998). The patients who came
to the ashram clinic were well aware of these problems and said they
trusted the Aghori to provide fresh and properly made medications.
Patients also cited their belief in the divine inspiration by which Aghori
renunciates modified the medication formulas and blessed the people
who manufactured and distributed them. Patients often expressed more
interest in the healing power of their providers than in that of the medicines themselves. Anything and everything, from ashes and sweets to
herbs and biopharmaceuticals, could be Aghor medicine as long as the
Aghori were the ones who provided them.

Emphasis on the provider over therapeutic substance is a general theme
among Indian approaches to medical pluralism. Speaking about medical
efficacy, Indians who use multiple systems often discuss the quality of
their healers more than the methods (Nichter and Nordstrom 1989; Kakar
1982; Beals 1976). I argue that this emphasis reflects the fact that the
practice of medicine in India is strongly informed by a cultural model of
food exchange, in which foodstuffs, especially foods that have been
cooked or highly prepared in some way, carry the qualities, both polluting and purifying, of the people who serve them (see Marriott 1976).
Most ashram medications required a great deal of preparation, and both

Aghori healers and nondevotee patients emphasized the importance of the character and intention of the people preparing and distributing them. This character and intention allowed the *duwā* of Aghor medicine to be faithfully transmitted from the most powerful renunciates to any and all who braved the skulls at the gates.

Patients of all persuasions spoke enthusiastically about the immense power *(shaktī)* and supernatural abilities *(siddhis)* of the Aghori. Everyone framed the efficacy of Aghor medicine in terms of Aghor *shaktī*. For nondevotees undergoing their first course of therapy, however, such proclamations of power were more hopeful than testimonial. As with the pilgrims of temples, the pilgrims of clinics placed their faith in certain authorities conditional upon the timely achievement of a positive result. If the desired result was not forthcoming, the pilgrim-patients were free to go elsewhere. If it was, then they not only referred others and returned for help with future problems, but some went on to become full-fledged devotees themselves (cf. Kakar 1982; Obeyesekere 1981).

Such was the case for nearly all the Aghor devotees whom I knew, who spoke of how they initially came to the Aghori for healing, or for solutions to practical problems. They testified about miracles performed and about the process in which their healer subsequently became their spiritual teacher *(guru)* over time. For patients under the guidance of a guru, the symbols and medicines of Aghor became much more than a dumping ground for problems; they were transformational devices to internalize and digest. Indeed, the metaphor of digestion was the most distinguishing feature of devotee-patient narratives, which likened the fires of digestion to those of the *dhuni* and *shmashān*.

Thus, we come to the second major question of this study: what is the role of ritual pollution and death in the acquisition of healing power and the attainment of nondiscrimination? The prevalent model of ritual pollution in India combines ideas of dirt and morality in a way that discriminates against people and justifies their lesser standing within a social hierarchy (Babb 1975; Dumont 1966). Pollution can be inherited according to the *varṇa* and *jāti* systems of caste, in which endogamous groups are ranked according to their degree of ritual purity. It can be transmitted from lower to upper castes through the exchange of coded substances, such as the previously mentioned foodstuffs, as well as through transactions involving money or gifts (Raheja 1988; Parry 1986). Pollution can also be acquired through association with bodily decay and disease, with infertility, skin diseases, and death being the most polluting conditions. The Aghori are famously associated with all three. Yet far from diminishing the Aghori's standing, these associations somehow empower the healers. How can we explain this fact?

The answer comes from a constructivist theory of social discrimination that is consistent with key elements of Aghor philosophy. It begins with cross-cultural analyses of pollution, deviance, and stigma as constructed realities designed to maintain boundaries within a given social order (Berger and Luckman 1966; Douglas 1966; Goffman 1963). The Aghori themselves view ritual pollution as a human construct designed to restrict people's actions within political and social hierarchies. They view human agency as a form of power. Similar to the liberation philosophy of *Advaita* Vedanta, the Aghor philosophy regards human nature as essentially good but corrupted by the illusions and attachments that people take on through socialization. Such is the case with pollution and purity taboos. Here, the Aghori take their constructivism a step further than Western social scientists do by asserting that these attributions restrict discriminators and discriminated alike. By transcending these taboos, the Aghori eliminate restrictions to human action, increasing their power as a by-product of nondiscrimination. For nondevotees who do not subscribe to this philosophy, or who are not yet ready to cast off their enculturated aversions, these transgressions and associations are more powerful still, for they represent the potential for human action in places where few dare to tread.

In his classic analysis of social power, Russell (1992/1938) describes how different forms of power—priestly, kingly, economic, and biological —can be converted and exchanged with one another in the human production of intended effects. Such exchanges abound in the history of Banaras, where generals and kings have sold protection to merchants and bankers, and all have gained legitimacy through religious and artistic patronage (Dalmia 1996; Freitag 1989; Lutgendorf 1989). That Baba Kina Ram and his successors rebelled against these power dynamics is hardly surprising, especially given the social inequalities that resulted. But neither is the fact that the symbolic power gained from Aghori egalitarianism would bring them considerable political and economic gains while furthering their power to heal.

Healing power was both helpful to society and enticing to would-be disciples. But once established in a spiritual practice, healing power was meant to be a by-product rather than an objective for the Aghori seeker. Associations with pollution and death were intended as exercises toward attaining a state of nondiscrimination. Chapter 6 explores these relationships between death and nondiscrimination while describing the methods and purposes of the old-style "practices." This chapter seeks to clarify the pervasive misconceptions about these practices and frame them within their appropriate cultural contexts. One can do so only by understanding the relationship between death and nondiscrimination in Aghor philosophy. I attempt this understanding with three major propositions. The first builds upon the lessons of socially stigmatized diseases, exploring the notion that disease discrimination is itself an illness, inclusive of its marked physical conditions. But though social and physical stigmatization can be closely intertwined, one should not confuse the victim with his or her perpetrator. Hence, the second proposition contends that the source of discrimination is the discreditor rather than the discredited. The source of the illness lies in the surrounding community more than in the patients themselves. The patients play a role only insofar as they stigmatize themselves (which they often do). This distinction between discreditor and discredited falls within the social-constructivist view of deviance as discrimination, but it often becomes lost in the emphasis on the mark itself. Stigma must be viewed as a process, not just a mark, to remain a viable topic of study within a constructivist framework. The Aghori are the ultimate social constructivists.

Having defined the illness and located the problem, the third proposition borrows directly from an Aghori belief that the fear of death is the root of all other fears and aversions, disease discrimination among them. This proposition resonates with the social psychology of Becker (1973), who argues that mortality anxiety and its subsequent repression are the primary sources of human neuroses, as well as the primary engines of human social institutions. But where Becker is optimistic about a healthy repression of death anxiety, the Aghori see such repression as a problem that one must eventually overcome. The Aghori have some support in Lerner's just world hypothesis (1980), which proposes that blaming victims is a coping strategy for human anxieties about vulnerability to tragedy. The Aghori seek to address this underlying problem by confronting it directly. Herein lies the answer to the second major question of the book: Aghor philosophy and practice are together a medicine against the illness of discrimination.

The concluding chapter addresses the degree to which confrontation with mortality and a transformational approach to Aghor medicine have brought the disciple community to a state of nondiscrimination. Drawing key examples from the Mishra family, I examine the challenges of sanskritization, Westernization, and material success to the traditional egalitarianism and austerity of Aghor. These challenges faced householders and ascetics alike. They also took on new meanings with the recent influx of Western disciples. Yet despite these changes, the Aghori have made modest but significant strides toward nondiscrimination that set them apart from their surrounding communities. As such, I argue that Aghor medicine constitutes a form of positive deviance, a culturally relevant solution to an important category of human problems.

CHAPTER I

The Cosmic Sink

The concentric mapping of microcosm to macrocosm is a dominant foundational schema in Indian religious traditions. The Ṛg Veda Saṃhitā (hereafter RV) tells how humanity and the cosmos are embodied in the anatomy of Purusha, the "Cosmic Man" (RV 10: 90). In the Caraka Saṃhitā (hereafter CS) the principal text of Ayurvedic medicine, the human body is a homunculus embodying greater cosmological principles (CS IV: 1). Similarly, Banaras is considered to be a microcosm of the divine world. As such, the city is thought to encapsulate all other centers of Hindu religious pilgrimage (Singh 1993). This concept is central in Diana Eck's comprehensive survey of Banaras's sacred geography: "The symbol that condenses the whole into the part is common in the Hindu world. The whole of the sacred Vedas, they say, may be packed into a single powerful mantra . . . or the whole of the universe may be depicted in the 'sacred circle' of a cosmic map called a mandala. [Banaras] is this kind of symbol, which condenses the whole of India into a great 'sacred circle,' a geographical mandala" (1983: 41).

Just as Banaras is a prototype for sacred India, her sacred features are prototypes for the divine roles of the city as a whole. Foremost among these features are the Ganga and the two famous cremation grounds *(shmashāns)* along her banks. Pilgrims commonly say that Banaras is like the Mother Ganga, who accepts and purifies anyone and anything that comes to her and transforms them into herself. Indeed, more than a million pilgrims visit Banaras each year for the same reasons that they

Figure 3. Banaras main bathing ghats along the Ganga River. Courtesy of the Sonoma Yoga Ashram.

bathe in the Ganga: to purify themselves of pollution and sin in hopes of better fortune in this life or the next, or spiritual liberation *(moksha)* from the perpetual cycle of rebirth.

For those desiring the latter, the Kāshī Kaṇḍa offers the promise of instant liberation for all who die within the sacred boundaries of the city (Skanda Purāṇa [SP] IV.1.30). Even people who die elsewhere can obtain an auspicious sendoff at the famous *shmashāns* at Manikarnika and Harischandra Ghats. Unlike most cremation grounds, which are typically located on the outskirts of Indian towns and cities, these *shmashāns* are centrally located in Banaras, along the bank of the river. Indeed, the *shmashān* of Manikarnika lies next to the purported site of cosmogenesis, the place where Lord Vishnu carved out the world with his discus. Manikarnika is named for the earring that fell to earth when Shiva shook with ecstasy over this earthly creation. To this day, Shiva continues to dance the *Naṭarāj* among the burning pyres of Marikarnika (SP IV.1.26). Lord Shiva is the ultimate ascetic of the *shmashān*. Banaras is the city of Shiva. So it is said that Banaras is the *mahāshmashān,* the Great Cremation Ground (Eck 1983).

Each of these features—the Ganga, the *shmashān,* and the city as a whole—functions as a kind of cosmic sink, a sacred dumping ground for humanity's physical and metaphysical refuse. Yet although people who work as sweepers and cremation attendants are socially denigrated for managing the excreta of humanity, the same stigma does not apply to these sacred geographic features. On the contrary, people believe that these places derive their divinity and ritual power from their ability to take on the pollution of any and all who come to them. Shakti takes the form of Ganga Ma. Lord Shiva takes the form of cremation ascetic. Both are as infinite as their capacity to absorb the sins of the universe.

These dynamics hold true for Aghor as well. The Kina Ram tradition asserts that Aghor is like the Ganga, accepting the purest streams from the Himalayas as well as the sewage of the cities. The Aghori consider Baba Kina Ram to be the manifestation of Lord Shiva; his *dhuni*, a cremation pyre; and the Kina Ram Ashram, the *mahāshmashān*. Like the city, the ashram and its namesake play the role of cosmic sink for the removal of pollution and sin from the many pilgrims and patients they receive. Significantly, this role is informed by the same models of purification that people use when bathing in the Ganga or offering the bodies of their ancestors to the fires of final sacrifice. These models of purification are the foundation for the practice of Aghor medicine. Thus, we need to understand their relationships to the history and sacred geography of Banaras.

BABA KINA RAM

The Kina Ram Aghor tradition emerged as an ideology of resistance to the pervasive social inequalities and power dynamics of Banaras during the British Raj. These dynamics have persisted through independence, and they continue to shape the context in which Aghor medicine is practiced today. The hagiography of Baba Kina Ram illustrates this fact well, though it has been filtered through the lens of the postreform Aghor tradition. His story has taken shape through oral legends recounted by Aghor disciples, published in tracts written by the Aghori, and illustrated on the many signboards hanging in Aghori ashrams (Ram 1997; Asthana 1994a, 1994b).

Although the Kina Ram Aghori have left more written records than the *kāpālikas* before them, a reliable history of the lineage before the 1950s awaits the discovery of sufficient primary source materials. Three potential sources exist for these materials, but such a historical project is beyond the scope and scale of this investigation.[1] I therefore represent the hagiography of the Aghori in the same way that I have operationalized

Figure 4. Statue of Baba
Kina Ram in the middle
of Krim Kund, 2000.

my definition of Aghor itself: that is, according to the stated beliefs of
my informants. Although this definition is biased toward a postreform
agenda, it is salient within the current Kina Ram Aghor tradition, its
social and medico-religious practices, and the image the Aghori projected
to the outside world. It follows the argument that one should evaluate
such hagiographies more for their ideological lessons than for their historical accuracy (Lorenzen 1995).

The Kina Rami tell of the miraculous circumstances surrounding the
birth and early childhood of their founder and namesake. According to
them, Kina Ram's parents were a childless elderly couple who lived in a
small village in the district of Chandouli near Banaras. Kina Ram was
conceived shortly after Lord Shiva visited his mother in a dream. Just
after his birth, the infant was visited by Lords Brahma, Vishnu, and
Shiva disguised as wandering sages, who whispered an initiating mantra
into his ear. As a young child, Kina Ram gave inspirational teachings to
his age-mates and lived a pious life. His marriage was arranged by the
time he was nine, but he correctly foresaw the death of his bride-to-be
on the eve of their wedding. The circumstances surrounding her death
were considered ominous, and the young Kina Ram was released from
the obligations of family life to become a wandering ascetic.

Such miraculous accounts of early childhood are common in Indian hagiographies, where they serve to establish the saint's supernatural power and religious vocation at an early age, but they are more common for saints of lower caste or untouchable origins for the likely reason that they serve to mitigate or deny their natal social status (Lorenzen 1995). In the case of Baba Kina Ram, however, divine conception would mitigate his *upper*-caste origins, supporting the argument that Aghor functions as an ideology of resistance to the entire schema of social hierarchy, not just to any caste or class within it.

As a young ascetic, Baba Kina Ram wandered India for many years before encountering Hinglaj Devi, a goddess associated with a legendary center of tantric worship in northwestern India. Hinglaj Devi directed him to go to Banaras, where she said he would find her once again, dwelling beside a sacred bathing tank that would eventually be known as Krim Kund. This message was reinforced by Lord Dattatreya, an antinomian form of Shiva closely associated with the cremation ground, who appeared to Baba Kina Ram atop Girnar Mountain in Gujarat. Considered to be the *adi guru* (ancient spiritual teacher) and founding deity of Aghor, Lord Dattatreya offered his own flesh to the young ascetic as *prasād* (a kind of blessing), conferring upon him the power of clairvoyance and establishing a guru-disciple relationship between them.

The young Kina Ram found his guru once again in Banaras. This time, Lord Dattatreya appeared in human form as Baba Kalu Ram, sitting in the *shmushān* at Harischandra Ghat. The guru gave three supernatural tests to his disciple. In the first, he fed grains to a group of chattering skulls. Kina Ram commanded the skulls to stop eating. Baba Kalu Ram then stated that he was hungry, so Kina Ram caused three fish to jump out of the Ganga. The disciple cooked the fish for his guru with wood left over from a cremation fire. With Kina Ram having passed these two tests, Sri Kalu Ram offered a third: he pointed to a body floating in the river. Kina Ram pulled the body ashore and brought it back to life. The revived soul was an Aghor disciple who later became known as Baba Jivayan Ram. Satisfied with the performance of his disciple, Sri Kalu Ram accompanied Baba Kina Ram to the dwelling place of Hinglaj Devi at Krim Kund.

Having reunited with the goddess, Baba Kina Ram established his *dhuni* (and thus, the seat of the Aghor lineage) beside Krim Kund. There, he became famous for his social activism and healing, the two dominant themes of his hagiography. The most famous story of Baba Kina Ram relates his confrontation with Chet Singh, the maharaja of Banaras.[2] The maharaja built a grand fortress just south of the *shmashān* to improve his physical presence within the sacred boundaries of Kashi. In celebration of its completion, he ordered a grand *yajña* (Vedic fire sacrifice) in the courtyard. The sacrifice was to be a very auspicious affair. A number of reputed Brahmin priests and *paṇḍits* were on hand to perform the rite, and the richest and most powerful men of Banaras were in attendance.

Baba Kina Ram was not on the guest list, but he nonetheless arrived at the ritual riding atop a donkey, an inauspicious way to show up at an orthodox ceremony.[3] When the maharaja and his priests berated him, the Baba responded, "Do you think that knowledge of scripture gives you the authority to decide what is holy and virtuous? Such knowledge is nothing special. Look, even my donkey can chant the Vedas." The donkey proceeded to chant the Vedas to an astonished court. Baba Kina Ram then cursed the maharaja, foretelling that his new fort would be occupied only by pigeons and that his family would never give birth to sons. Shortly thereafter, the British routed Chet Singh from the fortress. It has remained unoccupied ever since. Moreover, as Baba Kina Ram predicted, Chet Singh's successors had to adopt male children to maintain the lineage until the most recent generation.[4]

Although some scholars emphasize potential conflicts between the ritual authority of Brahmin priests and the worldly authority of their Kshatrya kings (Dumont 1966; Gupta 1995), the story of Baba Kina Ram's curse instead serves as an allegory of resistance against the collusion between these two groups. Such collusion has been a recurring theme in the history of Banaras, which has been as much a political and economic crossroads *(tīrtha)* as a symbolic one. The city arose out of a cluster of shrines and temples at the intersection of two key northern Indian trade routes, the Ganga and the Grand Trunk Road, sometime around the ninth century B.C.E. (Eck 1983). Because of its strategic location, Banaras became a major inland commercial capital, developing as a nexus of economic activity in parallel with its development as a religious center (Freitag 1989). This codevelopment of symbolic and material prosperity was evident in the activities of the Gossains, mendicant warriors organized around local temple networks, who protected traveling merchants and pilgrims by providing armed escorts, safeguarding merchandise, and enforcing trade agreements. The Gossains operated in small decentralized, feudal houses that concentrated religious, economic, and military power into more than three hundred local neighborhoods, or *muhallas,* through complex networks of patron-client relationships similar to the *jajmani* system of rural India (Beidelman 1959).

This complex and persistent web of local power relations made Banaras easily conquerable from without but totally untamable from within. The city's strategic location, auspiciousness, and wealth of resources have made it a key asset for political rulers, beginning with its emergence as one of sixteen Janapadas ("Great Kingdoms," literally "foothold of a tribe"), from the eighth to the sixth centuries B.C.E. Banaras was the capitol of the Gahadavala kingdom in the twelfth century C.E., before submitting to a long chain of Mughal and British colonial masters. Yet none of these authorities were able to control Banaras without close collaboration with its local centers of power. Such collaboration entailed careful and often problematic exchanges of symbolic, social, and material power.

The emergence of the maharaja of Banaras during the Mughal and British periods provides key examples of these problematic exchanges. The city's status shifted radically under Mughal occupation. Its religious and cultural institutions enjoyed generous patronage under Akbar, only to see these mainstays destroyed two generations later under the intolerant rule of Aurangzeb (Freitag 1989). These structures were partially rebuilt in the declining years of the Delhi Sultanate, for which Banaras remained an important source of revenue as well as a symbolic instrument for appeasing its Hindu subjects. To achieve the requisite local support for these objectives, the nawab of Awadh appointed the head of a prominent family of Hindu Bumihar landholders to serve as tax collector instead of a Muslim *zamindari*, as was usually the case. Through key alliances with the Gossains and nine families of merchant bankers known as the Naupatti, members of this Bumihar family became highly successful government revenuers, indispensable to Mughal and later British rulers, who granted them the title of raja, and then maharaja, in subsequent generations (Freitag 1989).

Despite his success, the maharaja held a tenuous position in Banaras. Lacking a royal pedigree and perched between potential war with colonial authorities and a revolt by the local population, the new maharaja was badly in need of symbolic legitimacy. He therefore adopted the same strategy of "sanskritization" that many of his merchant bankers had pursued.[5] He heavily patronized the city's temples, some with *mahants* of previously marginal standing. They, in turn, honored him in their words and ritual deeds. He patronized schools of traditional literature and music, which lauded him in their arts. He supported large religious festivals, such as the Ram Lila, a public enactment of the epic *Ramcharitmanas* (a popular form of the Ramayana), the largest of which had him

appearing before thousands to exchange salutes with the gods (Lutgendorf 1989). Without the need for a costly standing army, royal patronage of the arts increased under the British, resulting in more elaborate
festivals, expanded institutions of traditional learning, and a near monop-
oly in publishing (King 1988). Not surprisingly, the products of these
local institutions later served as templates for linguistic and religious
revivalism and nationalist identity in the half centuries before and after
Indian independence (see Dalmia 1996).

These historical relationships illustrate the classic struggle between
temporal and ritual authority that Dumont (1966) describes. Yet these
struggles never yield a clear winner, and the lines of defense are often
blurred. Instead, a dialectic of coercion and conflict emerges that persists specifically because it is never resolved (see Nuckolls 1996; Guha
1989). Baba Kina Ram attempted to break this dialectic by confronting
the maharaja, the priests, and their mutual patronage. The Aghori were
usually explicit about this confrontation when retelling the story—some
would even go so far as to trace the flow of money, power, and prestige
between the various interests—noting that that these overall dynamics
continue into the present day.

At a religious level, the curse of the maharaja closely parallels the
Puranic tragedy of Daksha's sacrifice. As the reluctant father-in-law of
Lord Shiva, Daksha disapproved of the ascetic activities of his new son
and his association with the *shmashān*. Daksha therefore excluded Lord
Shiva from a great fire ceremony, a *yajña*, to which he invited all the
other gods (SP IV.2: 87). In the end, the gods berated Daksha for his
omission, and his daughter jumped into the fire as an act of protest (SP
IV.2: 87–88). Daksha's sacrifice also has a more direct symbolic link to
Baba Kina Ram. After the tragic death of his consort, Shiva wandered
the earth, carrying his wife's corpse until Vishnu eventually cut her body
into many pieces with his fingernail. The places where these pieces fell
became Shakti *pīthas*, major centers of power and tantric worship
throughout India. Hinglaj, the place where the crown of the daughter's
skull fell to earth, is one of the most mythically prominent of these centers. Her namesake is the goddess at Krim Kund (Ram 2000).

Both of these stories depict their protagonists as sincere but mis-
understood figures with close ties to the cremation grounds. The antinomianism of Lord Shiva and Baba Kina Ram incurs the disapproval of
the landlords and priests of the Brahminical orthodoxy, who exclude
them from Vedic rituals. Consequently, these rituals are rendered inauspicious, the leaders of the orthodoxy are stricken with tragedies, and

their underlying hypocrisy is exposed. The protagonists, Lord Shiva and Baba Kina Ram, prevail as social revolutionaries against the powers-that-be in Banaras.

Many other tales reinforce Baba Kina Ram's role as an advocate against social oppression. In one, he rescues his first disciple and successor from the violence of a brutal *zamindar* (feudal landlord) by correctly telling the latter that he can find more than his share of rent buried right beneath his feet. In another story, Kina Ram poses as a beggar and has himself arrested in a town where the nawab (Muslim ruler) has punished begging with hard labor at his mills. Kina Ram forces the millstones to turn by themselves, thereby attaining from the frightened nawab the release of his fellow prisoners and a pledge of alms for all beggars. Kina Ram also stops a group of men from killing a young widow for giving birth to an illegitimate son. The men skulk away after Baba Kina Ram suggests that they kill the father of the child as well, a member of their group whom he is fully prepared to reveal. He finds employment for the widow as the resident caretaker of an auspicious *samadhī* shrine, the burial site of a famous saint.

Baba Kina Ram's social activism extended to his healing practices as well. He particularly reached out to women with socially discredited health conditions such as infertility or leprosy. Some people say that Baba Kina Ram conferred fertility upon barren women in the same manner that Lord Shiva brought fertility to the baba's own mother. Once, after Kina Ram blessed a barren woman with four children, another saint asked his guardian deity for the secret of this power. The deity demanded that the saint offer a piece of flesh from his own body for the knowledge. The saint was unwilling to make such an offering. Yet when the deity directed the saint to obtain flesh from the body of Baba Kina Ram, the latter readily cut a piece from his thigh. The deity stated that this willingness for self-sacrifice enabled Baba Kina Ram to perform such miraculous deeds.

The allegory of healing as self-sacrifice addresses two important challenges to the traditional practice of medicine in Banaras. The first is the importance of establishing the sincerity of the Aghori healer among a larger population of charlatans. Banarsi have a common saying: "Raṇ naṇ siṭī sannysā, ānse baché sévé Kashī" (Widows, bulls, steps, and *sadhus*, save [yourselves] from these [in order to] enjoy Kashi). Bulls can be unpredictable. Stairs can be steep. But gurus can be the most dangerous of all, for the corrupt among them can poison their disciples, just as the most sincere can be their salvation. The same is true of healers, who are commonly revered as gurus in their own right, regardless of any other claims to religious authority. The outward expression of self-sacrifice can help establish the underlying motivation and qualities of the healer. We will soon see how many patients of the Aghori come to value these qualities more than they value the medicines themselves.

The most famous of Baba Kina Ram's miraculous cures established Krim Kund as a place of healing. A desperate mother approached the Aghori in search of a cure for her dying son. In response, Kina Ram charged a few grains of rice with the *Krīm* mantra, a seed mantra associated with Kali and other fiery manifestations of the divine feminine. Kali is the fiery goddess who is often seen "dancing" upon a supine Shiva. She wears an apron of human arms and a necklace of human heads. Blood drips from her extended tongue as she holds a scythe and severed head. Yet despite her ferocious appearance, Kali is often considered to be a loving mother who helps the spiritual seeker break away from worldly attachments and limitations.

Kina Ram cast the mantra-laden grains into the water and instructed the mother to bathe her son there on five consecutive Sundays and Tuesdays. The mother did as instructed, and the boy was cured. Shortly thereafter, a courtesan was cured of leprosy by bathing in the *kund*—despite the double stigma of having been a prostitute afflicted with the most untouchable of human diseases. News of these cures quickly spread, and more people began bathing in its waters. Baba Kina Ram proclaimed, "This *kund* shall live as long as the Ganga remains in Kashi." Like the Ganga who fed her waters, and the Aghori who charged them, the Krim Kund acquired a reputation for great power in the context of limitless nondiscrimination.

GANGA MA

When I asked Agania Devi, a longtime Aghor disciple and retired schoolteacher, about the healing powers of Krim Kund, she began discussing the Ganga. "'Ganga' means holy," she said. "There is no kind of evil in her. All rivers flow into her and meet in her, and Ganga takes all into her. Even so, her purity remains. In the same way, are these Aghor saints." Her companion, Sangita, expanded on this idea: "There is no darkness in it. It has taken everything in it, meaning all things should be all right [i.e., no discrimination against anything]. [One should] stay away from discrimination, have a simple nature, and live one's life with simplicity." These women spoke of the *kund,* the Ganga, and Aghor interchangeably.

Sangita had previously bathed in the *kund* for a variety of ailments, and she claimed to have good results. We first met when she brought her son to bathe for an undisclosed "personal problem" within the family. Her son summarized the situation as follows: "Now we have put the burden of [these] problems on Baba. He will do it." He used the verb *ḍālnā*, meaning "to pour" or "to cast," verbalizing a hydraulic model of purification that frequently arose in the explanatory models of patients at the ashram and elsewhere. The healing modalities of Aghor medicine in general, and Krim Kund in particular, were informed by such cultural models of purification, for which the Ganga is a major prototype. One could therefore learn a great deal about the dynamics of healing in Aghor medicine by examining models of pollution and purity with respect to this holy river.

The Ganga is the foremost of India's seven sacred rivers, winding fifteen hundred miles from the glaciers of the Himalayas through twenty-nine cities and seventy towns of the northern Indian plains and exiting into the Indian Ocean through the great delta that feeds into the Bay of Bengal on the eastern coast. The river is the primary source of irrigation and alluvial deposits for the agrarian economies stretching out from her banks. For many centuries, the Ganga was a major route for trade and transportation. In recent decades, she has become a dumping ground for untreated sewage, industrial waste, fertilizers, pesticides, and detergents —in addition to an increasing number of animal and human bodies (Kumra 1995). The Ganga is also a pilgrimage destination for the hundreds of millions who bathe in her waters to remove the accumulated karma of many lifetimes, make offerings to deities and ancestors, and offer themselves as the ultimate sacrifice at the time of death. For these latter reasons especially, the Ganga is more than a river. She is the Holy Mother. She is Ganga Ma.

The story of the Holy Mother's descent to earth has been recounted in numerous oral traditions, as well as in the Epic and Puranic literature. Through the single-minded austerities of the pious King Bhagiratha, Lord Brahma granted a boon that Ganga Ma would descend upon the earth so she might carry sixty thousand of his cursed ancestors to the netherworld. Her fall was broken by Shiva's matted locks, which prevented the earth from being destroyed by her impact, and the locks channeled her downward flow from the Himalayas. Once upon the plains, Ganga Ma sought out King Bhagiratha in Banaras, who led her to the remains of his ancestors in Bengal, where she swept them along to the other world (Darian 2001; Eck 1983).

Although any point along the Ganga can serve as a pilgrimage site, a number of especially powerful *tīrthas* (sacred crossings) along her banks allow pilgrims to cover multiple spiritual bases with a single visit.[6] Banaras is the largest and most visited of these *tīrthas*, presenting itself as Kashi ("the Luminous"), an otherworldly abode that rests upon Shiva's trident and grants instant liberation to all who die within its boundaries (SP IV.1.26: 80). The Ganga forms the eastern boundary of Kashi, delineating the auspicious from the inauspicious, for people say that those who die on her far shore are destined to be reborn as donkeys (Eck 1983). One might therefore expect that such a border would occupy a peripheral position in this sacred space. Nevertheless, the Ganga is a central symbol and geographic feature of Kashi.

Most pilgrims begin their visit to Banaras with a ritual bath in the Ganga. Ideally, they bathe just before dawn, when the river waters are offered to the rising sun while reciting the Gayatri Mantra.[7] Although the bath is a *pūjā* in itself, pilgrims may make other offerings of lamps, flowers, incense, rice, and prayers, just as they would in a temple or shrine. The ritual structure of these offerings can range from personal formulas to complex rites performed under the direction of Brahmin *paṇḍās*, ritual specialists who hawk their services from umbrella-covered platforms along the bathing ghats.

Ritual bathing is the prototypical interaction with Mother Ganga. Yet amid the sacred ablutions, washerpeople *(dhobīs)* scrub and pound the city's laundry. Herders bring their buffaloes to cool themselves in the midday sun. Pilgrims throw plastic bags full of flowers into the river, and people everywhere urinate and defecate along her banks with the full knowledge that the next rain will wash their excreta into the waters below. The Ganga is also a dumping ground for the dead. The unburnt remnants of more than eighty cremated human corpses are put in the river every day (Parry 1994), and the remains of cows, buffaloes, and other animals float down the river like an endless convoy of bloated barges. But even these insults are dwarfed by the 125 million liters of wastewater that the city generates, 84 percent of which it dumps untreated into the river every day (Ahmed 1995). As a consequence, this river of spiritual purification has a fecal coliform count that is two hundred times greater than the World Health Organization's recommended limit for safe swimming (Mishra 2000).

The Ganga is often cited as an example of the apparent incongruence between Indian religious models of ritual pollution and scientific models of biological pollution. However, conversations with people along the ghats reveal a more complex and ambivalent relationship between these two models of contamination. Despite local awareness of river pollution, I found mixed interpretations of its implications. After hearing countless opinions and anecdotes, I decided to formally interview two dozen people on the riverbank on the subject. A couple of cosmopolitan-looking young men told me (in Hindi) after their bath that "the Ganga is certainly pure. Mother Ganga is giving salvation to the whole world, be it cattle, be it sparrows, be it dogs, be it man." Then (in Bhojpuri) they said, "Certainly [the Ganga] is polluted. You are seeing it, aren't you? You have the proof." On another day, a fisherman spat a large mouthful of *pān* into the river so that he could more clearly give me the opposite answer in similar terms: "Certainly the Ganga is pure. Can you not see it?"[8] I replied on both occasions with a sideways nod: "Yes, certainly. I see."

These statements reveal the range of models by which people understand the purity of the Ganga. Their use of different languages to describe these models is a common example of situational code switching among local speakers of *Banarsī bolī* (Simon 1993). It is reminiscent of other societies, such as in Samoa, which use multiple speech registers to affirm or deny categories of cultural behavior (Shore 1996). Yet even in the same language, the nearly simultaneous use of apparently conflicting models is not unusual in Indian metaphysics, which O'Flaherty describes as a suspension of opposites (1976).

At the same time, one should consider the different relationships that people have with the river and how these relationships might prompt the use of one model over another. For example, the fisherman above, using the same dialect and nearly identical sentence structure as the two young men, cited the same empirical evidence to support an opposite claim. Yet his adamant denial of pollution in the Ganga, on any level, was shared by many who earned their living from the river, whether by fishing, washing laundry, or watering their animals. If the Ganga could be dirty, even if only in a physical sense, then no one should put anything dirty in it nor eat anything dirty from it. The fisherman, like the washers and herders, would therefore have to choose between financial ruin or karmic disaster. In contrast, those who used the Ganga solely for ritual purposes could afford to be more philosophical about the coexistence of physical pollution with spiritual purity.

There may be nearly as many cultural models for the purity of Ganga Ma as there are people along her banks. Yet most of these models fall into at least two generalized patterns, or schemata, of purification. These

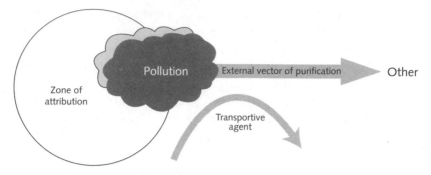

Figure 5. The transportive schema of purification.

schemata inform not only ritual purification within sacred spaces but also the manner in which people clean themselves and their environments on a daily basis. They include any means of dealing with physical or metaphysical pollution within a particular *zone of attribution,* an area in which a coded substance may bring negative social consequences for a person or group of people.

The first category is a transportive schema of purification, entailing the transfer of pollution from one zone of attribution to another. This schema describes a process of externalization, of excretion from the inside out (figure 5).

The transportive schema emphasizes the dynamic properties of water, an example of which is the common belief that a person can be properly cleansed only by running water (Babb 1975). Likewise, Banarsis often note that the relatively still waters of the city's sacred bathing tanks are replenished, albeit inadequately in many cases, by underground springs originating from the Ganga. Krim Kund is one such tank, and ashram residents affirm that it is constantly replenished by a spring that links it to the river. Even when people draw bath water from a relatively stagnant source, such as a well or container, they make it dynamic through a pouring action *(ḍālnā)* from the top of the head to the bottom of the feet. Likewise, bathing in the Ganga involves a series of vertical bobs in which the bather submerges his or her entire head. These practices evoke a top-down hierarchy from the auspicious to the inauspiciousness that is embodied in gods and humans alike (Babb 1975).

Significantly, the Ganga herself has a vertical orientation, flowing from the realm of the gods far up in the Himalayas to the netherworld below (Eck 1983). One elderly woman stated that "from where the Ganga originated is pure in itself," noting that the river *descended* from a pure source.

Another woman's version of Ganga Ma's descent emphasized the height and purity of the river's source in the Himalayas (while typically conflating the Ganga's heavenly origins with her earthly source). Therefore, "all the sins are washed away. Even the sins of gods are washed away."

Where is this "away," and what does the Ganga do with the sins once she receives them? Several people stated that the pollutants are washed into the ocean, but the more popular destination was *bāhar*, meaning "outside." *Bāhar* illustrates transportive purification as a process of externalization: excretion from the inside out. Through externalization, pollution flows from one zone of attribution to another. Thus, transportive models by necessity emphasize trajectory over destination. The destination of ritual pollution is not important so long as its general direction is *other*, moving toward someone or somewhere else.

Similar dynamics appear in the exchange of gifts for ritual services between people of different ritual status. For example, donations to high-status ritual specialists may carry with them the sins of their lesser-status patrons (Raheja 1988). Similarly, pilgrims drop rice and coins into the hands of beggars as a means of shedding some of their sins before entering temples or of getting a head start on their ablutions in the Ganga. The relative ranks of priests and beggars could not be more different, yet their roles are essentially the same: the removal of karma in exchange for material resources that function as a medium of transmission.

As with human sins, so too with human waste. In Banaras, a child may urinate or defecate in the street or open sewer just outside (and facing away from) the home. An adult male might urinate in the street or in an open sewer (facing away from everywhere else) that is not in front of a home entrance or storefront. And anyone can relieve himself or herself in an unoccupied lot, empty alleyway, or railroad embankment.[9] The liminal areas where excretion is socially sanctioned in Banaras even extend to the banks and ghats leading to the Ganga. Although defecating directly into the Ganga is a sin, many defecate just beside the river.[10] They do so despite the obvious fact that, in a very short time, rains, erosion, and the workers who clean the ghats will inevitably sweep the waste a few feet down into water anyway. Here, the responsibility for pollution does not rest upon the polluter, but rather its final recipient. In special cases in which the act of polluting is considered a sin in itself, only the person who performs the deed directly acquires its karma. As such, the people who clean the mud from the ghats with high-pressure hoses at the end of monsoon season are the ones who acquire the karma of defecating in the river.

On a larger scale, transportive models play out in the waste-management practices of the city as a whole. Although Banaras's dense urbanization and poor infrastructure have left few options for waste disposal, these constraints are not sufficient to explain the behaviors that take place before waste is flushed into an open sewer or swept into the street for professional sweepers, who pick it up by hand and cart it away to neighborhood holding areas.[11] Until then, people treat waste like a hot potato. They handle it as little as possible and quickly pass it to the most available person with the lowest status: a female or servant within a household, a peon within an office, or, in many cases, a child laborer working in a small shop or factory.[12] Trash receptacles are rare, so waste material is either burned or left for someone (or no one) to sweep up. Trash is thrown over a wall or out of a window; dumped in a pile just outside the home or workplace; or thrown on the street, into an empty lot, or into a space between two buildings. Trash is typically dumped in the closest available *outside* space (that is, a liminal space apart from the polluter's network of social relations) beyond the handler's zone of attribution.

From the householder to the servant, the sweeper, and then the sewer, polluted substances travel down a gradient of inauspiciousness, with little or no change to the relative (in)auspiciousness of the substances themselves. This conservation or immutability of attribution is another fundamental characteristic of the transportive schema of purification: the negative attribution is intrinsic to the pollution itself. If one cannot destroy or change pollution, then one must somehow transport it to another location.

The transportive schema also informs the daily dumping of untreated sewage into the river. Because of the near absence of water treatment, disposing of waste in sewers is little different from disposing of it directly in the Ganga herself. But conceptually, a distinction does exist, for the sewers are the elements that perform the final deed. Even those officials who may have pocketed money earmarked for water treatment can wash their hands of whatever happens to the water after their negligence. The sewers of Banaras are small rivers in themselves, carrying away the city's pollution from "self" to other.[13]

The dynamics of transportive purification beg further questions about the Ganga's role in pollution and the attribution of blame. The sewers of Banaras are not auspicious, even if they do act as little rivers. The same is true of the professional sweepers who tend the sewers and clean the streets. In both cases, the close association with pollution is very stigma-

tizing. Dirt and sin are inseparable entities that flow downhill. The far-
ther down the transport chain that the pollution passes, the more tinged
its handlers become, not because they passed it along, but because they
received it in the first place. Likewise, the Ganga herself could not maintain her purity simply by "passing the buck," especially if she were the
last recipient of pollution and sin in all of Banaras.

One explanation reinforces the idea that the Ganga is as immutably
pure as sin and dirt are immutably polluted. Nuckolls (1996) describes
a situation in which one of his American students presented a paper to
a professor at Banaras Hindu University (BHU) on pollution in the
Ganga. The professor rejected the paper on the grounds that Mother
Ganga is ever pure and therefore can never become polluted. The student
subsequently revised her argument to state that "the Ganga is indeed
most pure . . . but what is put *into* her is polluted." The professor understandably accepted this revision. Transportive purification entails the
conservation (i.e., the indestructibility) of pollution, such that the insult
itself never becomes purified; it only transfers from one location to
another. This model also entails the possibility that an intrinsically pure
solvent can never become contaminated but can merely be shifted about
or displaced by the polluted solute. Within this model, the mixing of the
immutably inauspicious with the immutably auspicious literally results
in a suspension of opposites, in line with O'Flaherty's characterization
(1976). Pollution in the Ganga is like oil in water.

Another explanation for the Ganga's persistent auspiciousness is a
schema of purification in which pollution and purity are not immutable
but interchangeable states dependent on their contexts. This transformative schema emphasizes the re-creative power, or *shaktī*, of certain
substances as agents of change, which either transform negatively coded
substances into those with neutral or positive attributes or eliminate the
substances altogether. In contrast to the transportive schema, in which
the vector of purification is externally oriented, from inside to outside,
transformative purification involves the internalization of a change agent,
from outside to within (figure 6).

An interesting application of this schema is the recurring explanation
that the Ganga is purified by the pious just as she is contaminated by the
immersion of sinners in her waters. A Brahmin *paṇḍā* sitting beneath an
umbrella beside the river told me that "this filth that is dumped [*ḍālnā*]
in Gangaji—not just from today, from a long time—just see: [when] some
sadhus/mahatmas die then they are immersed in Gangaji. By that, Ganga
water does not become polluted." An outspoken elderly woman sitting

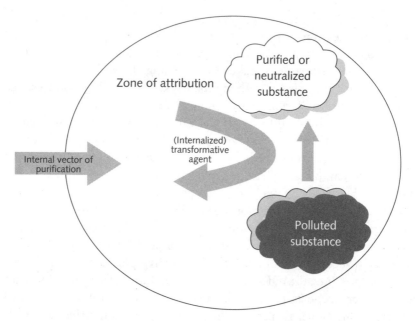

Figure 6. The transformative schema of purification.

beside him—the one who said that the Ganga washes away even the sins of the gods—made the same case in the following tale: "When Ganga was brought to Haridwar, then all the Gods asked: 'We wash all sins, but who will wash us?' Ganga said this to Lord Vishnu: 'Lord Vishnu Bhagwan, tell us, what should we do?' Then the Lord said: 'As many *sadhus* and saints are living in this world, every time they will bathe in Ganga, all your sins will be washed [automatically].'"

The proportion of *sadhus* (renunciates) who bathe in the Ganga is much smaller than the rest of the population, and the sincerity of even this small fraction is often regarded with skepticism. As such, a few great souls must go a long way toward keeping the Ganga on the auspicious side of the balance sheet. Such asymmetry is consistent with transformative models of purification, even among the much greater set of explanations that view the Ganga as intrinsically pure. By and large, both transportive and transformative models laud the Ganga's unlimited powers of purification. However, they do so with inverted proportions of the purifier and purified. When the Ganga purifies by transport, she functions as a vast solvent receiving a relatively small amount of polluted solute. When she purifies by transformation, she is a minute solute transmitted into a much larger quantity of polluted solvent.

A popular story in Banaras tells of a scientific study in which "a single drop of water from the Ganga" purifies gallons of brackish water, leaving (usually Western) scientists scratching their heads in puzzlement. Some people state that anyone can perform these experiments. A third of my informants in the ghats told me that one could place Ganga water and ordinary water in containers and compare their qualities over time. "It has been observed that if you store Ganga water [over some time] . . . it will not give off a bad smell," said a middle-aged renunciate. "[But] if you store ordinary water in a bottle, then after a few days it will start giving off a bad smell." There is a common saying that "even a single a droplet of Ganges water carried one's way by the breeze will erase the sins of many lifetimes in an instant" (Eck 1983: 217). Given this perspective, some resident bathers carry Ganga water back to their homes in brass pots to purify their family altars, not just by bathing the lingams and idols but also by combining the water with food and other waters in the household. Likewise, nonresident pilgrims collect Ganga water in sealed containers to take back to their friends and family in their home communities. According to the *paṇḍā* under the umbrella, "Place Ganga water in a bottle [and] suppose you go to the village or countryside. If you do *pūjā-path* [ritual worship] [and] do not find Ganga water there, then you have already kept [Ganga water] in a bottle. So mix it [with plain water] and then it becomes Ganga water." People can also purchase Ganga water in sealed pots and packages from local shops.

Unlike the transportively informed, externally oriented models of excretion, in which polluted substances (often plural) are taken out and away, transformative models usually involve the deep internalization of a purifying substance (often singular). Whereas transportive models often entail purification by excretion, transformative models typically entail acts of ingestion or digestion. For example, in the *achmāni* rite, the celebrant sips a small portion of water to purify himself or herself before performing a sacred rite, such as a *pūjā* or ritual bath. During the *achmāni,* the participant cradles water in the palm of the right hand in a particular posture *(mudrā)* and sips the water just after *praṇava,* voiced recitation of a simple mantra such as *Aum Tat Sat.* The mantra charges the water with sacred power before ingestion. Yet although the *achmāni* is common in Banaras, I have been told that the mantra is more for the benefit of the recipient than for the substance when the water is from Ganga Ma, because that water comes preloaded. People often link this preloaded quality of the Ganga, the independent variable of her auspiciousness, to her intrinsic creative power, or *shaktī.*[14]

Eck describes the creative power of the Ganga as "liquid *shaktī*," evidenced by the fertility of fields along her banks and her position as a second consort and active principle of Shiva. Citing the Gāṅgā Māhātmya of the Kāshī Khaṇḍa, she states that "one should not be amazed at the notion that the Ganges is really power, for is she not the Supreme Shakti of the Eternal Shiva, taken the form of water?" (1983: 219). The idea that *shaktī* is within the Gaṅga is consistent with all the models that I have heard of and observed, regardless of the degree of transportive or transformative influences. *Shaktī* is present in the dynamism of the Ganga's currents as well as in the heat of her creativity. This power is closely associated with her procreative status as the Holy Mother. It is also linked to her maternal attitude of nondiscrimination toward whom and what she meets. An elderly woman sitting beside a Brahmin *paṇḍā* said it best: "The mother keeps the baby in the stomach for nine months and then gives birth. She cleans his excreta and urine, and the child is [always] in this when he is small. Then that is [how] the mother takes care of the baby, doesn't she? So she is Ganga Ma. All this trash, good things, bad things, everything, is in her. So she will never be impure. The mother is never impure."

In discussing the unlimited grace of the Ganga, Eck cites a common Indian saying that "no child is too dirty to be embraced by its mother" (1983: 216). Indeed, Mother Ganga embraces everyone and everything that is put into her (or that she enters). The same is said of the Aghor guru. A prominent sign in the Kina Ram Ashram states that "the guru is always in the form of a complete mother. The physical mother raises the child by nurturing the physical body. The guru, through his motherly love and secret methods, nurtures the mind and soul."[15] Ironically, this maternal message hangs above one of the giant skulls under a peepal tree in the Kina Ram Ashram. Aghor may be nurturing, but one must overcome major aversions to partake of it, especially those aversions pertaining to human mortality.

MAHĀSHMASHĀN

Banaras and the Kina Ram Ashram share the epithet of *mahāshmashān*, the "Great Cremation Ground." The cremation pyres of Harischandra and Manikarnika Ghats are prototypes for the liberating function of all sacred spaces in Banaras. Just as the Ganga is a prototype for purification by ablution in Krim Kund, so are these *shmashāns* prototypes for the flame that burns in Baba Kina Ram's *akhand dhuni* (perpetual fire).

Figure 7. Kamleshwar Baba worshipping at the *akhand dhuni*, 2000.
Photograph by Victor Balaban.

But whereas the *shmashāns* carry the hope of liberation after death, this
diminutive pyre holds the promise of *jivanmukti*, spiritual liberation
within one's own lifetime, and the promise of healing that this kind of
liberation entails.

The *akhand dhuni* burns within an enclosure on the eastern side of
the courtyard flanking Krim Kund, just before the seat of the lineage.
Every day, scores of Aghor devotees pay their respects and offer mantras
to this sacred fire. Hundreds of nondevotees also visit in hopes of healing or finding solutions to socioeconomic problems. All seek the grace
of the sacred fire through its *darshan* (auspicious sight) and the *vibhuti*
(blessing) of its ash, which they use for a variety of ritual and healing
purposes.[16]

In a general sense, the *dhuni* is not unique to the Aghori. *Dhunis* are
common features among guru-based traditions, and traveling renunciates will often use them to establish their presence in a particular place,
whether temporarily or permanently (Gross 1992: 357–69). Indeed,
one can see millions of these fires burning though the night during the
Kumbha Mela, a great religious festival held in one of four sacred cities
along the Ganga every four years (Rai 1993).

The *dhuni* is a gathering point for disciples and pilgrims who seek the reunciate's blessings and advice. Visitors may use it for cooking, warmth, and illumination; but always with the understanding that the benefits of the fire are the *prasād* (sacred remnants) of the guru and his or her presiding deity by way of the *havan,* or fire ceremony.

Derived from the Vedic *yajña* (fire sacrifice), the *havan,* or *homa,* is a ritualized sequence of offerings to the gods through the medium of Agni, the deity of fire, via Svaha, his consort. Its Vedic predecessor, the *yajña,* was the prototypical rite of ancient Hinduism. The elaborate ritual prescriptions and proscriptions of the *yajña* were outlined in an oral tradition of hymns that eventually formed the corpus of the Vedas. As the greater mirror of humanity, the gods themselves perform the *yajña* in the Epic and Puranic literature (Vesci 1985). Indeed, the Vedic myth of human origins and even the origin of the sacrificial act itself is described in the self-sacrifice of Purusha, the Cosmic Man (RV X: 90).

In ancient times, the *yajña* was an extensive series of rites conducted by a team of ritual specialists over several days. The rites took place in a temporary temple that was destroyed upon their conclusion (Staal 1983). The *yajña* mandated that its celebrants be of the highest ritual purity, a requirement that has often been invoked to justify social segregation and pollution/purity taboos, particularly among the upper castes of orthodox Hindu communities (see Dumont 1966). Moreover, the considerable human and material costs of this rite restricted its sponsorship to the wealthy and powerful.

In strictly Vedic terms, the *yajña* was supposed to be the primary means of communication between the human and the divine. Yet common people did not have the knowledge and resources to conduct or sponsor a *yajña* themselves. They had to rely on the ritual patronage of the powerful within their own communities, who performed the rite on their behalf in exchange for essential but labor-intensive and sometimes ritually polluting services.

Following the rise of Hindu devotional movements, the *havan* arose as an inexpensive and simpler alternative to the *yajña.* Henceforth, people of all classes and backgrounds could perform the rite, with only minor preparations. Even when led by a guru or priest, the *havan* allowed as many people to make their own offerings as could fit around the fire. This approach was in the spirit of many tantric and Bhaktī devotional movements, which encouraged a direct relationship with the divine without the need for hereditary ritual specialists (see Urban 2003; Lorenzen 1995).

Instead of having to master complex formulas, *havan* celebrants typically offer a series of praises and mantras through the medium of grain or seed mixtures and a liberal amount of ghee. These offerings are transmitted to Agni, the fire god, through Svaha, his consort. Agni may then pass on these offerings to designated saints, ancestors, or other deities. The spirits who receive them imbibe the ethereal qualities of the offerings, leaving behind the material remnants for the benefit of their human hosts. Because the divine exist on a much higher plane, this "backwash of the gods" is *prasād* for humans, a blessed return for their sacrifices. In this manner, the human and the divine exchange power through the media of language, food, and fire. As we will see, this schema of exchange, modeled in the prototype of the fire sacrifice, also informs exchanges between patients and healers in Aghor medicine.

Like other *dhunis,* the *akhand dhuni* of Baba Kina Ram provides a medium for divine exchange and the occasional *havan*. Its special relationship to the *shmashān*, however, adds significance to these roles. Since its establishment three centuries ago, the *akhand dhuni* has been fueled by leftover wood from the cremation pyres of the nearby Harischandra Ghat, purchased for a token sum according to an old agreement with hereditary funerary attendants of the Dom community. These days, trucks deliver most of the wood, but Aghor devotees occasionally carry a few logs to the ashram as a ritual duty. The ash from this fire is the main *prasād* distributed from this ashram, a substance that would ordinarily be considered untouchable because it carries the pollution of death. Yet in this case, both devotees and non-Aghor pilgrims consider it to be a blessing imbued with tremendous power for healing and salvation.

During my time in Banaras, Aghor disciples often spoke of the *dhuni* and the *shmashān* interchangeably when discussing Baba Kina Ram's sacred fire. This conflation was usually deliberate, just as it was for the *kund* and the Ganga. Prem, an unmarried resident of the Kina Ram Ashram in his early twenties, stated that, while meditating in front of the *dhuni*, he felt that his body was like a corpse with the real power burning in front of it. "It seems that everything that is here is a corpse. Meaning, just before you it is burning," he said. Prem believed that this power derived not only from the confrontation with death but also from confrontation with the entire cycle of human existence. "There is also a form of *shaktī* over there. Everything is coming to an end there. It notes the whole time as well. Another time is coming to an end and increasing. So, in other words, it is a complete form of culture there. People come and go—one complete life cycle; it is a life cycle. People come . . . [are] born

. . . then [are] young and then dead, then again [they are] born. In this way [we] visit a complete life cycle there."

The *shmashān* speaks to the power of death as a universal human experience that equalizes social differences. Lakshmi, a young college student and resident of the ashram, asserted that everyone burns the same way in the *shmashān*. She stated that "there is . . . no poor. There is equality. No difference there. In society we have difference between he [and me] . . . I am poor. He is medium class. We have a lot of categories here. But in that fact place, the reality place, we don't have any difference. That is the point," she laughed. Prem spoke similarly of the power of the *dhuni/shmashān*:

> What is the reason that [the wood for the *dhuni*] comes from the *shmashān?* . . . Our relation is that we people connect our life with that place. So that *shmashān* is also a very big part of our life. The meaning of *shmashān* is *"sam asan,"* "equal position" [sic], where everything is given equal position. This is my thinking. The meaning of *shmashān* is that it is a place where everybody is given equal position. So that is a holy ground where one . . . in a *havan kund,* we burn our whole body. So we call it the biggest *pūjā*. In the other *havans,* we offer everything. But in that *havan kund,* we dump our whole body.

The funeral pyre is the prototype for Baba Kina Ram's *dhuni*. It marks the establishment of the Aghor lineage and marks Aghor itself as a spiritual state of nondiscrimination that one achieves through confrontation with mortality. In Hindu life-crisis rituals (*saṃskāras*) the rite of cremation is often seen as the ultimate fire sacrifice. We can therefore understand why the ultimate sacrifice in the cremation pyre extends into the more diminutive offerings of the *akhand dhuni*.

The funerary rites, or *antyeshṭi saṃskāras,* are the last in a sequence of life-crisis rituals that take place from conception to death in Hindu religious traditions. Although the Hindu *saṃskāras* share with each other elements derived from the Vedic fire sacrifice, particularly those of the fire itself (Pandey 1969), the rites of cremation are unique in that the fire is more than a witness to the worldly development of the person. In cremation, the fire is the active participant, the deceased is the sacrificer, and his or her body is the chief offering to Agni. Many authors have described this powerful cultural model of cremation as the ultimate sacrifice in which the body becomes the material element of sacrificial food to be consumed by fire, whereas the ethereal soul is released as the vital breath, or *prana,* from the top of the skull (Filippi 1996; Parry 1994; Pandey 1969). Indeed, the meaning of the Sanskrit word *antyeshṭi* is "final sacrifice." The ritual elements of the *antyeshṭi saṃskāras* are modeled upon the death of the extended family's patriarch and the succession of his eldest son. When the patriarch dies, his adult male kin wrap the body in a shroud and carry it to the *shmashān* on a wooden litter, chanting "Ram nam satya hain" (God's name is truth). Upon arriving at the *shmashān*—which is ideally next to a riverbank—the relatives place the corpse feet first in the river and give it a bath while placing camphor in the mouth. Family members negotiate for the wood and the services of the professional funeral attendants. They place the body upon the pyre and give offerings of wood, incense, ghee, and parched grains, much as they would during a *havan,* except that the family members make the offerings before the ignition of the fire. Once the offerings are made, any accompanying women and children return home while the adult males retreat to the sidelines—all, that is, except for the eldest son, who remains behind in his role as chief mourner and cremator.

The eldest son usually has the task of cremating his father's body, and he assumes the role of family head at the conclusion of the rite. Similarly, when the guru of a religious lineage or school of traditional knowledge dies, his successor (again, usually a man) is often designated to cremate his teacher.[17] If the head of a family or teaching lineage wants to change the line of succession, he designates someone else to cremate his body. In these prototypical instances, the cremation is as much a rite of succession as one of death, and it is fraught with social and spiritual hazards. Thus, the circumstances surrounding death and cremation must be as auspicious as possible.

In preparation for the cremation, the eldest son has his head shaved (except for a small lock in back) and dresses in a white cotton shawl. In this manner, the son undergoes a kind of temporary ritual death not unlike that of the religious renunciate who marks his death to the world by tonsure and the wearing of a funeral shroud. Parry discusses how the son undergoes a temporary symbolic death concurrent with his father's, entailing a process of regeneration within these funerary rites. In this patriarchal prototype, "the father repays his debt to the ancestors by siring a son; the son repays his debt to his father by giving him birth on a new and higher plane, and this newly created ancestor in turn confers fertility and material prosperity on his descendants" (1982: 151). Death marks the turning of the wheel of *saṃsāra,* of regeneration and rebirth.

Once the family retreats to the sidelines, the son circumambulates the pyre while carrying embers in a sheaf of grass. When the grass is aflame, he ignites the pyre and stands by to attend the fire for the duration of the cremation. For this task, he usually receives more than a little assistance from the professional funeral attendant.[18] The cremation usually lasts between three and four hours. At a key moment in this process, the son breaks open his father's skull with a bamboo staff to release his *prāṇa* (vital energy) from the chakra (energy center) at the top of his head. Once the soul has separated from the body, the latter burns into a small remnant about the size of two fists. The attendant picks up the remnant with a pair of tongs and throws it into the river. The remaining ashes are gathered into a clay pot. The chief mourner holds this pot on one shoulder, turns his back to the river, throws the ashes over his shoulder and into the water, and then walks away without looking back. This act concludes the cremation rite.

As with ablution in the Ganga, the final sacrifice of cremation is an opportunity for ritual purification for the living as well as the dead. However, purification by fire has distinctive attributes, not the least of which is that cremation confers a temporary but significant degree of ritual pollution on its living participants. Mechanisms exist for removing this pollution, which, like the Ganga, are informed by transportive and transformative schema of purification.

Two major aspects of the *antyeshṭi saṃskāras* lend themselves to transportive purification. The first is a cultural model of fire as the reducer of both pure and impure substances to their primary constituents. The prototype for this kind of reduction is the immolation of the corpse. Despite having been ritually bathed and decorated, the corpse remains a highly polluted vessel of the human soul and becomes a fitting offering to the divine only after its somatic attachments to worldly existence (and the sins therein) have burned away. Prem spoke earlier of offering one's whole body as sacrifice to the funeral pyre. He also extended the *dhuni*'s purification function to the removal of sin. "My concept about the *dhuni* is [that] . . . here, our bad deeds are destroyed. . . . It can even be seen in a small form." Here, the *dhuni* is the "small form" of the *shmashān* that removes (i.e., transports) the pollution of human sin in the way that cremation separates out the polluted remains of the human body.

The *antyeshṭi saṃskāra* also provides opportunities for the transportive purification of the surviving family. Family members usually undergo a period of death pollution (often twelve days) in which they must abstain from many ordinary social functions. Parry (1994) describes this period as a ritually hazardous time for the family, one that determines whether the soul of the dead person departs the world as a friendly ancestor or remains a malevolent ghost to impede the fortunes of his/her descendants.

This period can also be hazardous in a structural sense, in that the death of the family patriarch entails the succession and reorganization of roles within the lineage (cf. Douglas 1966). The structural hazards of this transition are evident in cultural models of auspicious and inauspicious deaths, with the ideal of the former being the natural demise of a long-lived, financially successful, pious, and prolific patriarch (see Justice 1997). Such ideals are rarely achieved in reality, so families must find other ways to make the transition of death as auspicious as possible. The rites of the *antyeshṭi saṃskāra* can compensate for any shortcomings by ensuring that a bad death does not linger around the family. They do so by providing for a temporary period of asceticism involving ritual ablutions, tonsure, and postmortem offerings to ensure proper transport of the dead away from the living (Parry 1994).

The transformative schema of purification exists within the *shaktī* of the fire itself. For some, this heat has the power to destroy negatively coded substances, but only when the *shaktī* of the transformative agent exceeds that of the ritually polluting entity. The *shmashān* must therefore be associated with the most powerful manifestations of this contra-negative destruction: Shiva the Destroyer and fierce goddesses such as Kali and Tara. Significantly, the power of these deities is internalized in the fires of digestive transformation.[19] For example, Shiva, the lord of cosmic destruction, becomes the lord of worldly medicine by ingesting deadly poison and transforming it into a life-sustaining substance within his esophagus (Eck 1983).

This latter myth is important to Aghor medicine, and we will see in later chapters that those who take the most transformative approach to cremation as purification, the Aghori themselves, make a conceptual link between fires of the *dhuni* and *shmashān,* and the fires of their own digestion. The use of cremation wood in Aghor *dhunis* is symbolic of this connection between death and digestion, with not only the Aghori but also their patients ingesting the products of ritual sacrifice—offerings of food and even the ash from the wood (see Parry 1982). Along these lines, Prem spoke of imbibing ash as a blessing: "It is like this. . . .We apply [the ash]; that is for the peace of our heart; for our own mental peace, and that which has burned itself. From that, I feel something different in myself. For instance, we are very cruel. With that *dhuni* . . . because that is burning outside, that is a different process. One is burning inside. They [these two fires] have the same relation."

Such acts of ritual ingestion represent a kind of "tantric homeopathy," purification and healing by confronting the source of the pollution. When the pollution involves death, this digestive transformation represents an intimate confrontation with mortality. We will further examine these dynamics in the next chapter through a popular ritual-healing sequence that contains key elements of the *antyeshṭi saṃskāra,* and we will see how these models of purification inform the ways that patients and healers approach Aghor medicine.

CHAPTER 2

Fire in the Well

Anil had filled in the white patches on his son's arms with a ballpoint pen. Although the black ink was a noticeable contrast to his son's "wheatish" complexion, it was not as socially discrediting as the patches beneath. Despite the fact that the condition is noncontagious and completely harmless, people commonly consider the patchy depigmentation of leukoderma (cf. vitiligo) to be a kind of leprosy, with all the accompanying social penalties: a lifetime of ostracism, job discrimination, and few if any prospects for marriage or a family of one's own.[1] The disease was a tragic sentence for an otherwise handsome and healthy twelve-year-old boy, and his father was desperate to find a cure.

Father and son were in good company at Krim Kund. Their problem fell into the two most common illness categories, pediatric and dermatological, for which people sought Aghori healers at this ashram. For most visitors to the ashram, the Aghori were an option of last resort after many unsuccessful visits to doctors, healers, and astrologers. As with all the other healing traditions, people knew little or nothing about Aghor, save that the ashram and its people might have the power to solve their problems. For this possibility alone, they were willing to pass through the skulls at the gate, bathe in the *kund*, ingest the ashes of leftover cremation wood, and follow whatever additional instructions the Aghori gave them.

In chapter 1, we saw how the Ganga and the *shmashāns* of Banaras serve as ritual prototypes for Krim Kund and the *akhand dhuni*, the primary features of the Kina Ram Ashram and the lineage as a whole.

The *kund* and *dhuni* are also the chief features of a cremationlike sequence of bathing and fire sacrifice that is the central rite of Aghor medicine. Within this rite, the Ganga and *shmashāns* provide a template for common interaction between Aghori healers and their non-Aghori patients. Yet although healers and patients go through many of the same motions, the significance of their actions is often very different. For many patients, Aghor medicine occurs within a transportive schema in which the ashram is a transfer point, or dumping ground, for their problems. The Aghori, in contrast, see these problems as opportunities for the practice of non-discrimination and transformation into further healing power.

THE HEALING SEQUENCE

Most patients know little about Aghor when they first enter the ashram gates, but they soon pick up the basic elements of ritual bathing at Krim Kund. They learn the story of how Baba Kina Ram charged the *kund* with the Kali Mantra via a few grains of rice, and they learn his prescription for bathing on five consecutive Sundays and Tuesdays, shedding old clothes and donning new attire after the first bath. Following each bath, an Aghori ritual specialist provides them with sacred ash and instructions for additional tasks, if needed. After performing these tasks, the patients worship in front of the *akhand dhuni* before departing. If they achieve a favorable result following the five-day sequence, the patients return to offer a ritual feast of fish and rice for the entire ashram. The feast is consumed only after it has been offered to the *dhuni*, thereby converting it into *prasād* of the cremation pyre.

The people who came to the ashram while I was there conducted these rites for many reasons. Like Anil and his son, many had run out of options for chronic and otherwise incurable conditions: skin diseases, rheumatic and autoimmune diseases, developmental disabilities, and neuropsychiatric disorders. Families came to resolve conflicts and improve finances. Merchants came to increase business, and students came to maximize their performance on important examinations. Yet the most common reasons by far were matters of perinatal and child health, and a broad category of skin diseases that included leprosy and leukoderma.

Without diminishing the Aghori's own models, I suggest an additional explanation for the predominance of pediatric and dermatological conditions at Krim Kund. Eck (1983) notes that many of the holy tanks of Banaras were built around naturally occurring ponds and springs that had long been used for sacred bathing. Similarly, Aghori legends admit the preexistence of the *kund* as a sacred location where other renunciates dwelled. Similarly, I suggest that Krim Kund functioned as a solar tank (i.e., a man-made pool dedicated to Surya, the sun god) for the healing of infertility and skin diseases long before the arrival of Baba Kina Ram. The relationship between Krim Kund and the nearby tank of Lolark Kund supports this hypothesis. Like Krim Kund, Lolark Kund is known for its ability to cure skin diseases and infertility. The most common explanation is that Lolark Kund was a solar tank and that the sun could reduce the severity of these two conditions (Pathak and Humes 1993).[2] Significantly, fertility bathing at Lolark Kund closely resembled that at Krim Kund, with people discarding their old clothes and putting on new ones following their first bath.

Ritual bathing occurs throughout the year at Lolark Kund, but people believe that on one day in the year, the tank is at its maximum power for instilling fertility. On this day, thousands of couples come to bathe in the tank, known as Lolark Chāth in honor of a legendary king who discovered the healing powers of its waters after it cured him of leprosy. This day corresponds to the anniversary of the naming ceremony for the infant Baba Kina Ram, the largest annual gathering of the Aghori in Banaras and one in which thousands gather to bathe at Krim Kund.

The Sunday and Tuesday baths prescribed by Baba Kina Ram are respectively associated with the sun and moon in Vedic astrology (Frawley 1992), further suggesting a solar connection to Krim Kund. Finally, a stone Surya Yantra (a geometric representation of the sun god) was discovered at the bottom of Krim Kund when the tank was dredged in 1989. The *yantra* has since been prominently displayed, and many bathers make offerings to it before entering the water.

Despite its early origins and recent revival, the solar element has played a relatively minor role at Krim Kund. Confrontation with mortality is the main ritual objective of the bathing sequence. Whether patients are Aghori or not, they have to deal with the symbols of death that pervade the Aghori healing rituals. And though most patients are more concerned about the power than about the meaning of the symbols around them, the purification models underlying their pragmatism are complementary to those of their Aghori healers.

THE AGHORI AT THE WELL

Kamleshwar Baba was a key resource and gatekeeper during my months at Krim Kund. Although not fully recognized as an ascetic or official leader in the Kina Ram lineage, Kamleshwar Baba was nevertheless a key figure for patients, pilgrims, and residents of the ashram. A retired agricultural engineer, Kamleshwar Singh had become the resident ritual specialist *(mahant)* of the ashram. He oversaw most of the ritual activities at the *kund* and *dhuni,* conducted the regular morning and evening *āratī* celebrations, and dispensed ashes and advice to all who approached him. He taught newcomers about the meaning and mechanics of the healing rituals and made referrals to the ashram physicians, to the dispensary, or to other medical resources in the area. He was the primary liaison between the bathers and the Aghori at the Kina Ram Ashram.

My assistant and I spent most of our Sunday and Tuesday mornings sitting beside Kamleshwar Baba in the veranda between the *kund* and *dhuni,* surveying the scene around us and making small comments to one another. Even with Kamleshwar Baba's help, we needed time to make sense of all the people and activities at Krim Kund on a typical bathing day. To begin with, we noted considerable seasonal variation, with the number of bathers ranging from fewer than forty in the winter to more than two hundred in the summer, with the highest peaks during major religious festivals.[3] The ritual activities also varied greatly in any given season. In addition to observing the *kund-dhuni* sequence, one could find people lounging on the veranda, circumambulating the *samadhī* shrines, taking *darshan* at the seat of Awadhut Baghwan Ram, and cooking *bhojans* in celebration of fulfilled wishes. People came alone, with their families and friends, and sometimes with guides. Pilgrims intermingled with devotees; residents with nonresidents; ascetics with householders; and the psychotic and intoxicated with the more sane and sober.

Everyone had his or her own agenda and routines, some of which were at considerable variance with the established practices of the Kina Ram tradition. Some received corrective guidance and information with subsequent visits. Others, especially those who had a self-proclaimed expert in the group, were less receptive to advice. Kamleshwar Baba usually took a passive approach to these latter cases, as long as they did not interfere or distract the people around them. He offered advice to those who would listen and pretended to ignore everyone else. I qualify this last statement because, not long after Kamleshwar Baba and I first began comparing our observations (one of our favorite activities together), I developed a strong appreciation for how little escaped his gaze.

After seeing me spend time with Kamleshwar Baba, some patients became interested in talking with me as well. Kamleshwar Baba encouraged them to do so, and in time, my research assistant and I found a way to gain a degree of trust among returning patients and to interview them fairly unintrusively.[4] The interviews provided an important glimpse into the lived experiences of nondevotee patients who sought Aghor medicine.

SUFFER THE CHILDREN

Kamleshwar Baba often quizzed me to see if I could guess why certain people had come to the *kund*. We usually made the same predictions for infertility, and when we had an opportunity to validate them, our predictions usually turned out to be correct. People with fertility problems usually came as a couple; they were young, newly married, and often accompanied by an older maternal figure. They were often disoriented and shy, their eyes displaying an underlying sadness mixed with anxiety and desperate purpose. They rarely talked about their problems, even to Kamleshwar Baba. They behaved as if talking about infertility would make their situation all the more real and thereby seal their fate. Infertile couples were the most difficult people to approach at Krim Kund. I rarely talked with them, except on a few occasions when they initiated the conversation.

We could talk far more easily with would-be parents whose fertility concerns were limited to a desire for male children. Indian societies are strongly patriarchal, and the prevalence of dowry in this part of northern India further increases the value of sons over daughters (Dube 1996).[5] In this region, people often say that a new bride has no real status in her husband's family (and perhaps not even a real marriage) until she bears a son. At the ashram, couples without sons appeared to be less desperate than those without any children at all, but their anxieties became apparent when we talked with them.

People who desired sons were usually very discreet when seeking the Aghori. Kamleshwar Baba would prescribe the usual course of five biweekly baths plus a special preparation of Ayurvedic medicines from the dispensary if the couple could afford it. Like most Aghori, however, Kamleshwar Baba was sensitive to the Western critique of Indian androcentrism. He therefore downplayed his prescriptions when I was around. Yet despite this discretion before the fact, those who achieved success were very public afterward. Like many of the people who made contracts with "lesser" deities to gain solutions to worldly problems (cf. Obeysekere 1981), families usually agreed to conduct *saṃskāra* ceremonies for their sons, especially the *muṇḍan* (first tonsure), in conjunction with a fish *bhojan* for family, friends, and residents of the ashram.

Occasionally, however, families performed the *muṇḍan* for a girl, partly out of gratitude for a healthy baby and partly as sympathetic magic for a future boy, by celebrating for a daughter as if she were a son. Sita's family was one such case. Her parents performed two *muṇḍans* for her birth: one at Krim Kund, the other at Vindhyachal, a mountainous pilgrimage site where a famous Aghori saint and reformer once sat in meditation. "My niece had a son," she said. "So my sister-in-law's family promised if a boy was born then they would do *muṇḍan* [at those places]. Then they got a boy." Although apparently happy with her daughter, she also emphasized that she made this ritual display of gratitude at least partly out of duty and hope for a different outcome next time.

Rajesh's family presented the classic example of such a post hoc celebration. For three generations, the senior males of the family proudly gave offerings of fish and rice after the births of their sons. The family claimed relations with an Aghori baba several generations back, who directed the infant's great-grandfather to perform the *muṇḍan* at Krim Kund for all subsequent male heirs.[6] The grandfather was very happy and very willing to talk with me. He explained, "When I had two granddaughters, then I made the *manotī mangī* [a kind of divine contract] that if my daughter-in-law has a son, then I will come here to make an offering."

Rajesh's family hired a barber to perform the *muṇḍan* on the west bank of the *kund*. Afterward, the parents dipped their son five times in the tank—bathing on five separate days was necessary only for illnesses or other problems. Then they took the boy to worship at the *akhand dhuni,* after which he received ash from Kamleshwar Baba. They purchased enough fish and rice to feed themselves and most of the ashram residents, about forty people in all. The resident cooks oversaw the purchase and prepared the fish in the same large kettles they used to prepare the ashram's medications.

Kamleshwar Baba offered the first plate of food to the *akhand dhuni,* placing half of each item into the fire along with offerings of incense and a silent mantra. He waved the plate with the remaining food over the fire and returned to the kitchen, where the cooks blended the food back into the kettles in order to transform all the food from the *dhuni* into *prasād.* The family then assisted in feeding the residents, attendant guests, and finally themselves. Like most *bhojans,* the meal was eaten with a combination of solemnity and happiness. It was a sacred rite at Krim Kund: an acknowledgement and partaking of the power of Aghor. It was also a happy moment for both the family and the ashram residents:

a healthy baby among the former and a chance for the latter to eat something other than lentils that day.

As in many other countries with recent histories of high childhood mortality, young children in India are not afforded much of a social identity until they pass some risky developmental thresholds. Consequently, most of the Hindu *saṃskāras* cluster around major milestones in early childhood such as the sixth-day naming celebration, the infant's first intake of solid food, and the first tonsure, between one and two years of age (Jayaraman 2005; Pandey 1969). Significantly, these rites coincide with periods of high childhood mortality. If a child is sick during the textually prescribed times for these rites, the family delays the rites until the child is well again. One can therefore argue that Indian models of fertility are not only gendered (with a male-child preference), they are also closely tied to anxieties about child survival. Just as death entails another life in an endless cycle of rebirth, so birth entails the possibility of an early death, especially under the worldly conditions of poverty and inadequate health resources.

Parents seeking the prevention and treatment of childhood diseases were the largest group of visitors to Krim Kund. They were usually women from surrounding villages, huddled in groups, with saris covering their heads and mouths as they spoke rural Bhojpuri. For many of these women, the bath at Krim Kund was a postpartum follow-up to an earlier bath at Lolark Kund. The first bath was for the ability to have children in the first place; the second was for the children's continued survival. As with the post *mundan* celebrations, these prophylactic baths consisted of five complete immersions of the children in a single visit. The children emerged coughing and sputtering only to be quickly toweled off and held upside down for a head touch before the *akhand dhuni* and Kamleshwar Baba, at whom they stared in puzzlement while dirt-flavored ash dribbled down their chins. Such was the plight of healthy children at Krim Kund.

Except for colicky infants, the sick children were disturbingly docile. Most were emaciated, with the poor skin turgor and depressed fontanels indicative of severe dehydration. They put up little resistance when bathed, and their cries were usually weak and tearless. The parents referred to their condition as *sukhāṇḍī,* or "dryness," an apt description for infant dehydration and failure to thrive caused by enteric infections and diarrhea. Diarrhea is the second leading cause of childhood mortality worldwide, accounting for 15 to 30 percent of all deaths among

Figure 8. Man bathing
his grandson in Krim
Kund, 2000.

children under five years old around the time of my research (Enzley and
Barros 1997).

Many of the parents who brought their children to Krim Kund for
sukhāṇḍī subscribed to an etiological model of *nazar lagna* (to be
touched by the evil eye). This model was evident in the words of Vinay,
a middle-aged shopkeeper from a village just outside Banaras who came
to Krim Kund with his emaciated son at the urging of his uncle:

> I am not a doctor. Women say these things in the countryside. Some women
> say that if the child is not eating while being fed and he is not drinking or
> eating, this means that some spell has happened to him. That is why he is
> not eating, no? The main reason is, if another's child is sick, [then] for the
> welfare of that child, they [cast the spell] to another's child so that their
> child will become completely healthy. [Another reason is if] some woman is
> menstruating. If she is, then in that condition [if she] touches the child, then
> the child will be affected.

Figure 9. Man feeding
vibhuti ash to his grandson beside Krim Kund,
2000.

Although the Kina Rami did not subscribe to models of menstrual
pollution, they were equivocal about matters of sorcery. Sensitive to my
Western scientific upbringing, most Aghori were bashful about these
issues. They spoke of their treatments as placebos, explaining to me that
they were healing patients in the terms of their own beliefs. Kamleshwar
Baba tried to sound me out on my own beliefs whenever he mentioned
ghosts or spells. He often beamed at me to see if I would respond with
a look of amused disbelief. In those moments, I tried to convey as much
neutrality as I could muster. In time, Kamleshwar Baba confirmed that
his beliefs coincided with the explanations he gave to his patients.

Speaking about a five-month-old boy whose grandmother brought
him in from Bilaspur, Kamleshwar Baba said, "He got the *nazar lagi*."
He explained how a barren woman could cast the evil eye when she gazes
enviously upon a beautiful child. In this manner, the stigma of infertility

can be as contagious as a bacterial infection, taking the form of a "courtesy stigma" (Goffman 1963). Such contagion is also a common theme in other societies that link infertility to a notion of the evil eye (Reissman 2000; Inhorn 1994; Ngubane 1977). It is no wonder that infertile couples would be so secretive about their problems.

Yet the model of *nazar lagna* did not exclude an empirical and pragmatic approach to health seeking among the fertility patients at Krim Kund. Most of these patients had previously sought professional medical services, and many continued medical treatments concurrent with their ritual bathing at Krim Kund. Vinay explicitly articulated this pragmatic approach:

> Our child's condition is getting better. That is why we are coming. Otherwise, why would we be coming here? We come here to be cured. If our child will have some benefit, that is why we come here. . . . [If] our child has a fever, [then] OK, I will go to the doctor. As he has a one-hundred-degree fever and the doctor gives him medicine and injection. Then his fever goes down. So we feel that the medicine of [this Aghori] doctor has worked for our child. So we are coming here.

Such pragmatism and willingness to engage in multiple-use strategies are common in India's highly pluralistic healing environments, where particular help-seeking strategies often stem from poor geographic and financial access more than from particular health beliefs or explanatory models (Nichter 1992a; Minocha 1980; Beals 1976). Sunita gave her eighteen-month-old son medicines prescribed by a homeopath while bathing him at Krim Kund. But she emphasized that the medicines were not homeopathic: "There is a homeopath below our house," she said. "So he prescribed a syrup. It has come from a medical store. It has come from an English [i.e., biomedical] medicine store. He has not treated him with homeopathy." Further discussion with Sunita revealed that, although she would prefer to see an allopathic doctor, her financial situation limited her medical options. She was estranged from her adulterous husband, and her father-in-law was deceased. Sunita and her mother-in-law were struggling to raise her children with miniscule resources. She saw her approach as the best combination of treatments within the limits of her finances and available information.

Laxmi, the grandmother of the five-month-old boy suspected of having *nazar lagi,* stopped taking him to an allopathic doctor after spending most of her money on expensive massage oils and medications with little result. "I had so much medicine. Everybody comes to get strength from this medicine. Eighty rupees for two hundred grams in this much of a box," she said, indicating the amount with her thumb and middle finger. "I have already applied four/five boxes of this medicine. We did not get any benefit. Now he is feeling good [from the bath]. Yes, God is very kind."

Most parents with dehydrated children did not seek the services of the ashram clinic itself, nor did they purchase medicines at the ashram dispensary. Most could not afford such medicines, although Kamleshwar Baba insisted the preparations were not effective for dehydration anyway. Instead, he gave family members the *vibhuti* ash with a generous dose of advice: "Do not force feed the child while s/he is sick. . . . Make sure to give him/her water that is boiled. . . . Keep the household clean." In this manner, *kund* and *dhuni* were vehicles for preventive medicine as well as for the blessings of Aghor.

THE LEPROSY OF LEUKODERMA

Skin conditions were the second most common problem among the patients at Krim Kund. Like the infertile couples, patients with these conditions were identifiable by their efforts of concealment. They bathed in the manner of most Indians, changing their clothes beneath large pieces of cloth, but they were much more fastidious about covering their skin. They concealed as much as possible beneath long sleeves and Western-style shoes. They covered any remaining lesions by makeup or filled them in with black ink, as Anil did for his son.

Leukoderma was the most common skin problem for which people bathed at Krim Kund. Commonly associated with the subcategory of vitiligo conditions, leukoderma is a progressive depigmentation of the skin that begins with small whitish spots, *phūl* in Hindi (white spots; literally "flowers"). The condition is more difficult to notice among lighter-skinned people, but the contrast can be striking on people with darker complexions. Even within the Indian ideal of "wheatish" complexion, leukoderma presents significant camouflagelike patterns that can break up the symmetry and outline of facial features. Leukoderma is an idiopathic condition with multiple potential etiologies. Contributing variables can include autoimmune responses, contact with industrial solvents, and prolonged exposure to ultraviolet radiation. Leukoderma has a small but statistically significant tendency to run in families (Gawkrodger 1997; Pasricha 1991).

At present, the medical community has no effective biomedical treatments for leukoderma. Yet aside from causing increased sensitivity to

sunlight, the condition is benign and completely noncontagious. Nevertheless, Ayurvedic medicine places these conditions into a category of progressive skin conditions known as *kushṭh* that includes chronic eczema,
psoriasis, and Hansen's disease (leprosy). Although these conditions
have no biomedical relationship to one another, people afflicted by them
share a common experience of stigmatization by which the conditions'
social morbidity and transmissibility are much worse than the biological conditions themselves.

A classic textbook of Ayurvedic medicine, the Caraka Saṃhitā, clas-
sifies eighteen kinds of obstinate skin diseases within the category of
kushṭh (CS VII). It places leukoderma within a subcategory of eleven
kshudra kushṭha (lesser forms of *kushṭh*), separate from the seven forms
of *mahakushṭha* (greater forms) that include Hansen's disease proper.
Yet despite this categorical distinction, the Caraka Saṃhitā asserts moral
etiologies for leukoderma that are similar to those of leprosy: "Untruth-
fullness, ungratefulness, disrespect for the gods, insult of the preceptors,
sinful acts, misdeeds of past lives and intake of mutually contradictory
food are the causative factors of [leukoderma]" (CS VII: 177). It lists a
large number of less blameworthy alternatives to moral transgression,
such as a number of dietary incompatibilities. Unfortunately, however,
the dominant models for *kushṭh* were based on the most socially dam-
aging of these alternatives (cf. Weiss 1980).

Among five Ayurvedic doctors who were well known for treating skin
diseases in Banaras, four supported the moral etiologies described in the
Caraka Saṃhitā, three of whom privileged these explanations over other
Ayurvedic alternatives. Among the most vocal of these supporters was
Dr. Shastri, a professor of Ayurvedic medicine at a well-known university,
who associated the Caraka Saṃhitā use of *kshudra* for lesser conditions
with the *shūdra* (peasant) castes, linking both with lesser moral deeds:
"As many *shūdra karm* [dirty work, literally, 'the work of *shūdras*'] that
people do—to tell a lie, to sin, to give pain/trouble; all these—. . . after
some days it is obviously seen. It gets on your face. [He touched his lips.]
It is seen to the people [as, for example,] 'Those are liars.' *Kushṭh* is often
seen to them. *Kushṭh* is hereditary. So the man who does bad deeds et
cetera, after some days, I mean, it seems obvious. I mean, obvious."

Dr. Shastri linked this moral etiology to a hereditary model that combines aspects of Mendelian genetics with karmic transference:

> For instance, the parents have *kushṭh*. They had three children. Two chil-
> dren did not get *kushṭh*, [but] the third one got *kushṭh*. Now, in that, [we]
> count his fault, karma, et cetera. Both [the two] did not get *kushṭh* because

the *dosha* and karma was fine in the previous lives of both. The third got it [because] it comes from "genes." The combination of the two "genes" was bad, but in the third generation, those two boys who did not have *kushṭh* et cetera, their boys get this in the third generation. It all comes because of previous life. All these things come.

In addition to linking the two moral etiologies, Dr. Shastri believed that allopathic physicians treat both leukoderma and Hansen's disease with the same multi-drug therapy (MDT) regimen.[7] Such unique conflations of Western and Ayurvedic medicine are well documented in studies of Indian medical pluralism (Nichter 1992c; Minocha 1980).

Although Dr. Shastri's hybrid viewpoint seemed highly idiosyncratic, his model of blame was little different from that of other biomedical physicians in Banaras. One of Banaras's most reputable biomedical dermatologists stated that, with the ready availability of MDT, the only people who get advanced leprosy are those who want to become professional beggars. A medical officer of a leprosy-treatment center in a neighboring town made a similar assertion in the form of a diagnosis: "leprophilia." Although neither physician cited the sins of previous lives, each favored an etiological model that clearly pointed to the sin of deliberate self-mortification in this life.

Written into classical texts, and reinforced by medical authorities of all persuasions, cultural models of blame have strongly influenced local attitudes toward people with leprosy and leukoderma. I interviewed twenty-eight shopkeepers in the Godaulia, Lanka, and Gandhi Chouk neighborhoods who provided essential services to people with these conditions. Although my group of interviewees was too small to comprise a representative sampling, these interviews revealed several common themes that reflected Ayurvedic concepts and categories.[8] To begin with, everyone used the term *leukoderma* interchangeably with *kushṭh*. Eleven considered *kushṭh* to be a single disease that begins as leukoderma and eventually progresses to leprosy. A thirty-five-year-old clothing vendor in the Godaulia market area described the progression of this hybrid disease, beginning with the *phūl* spots: "then sores on the fingers and hands, then slowly, slowly the fingers start going away." A forty-eight-year-old bicycle-parts shop owner in Lanka stated that leukoderma begins with the *phūl* spots, and "then the pus comes. The pus gets into the fingers. The fingers stop working. After the pus comes, the fingers get into a contracted position when they sleep."

Pus does not develop in vitiligo. It is not usually a feature of leprosy either, outside of untreated secondary infections. In fact, this criterion reveals more about local perceptions of poverty and disability than of any specific health condition. One college-educated shopkeeper referred to people with leukoderma as those who "live on the ghats and speak only to foreigners," stressing that "Indians would never speak to them." He was clearly referring to the indigent people with leprosy on Dashashwamedha Ghat and the Western volunteers (including me) who worked with them. Here, the street-dwelling beggar served as a cultural prototype for local perceptions of *kushṭh* conditions, as evidenced by a recurring theme of dirt and poverty in people's etiological explanations. Citing permutations of contagion, bad blood, heredity, and spells, these models described poor and unclean people living in poor and unclean conditions.

Such models carried the blame of self-neglect. A tailor in Gandhi Chowk stated that *kushṭh* happens when "people get injured and the wounds get infected. They get hurt and do not care for themselves." His attitude was revealed by his interchangeable use of *garīb log* (poor people) and *koṛhi,* an extremely derogatory term for people with leprosy. A man with a toy stand in Godaulia was more direct in blaming the *garīb log* for their leukoderma/leprosy. "Some people do not work, so the disease just happens," he said. "They don't take care of themselves because they are lazy. They just want to start begging."

Little conceptual distance separates general models of blame and neglect from Ayurvedic models of previous sin. As one person said, "Bad people get this disease. They have hurt people and burned people and whatever they did in past lives. Bad people get it. Good people don't get it." Moreover, the triad of poverty, dirt, and blame incurs a kind of untouchability that is independent of people's notions of contagion. A vegetable seller in Lanka stated that she did not think that leukoderma is contagious, but she nevertheless did her business with those afflicted from a distance. "We don't touch them, . . . just sell them the vegetables," she said. "Lowerclass people have it. We should not touch those people anyway." Indeed, even though most people stated that they were willing to trade with people who have *kushṭh* conditions, those who sold tea and foodstuffs emphasized that they use disposable clay cups and leaf plates when serving these customers. The rest were able to drop their products into bags or hand them to people while avoiding direct contact.

Finally, even when people stated that leukoderma is "just a disease" from which they felt no direct threat, they were nevertheless cognizant of community opinion, should their interactions with the afflicted appear to be different from their manner with the people around them. A particularly enlightened restaurant owner told me that, although he might serve a person with leukoderma in his restaurant (with disposable cups and plates), he would not invite such a person into his home for fear of sullying his family's reputation.

The most accepting of Ayurvedic physicians with whom I spoke echoed these concerns. Dr. Tripati asserted that leukoderma was a "nothing thing," a simple lack of melanin and tyrosine that was neither harmful nor contagious, "but there is a social importance," he said. "If somebody is having leukoderma . . . his family members are being discarded by the society." This kind of stigmatization by association, or "courtesy stigma," greatly amplified the discredit of leukoderma and leprosy, impeding changes in public attitudes toward these conditions, even among those with biomedically approved public-health knowledge. The question remains, however, why etiological models that blame the victim seem more popular than other available explanations for these conditions.

A large discrepancy exists between the physical experiences and social experiences of illness among Indian leukoderma patients, for whom a harmless and noncontagious depigmentation can bring a lifetime of untouchability. Leukoderma is biologically distinct from Hansen's disease, yet these kushṭhs share a similar social reality. Such was the case for the leukoderma patients who came to Krim Kund. They did not complain of physical discomfort. Neither did they worry about contracting leprosy; if they did not know already, the Aghori would inform them in the strongest terms that these conditions are in no way related to one another. But this knowledge alone could hardly solve their social problems, or quell their anxieties about further depigmentation.

Sanjay was an unmarried Rajput in his midtwenties studying for his BA degree at Banaras Hindu University. He looked a bit like Rajiv Gandhi, having a combination of chiseled features and boyish looks, the symmetry of which was interrupted only by white spots on his lips and forehead. The spots on his hands and feet were somewhat less apparent, for he had filled them in with a black ballpoint pen. Sanjay tried his best to appear relaxed and nonchalant during our only interview. Yet his underlying anxiety was as obvious as his unwillingness to share his feelings about the situation. I had no intention of pushing him. I let him relate the history of his condition; how he had first noticed small spots ten years ago but did not think of pursuing treatment until they became more socially visible, while he was at the university. "At the moment I am worried," he said. "I was thinking that somehow I should [take care of] this as soon as possible. Somehow I should remove it."

Tracking the trajectory of his condition, Sanjay had felt an increasing amount of subtle discrimination among his fellow students. It distracted him from his studies. "People do not say [things] in front of me, but they keep on talking about this. So it is not good," he said. With a prompt from Sujata, my assistant, he then related his anxieties about marriage with a change in tone and drop in volume, averting his gaze from us so that we could not see the tears welling up in his eyes. Sanjay was in his senior year at the university, the time when his family was supposed to be arranging his marriage. Despite all his other advantages, however, a marriage would most likely be impossible if the spots did not go away. Sanjay faced a lifetime without the companionship and social identity that would come from having a wife and family of his own.

Sangita was an eighteen-year-old unmarried homemaker with a middle-school education. Like Sanjay, she would have been considered an attractive young woman were it not for the depigmentation on her face and beneath the black ink on her hands. By the standards of her community, Sangita was at the prime age for an arranged marriage. Yet instead she still lived with her natal family. I often saw her in the neighborhood fetching water and taking care of her younger siblings. Her mother had a chronic illness, and Sangita, as the eldest of four children, had become the family caretaker. With no other prospects, this arrangement was likely to become permanent.

Sangita was accompanied by an older male cousin who tried to interject as much as he could into the conversation. Although modest in her demeanor, Sangita was assertive enough to hold her own on matters that she felt were important. She initially denied that people in the neighborhood treated her differently from anyone else, but she later admitted that other girls in her neighborhood teased her. They did not call her names directly. "They do not say it with my name," she said. But they would ask about her condition in a strange kind of way that made her feel uncomfortable. When Sujata asked her about her marriage concerns, she replied that she was not worried about marriage because she knew that it would never take place. "It will not happen. Who will marry me?" She made this statement with such resignation that Sujata suddenly became tearful and could no longer speak. Sangita, however, was not tearful. Evidently, she was long past tears.

Sangita lived just down the street from me, and we ran into each other from time to time after the interview, exchanging nods and *namastes* (greetings) when no one else was looking. I had several opportunities to see her interactions with other women in a local alleyway where mothers often congregated while their children played. Sangita always sat quietly in the shadows beside her household doorway. I never saw her smile.

The stories of Sanjay and Sangita illustrate the two most common forms of discrimination described by the *kushṭh* patients with whom Sujata and I spoke at Krim Kund. One was a subtle form of social ostracism. Only a few patients described overt acts of verbal or physical abuse, but nearly all described the subtle cues of social distancing and the persistent sense that people were talking about them behind their backs. Agania Devi, an elderly indigent woman from a nearby village, described the experience as being displeasing to others. "I am a little bit shy. I feel shy. Some people feel bad," she said. Rakesh, a middle-aged policeman from Bihar, stated that while nobody said anything to his face at work, he felt that people looked down on him. Because of antidiscrimination laws, people did not say anything outright, but he felt a change in his work relationships, and he was definitely ostracized by some people.

Marriage discrimination was by far the greatest concern of unwed young adults and children with leukoderma and their relatives. Anil made this concern plain when Sujata and I asked about his son's marriage prospects. In contrast to the optimism he projected during visits to the ashram, Anil's response was immediately fatalistic. "Yes. Yes!" he replied. "Marriage does not happen. Actually, nothing happens." He made this announcement with the same finality and hopelessness that Sangita had shown.

The courtesy stigma of leukoderma was enough to doom the marriage prospects of an entire family, even if no family members beyond the afflicted one showed any sign of the condition. For this reason, Agania Devi hid her leukoderma from her children's prospective in-laws until the marriages were complete. Similarly, Rakesh sent his eldest sons to arrange his daughters' marriages, giving the excuse that he was on special assignment in another city. Although he denied having subsequent problems with his affines, he nevertheless avoided further visits so as not to obligate other people to interact with him. Rakesh's willing segregation from his daughters' families was a common response that patients more often implied than directly stated during the interviews. People with leukoderma tended to self-isolate, either to prevent social penalties against themselves or their families or to minimize untoward social interactions once they incurred penalties. These strategies of stigma disavowal are known, respectively, as sheltering and covering (Jones, Scott, and Markus 1984; Goffman 1963).

Anil struggled with these issues. When we asked if his son had problems with other boys when he went outside to play, Anil replied, "No, no. I do not let [him] go play with anyone else. Times are not good. Society is bad. We keep our child inside the house. We like to keep him inside the house. I have a small studio. We just go there." We learned that Anil had multiple and complex motives for sequestering his son. During his many subsequent visits, Anil related his concerns about his son's feelings in the light of community discrimination; the further effects of ultraviolet radiation, which many doctors had explained to him; and the threat of courtesy stigma to the rest of his family while he still had a chance to arrange decent marriages for his two other children.

Anil displayed a great deal of affection for his son. Yet one could reasonably expect that Anil's efforts to conceal his son's condition and sequester him from the community would have a profound impact on the boy's self-image, especially as he grew older. Social discrimination can be deeply internalized through early socialization, especially when a child experiences the effects of dominant cultural beliefs and attitudes before he or she acquires, or is fully aware of, a stigmatized condition (Goffman 1963). This presocialized internalization explains how people with Hansen's disease learn to become "lepers" [sic] in some (but not all) societies (Waxler 1981). Likewise, it is not surprising that many of the kushṭh patients at Krim Kund shared many of the attitudes and models held by the physicians and shopkeepers we interviewed around Banaras.

Anil subscribed to a model of witchcraft that was common among parents with sick children at Krim Kund. He spoke of the possibility that his son had been cursed: "It happens like this these days, that many people feed something, and by way of a mantra, it falls on somebody. Then [it moves] on to any human . . . it happens." He explained how a curse could transfer from one person to another through the medium of food, just as it could attach itself to another through the evil eye. In his son's case, the curse could have been by someone who was jealous of his good looks or who wished to remove it from his or her own child by transferring it to someone else's child. Anil described leukoderma as a form of leprosy, using a derogatory term for the latter:

> *Anil:* This is a disease of several types. Somebody gets *khoṛi*. Somebody gets *phūl*. Somebody gets it in his whole body. [My son] has a lot. Many people say that he is sick. Many people say that he has been fed.
>
> *Sujata:* What do you think?
>
> *Anil:* I think that someone has fed him. Someone has fed him.

Anil acknowledged commonly held beliefs about leukoderma and leprosy in discussing his son, even when these beliefs contradicted what Kamleshwar Baba had been telling him. He then used these same models to blame the person who had cursed his son. Likewise, Sanjay used a model of contagion to identify a close friend with leukoderma as the source of his condition. Whether assuming that the condition came about by witchcraft or infection, everyone was trying to pass along some model of blame.

No one questioned whether leukoderma should be a stigmatized condition in the first place. And though no one talked about the dirt, poverty, or laziness that the merchants described on the street, neither did anyone offer less blameworthy models, such as the dietary incompatibilities that abound in Ayurveda. Patients who relied on Ayurvedic models emphasized the intrinsic constitution of one's self or family. Rakesh's narrative was ambiguous about the distinction between heredity and contagion in believing his father to be the source of his condition. Likewise, Sangita's cousin did not question the model of "bad blood" presented by a (nonphysician) university lecturer: "In [our university] . . . Dr. Mishra used to teach us . . . regarding this disease—I mean, who can get leprosy et cetera and what all happens. I mean, all that *bhūt pret* [superstitious stuff; literally 'ghosts'] are not [true]. For this infection only happens from the decomposition of blood."

Whether by heredity, contagion, or bad blood, these etiologies spoke of the intrinsic (and therefore moral) constitution of these people's families in the absence of any other defense. No such defense was forthcoming among the leukoderma patients at Krim Kund. They sought to eliminate their marked conditions rather than the bigotry itself, to heal the illness by healing the disease. Understandably, they took a pragmatic approach; as was clear by the hierarchies of resort by which they made particular treatment decisions. Significantly, the Kina Ram Ashram was never the first choice among the leukoderma patients with whom we spoke. Nine out of the ten patient-family groups we interviewed first sought allopathic doctors for professional treatment.

Rakesh saw an allopathic doctor in Patna (the capital city of the adjacent state of Bihar) just after the first white spots appeared on his skin. Despite three years of treatment, the spots had worsened during the hot season and steadily increased with each passing year. He tried a series of homeopathic, Ayurvedic, and allopathic physicians, with no success. Sangita initially sought allopathic treatment for her leukoderma at Banaras Hindu University (BHU), just as her family did when someone was very

sick. She then tried a six-month combination of homeopathic and Ayurvedic treatments, also with no result. Sanjay, because his father worked
at the hospital, almost always used the biomedical services at BHU. Even
Anil, who strongly believed that his son had been cursed, sought allopathic treatment at BHU a year before coming to Krim Kund.[9]

These patients did not consider the Aghori their first choice of treatment, but they also did not consider Aghor medicine to be incompatible
with any subsequent treatments. Sanjay thought that bathing at Krim
Kund would complement his visits to the dermatologist. Although he
believed in the *dawā* (medicine) of the dermatologist, he had faith in the
duwā (blessing) of this place. "If there is no belief, then what does a person have?" he said. "What is in this world? Only belief. I have belief.
That is why I come here."

Sangita spoke in similar terms, although she expressed more faith in
the *dawā* of the Aghori than in their *duwā*. Rakesh also affirmed his belief
in the *dawā* and *duwā* of Aghor. He said that his previous physicians and
spiritual healers had emphasized only one form of healing at the exclusion the other. For Rakesh, the combination of *dawā* and *duwā* promised
much more than either by itself. But he already had a backup plan to see
another allopathic doctor if this combination proved ineffective.

These health-seeking patterns reveal an underlying pragmatism that
was both common among the *kushṭh* patients who came to the ashram
and independent of the differences between their stated etiological
models. Similarly, these patients showed little interest in the mechanics
of different healing modalities and did not focus much on whether they
believed in one model of treatment over another. In the religious and
medically pluralistic environment of Banaras, the relative legitimacy of
these modalities was less in question than their efficacy. The most important issue for these people was the possibility of losing their employment,
their families, and their status within the community. In the face of such
possibilities, people are more likely to seek a particular healing modality for its efficacy than for its underlying philosophy. Aghor medicine
was no exception in this regard.

THE SCHEMATA OF STIGMATA

Patients' varied approaches to Aghor medicine are most apparent when
the healing process involves a confrontation with human mortality. Death
is a major theme at the Kina Ram Ashram, the symbols of which extend
beyond the ashram's skulls and cremation ash. The central rite of the

ashram, the *kund-dhuni* healing sequence, follows the overall schema of
the Hindu cremation rites. In the *antyeshṭi saṃskāra,* mourners first bathe
the body in the Ganga before placing it on the pyre for the ultimate sacrifice. At the Kina Ram Ashram, pilgrims bathe their own bodies in Krim
Kund before making their offerings to the *akhand dhuni.* They already
understand that the *kund* is a metonym of the Ganga and that all the
sacred waters are Ganga Ma, just as "all the mothers are one."[10] And
soon they learn that the *dhuni* is a kind of cremation pyre. Most have
attended funerals and seen that only the corpse is bathed before the cremation; everyone else bathes afterward. Putting these elements together,
they come to see that the *dhuni-kund* healing sequence is a rite of symbolic self-cremation, one in which the pilgrim-patient ritually offers his
or her own self, not unlike the Aghori who meditates in the *shmashān.*
Though no patients volunteered this interpretation, one could not easily
ignore the comparison after five consecutive baths.

The bathing sequence notwithstanding, the *kund-dhuni* rite is distinguishable from the *antyeshṭi saṃskāra* insofar as people do not take
prasād immediately following the cremation of a relative. No self-
identified Hindu would think to apply or ingest the remnants of the
cremation, for to do so would constitute a form of cannibalism. Yet in
theory, such an act would complete the schema of sacrifice. The Ṛg Veda
describes how Purusha, the Cosmic Man, creates the prototype of sacrifice itself by simultaneously assuming the roles of agent, object, and
recipient of the rite (RV X: 90). As with other supposedly unorthodox
elements of Aghor *sādhanā* (spiritual practice), the taking of cremation
ash as *prasad* has some precedent in more mainstream Indian religious
traditions.

The ingestion of ash, like the bathing and shedding of clothes, sym-
bolizes a rebirth process that has strong precedents in Hinduism. The
foundational model of *saṃsāra* describes an endless cycle of (more or
less favorable) rebirths that is escapable only through a process of
moksha, or spiritual liberation. Within this cyclical schema, cultural
models of death necessarily entail those of rebirth. Parry (1982) discusses this death-rebirth schema in relation to Hindu cosmology and the
shmashān.[11] He relates the foundational schema of microcosm and
macrocosm to that of the human body and the cosmos, a recurring
theme in Hindu religious traditions. As in the cosmos, human life is
destroyed only to be re-created. The fact that the cremation grounds of
Manikarnika are juxtaposed with the site of cyclical cosmogony and cosmic destruction is no small coincidence (Eck 1983). Shiva dwells in the

shmashān, where he dances the *Naṭarāj* in his role as the causal principle in this cycle of destruction and re-creation (SP IV.1.51–65). In this
manner, death is linked to sexuality on both microcosmic and macro-
cosmic scales.

That this foundational schema of rebirth entails a connection between
mortality and sexuality finds additional support in the relationship
between the *kund* and the *dhuni,* which directly maps to that of Shiva
and Shakti, the divine manifestations of male inertia and female activity. These relationships, in turn, find their prototypes in the Ganga and
cremation fire. All sacred waters are Ganga, just as all the mothers are
one, for Ganga is mother to all (Baartmans 2000; Eck 1983). Although
Agni has his feminine consort, Svaha (the principle of oblation), he is the
one primarily associated with the element of fire, and he is the one considered to be the causal agent of sexual union (O'Flaherty 1973). These
two principles are intimately connected at the Kina Ram Ashram, where
kund and *dhuni* not only stand beside one another but are sequentially
linked within a healing rite of death and rebirth.

This regenerative principle also explains the Aghori's reputed control
over conditions of infertility. In addition to the story in which Baba Kina
Ram curses the maharaja's family with the inability to bear male heirs
for generations to come, many stories describe his curing women of barrenness and saving the lives of young children. In the most famous story
of the *kund,* Baba Kina Ram acts as an earthly avatar of Shiva, casting
his seed into the waters of Shakti as a fire into a well.

We began this analysis by examining the *kund-dhuni* healing sequence
at the Kina Ram Ashram as a symbolic rite of cremation. The juxtaposition of the rites of healing with those of death makes sense in light of
Aghor spiritual practice, which seeks to attain a liberated state by confronting one's own fears and aversions, especially those pertaining to
death. Cremation as healing also makes sense in light of the social deaths
experienced by people with leprosy and leukoderma. Although biologically unrelated, both conditions entail a progressive decomposition of a
culturally ideal body image: the secondary loss of extremities and facial
distortions in more advanced stages of untreated Hansen's disease; and
the breakup of visual symmetry through the camouflagelike patterning
of leukoderma. Insofar as the body is a material reflection of community and soul, leukoderma threatens to distort these established orders
and therefore life itself (cf. Larson 1993; Trawick 1991).

One can make a similar case for linking infertility and death. Early
child mortality and a lack of male children are both forms of infertility.

Along with barrenness itself, they are two of the most inauspicious forms of death that can befall a family. The death of an adult within a family is difficult enough, but the death of a child (or the lack of a child) threatens the perpetuation of the family over time. By means of continued infertility, the family itself may die. And insofar as the perpetuation of the family represents of the eternal cycle of *samsāra*, infertility within the family threatens the very schema of regeneration.

Kushth and infertility also entail the inauspiciousness of a social death. Given the importance of collective identities, such as the family and community "dividuality" that Marriott (1976) describes, the inability to have a family or social life because of the courtesy stigma attached to these conditions only amplifies their morbidity to cause a complete loss of family members' sociocultural identities. Death therefore occurs at the deepest psychological levels.

For surrounding communities, the relatively high prevalence of infectious diseases and child mortality in India can only heighten people's sense of vulnerability. This perceived vulnerability can, in turn, lead to discrimination and blame as coping mechanisms. As such, this situation seems to argue for safe segregation of these conditions—hiding them beneath a veil of untouchability and blame so that the average citizen need not worry, assuming that these tragedies befall only the people who deserve them. In this manner, a deformation of the body reflects a deformation of the spirit, and the curse of infertility can spread through the jealous gaze of a barren couple. To diminish the anxiety of vulnerability, people define both conditions as "other"—the curses of the undeserving and untouchable.

These coping mechanisms are manifestations of an overall fear of death—not the death that comes at the end of biological life but rather the loss of a life lived among family and friends in a social world. The death that comes at the end of life remains an abstract concept for a young person who is in relatively good health. Far more troublesome are the little deaths that lurk only one step away: poverty, disability, and all the family tragedies that threaten one's place in the ever-changing matrix of Indian society. Such little deaths are a pollution of which one must be cleansed.

PATIENT APPROACHES TO AGHOR MEDICINE

Earlier, I discussed the phenomenon in which discredited groups retain the same models of discrimination as the communities in which they have been socialized (per Goffman 1963). Clearly, the *kushṭh* patients of Aghor medicine held many of the same etiological models as the people we interviewed on the streets of Banaras. Not so clear, however, is the degree to which these patients also shared their models of blame. The shopkeepers spoke openly about their reasons for blaming the afflicted. Yet the patients were not so open about the discrediting implications of their health beliefs, and they were even less so about any negative self-assessments. Instead, they revealed their self-stigmatization indirectly—in statements indicating the polluting nature of their conditions and in reports of self-segregation. Anil's awareness of his son's stigmatization came through when he spoke of the possibility that his son would be cured: "It is light. He will begin to look clean and beautiful. All of these things should not be on somebody. Look, I am in this age; now I am in my fifties. I do not have any spots. Of course [my] skin has turned with time. But it is clean. All these things should be clean."

Anil's statement points to the popular Indian model of disease as a form of pollution for which the healing process is one of purification. This perspective is important in light of the fact that patients approach the *kund-dhuni* healing sequence in much the same manner as they approach other major sacred geographic features in Banaras. In chapter 1, I describe how foundational cultural models of transportive and transformative purification informed the way that people interacted with these sacred features. Insofar as the Kina Ram Ashram is a microcosm of Banaras and its features are diminutive models of the prototypical Ganga and *shmashān*, the pilgrim-patients might well apply these same foundational models of purification to Aghor medicine, regardless of their particular beliefs.

They indeed did so. Patients described the great powers of the ashram and the Aghori in terms similar to those they used to describe the sacred geography of Banaras. As with the Ganga, they attributed nearly unlimited powers of healing to the nondiscriminatory nature of the Aghori. Vinay, the merchant with leukoderma, summarized this attitude succinctly: "What I think is this: *Aughars* do not care about food restrictions. They consider whatever . . . comes to them as *prasād* and eat it. They do whatever [they want]. They consider country liquor as *prasād* and consume it. There is no feeling of untouchability for anything. Whatever comes to them, they just consume it. The one who does these things can be called an Aghori. They have *siddhis* [special powers]. They have tools through these *siddhis*. That is why they are called *Aughar*."

People made the connection between nondiscrimination and healing power for Aghor and Ganga alike. Meena, a retired schoolteacher who accompanied Agania Devi on her ablutions, stated that "Ganga is holy. There is no kind of evil in her. All rivers flow into her and meet in her, and Ganga takes all into her. Even so, her purity remains. In the same way are these Aghor saints."

Agania Devi affirmed this statement: "There is no darkness [i.e., sin] in it. It has taken everything in it, meaning all things should be all right [i.e., no discrimination against anything]. One should stay away from discrimination, have a simple nature, and live one's life with simplicity."

Given these beliefs, to what extent do non-Aghori patients actually adopt the attitudes and behaviors of their Aghori healers? A few people claimed to have undergone significant life changes as a result of their experiences at the ashram. Sanjay, a retired jeweler with advanced leukoderma, said that he came to the ashram after having a nightmare about snakes that suggested his misfortunes were the result of a curse. After visiting the ashram over several months, he believed that he no longer needed to fear such things, regardless of the outcome of his physical condition. Srikant, an elderly Brahmin and village leader, believed that he no longer needed to fuss so much about purity and pollution rules. His friend who accompanied him stated as such: "I told him, 'Leave all these things [purity and impurity] behind.' [Then] a lot of changes happened to him. Otherwise, he used to not eat the food touched by anybody at all and other things like this."

Nevertheless, only a small minority articulated such changes in attitude. Even these statements sounded more like formulas to please the Aghori healers or the Western researcher, referring more to ideals than to daily practice. Thus, I suggest that a better way to determine lasting attitudinal changes is to look at how patients approached the symbols of death in Aghor medicine. In particular, did they take a transformative approach to the healing process, internalizing its lessons in human mortality; or did they adopt a transportive approach, discarding the offending condition into a sacred sink with the power to whisk it away?

On the surface, patients certainly performed rituals that fit with a transformative schema of purification. This schema took shape in the way that people drank the water from the *kund* and brought it home to their family altars. It was expressed in people's willingness to consume the ashes of a cremation pyre after every bath, the *prasād* of their final sacrifice. So too was it evident in the ritual feast of fish, a creature chosen

for its indiscriminate consumption of everything within the Ganga
(including human flesh) and eaten only after participants had offered it
to the *dhuni*.[12]

In the previous chapter, we saw how the *dhuni* and the cremation pyre
lent themselves to a transformative model of purification, with these fires
resembling those of digestion and the heat generated by the austerities
of the practicing Aghori. A few patients articulated this connection when
they discussed the power of the *shmashān* and the *akhand dhuni*. Priya,
a young college student who had come in hopes of obtaining success in
her exams, described the transformative power of the *shmashān/dhuni*
in elemental terms:

> *Priya:* When a human dies, then he himself is made of ash and he goes into
> that ash. So in the form of ash, which is the form of a complete
> human being. So everything is from ash.
>
> *Ron:* So what happens when the body turns into ash?
>
> *Priya:* The body goes away from [the *shmashān*]. But just the soul from
> there because I believe this is the source. I believe that reincarnation
> happens, the soul transfers. So whatever he leaves behind that
> remains is this ash. [It is the place] where one becomes free. That
> is why this place is holy.

For Priya, the *dhuni* and *shmashān* were the loci of ultimate transformation: places where the soul was distilled from its physical form. Agania
Devi gave a similar explanation of the *dhuni*'s power, stating that "a
human is made of five elements." Having listed these elements in Sanskrit, she said that "out of five a human is born and he goes back to these
five." Like many others, she evoked the cycle of rebirth through the
transition of death and equated this transformation with the purifying
powers of the *akhand dhuni*.

Yet despite her transformational approach to these ritual elements, and
affirmations about a life of simplicity and nondiscrimination, Agania
Devi and her family took a strongly transportive view of Aghor medicine.
She said that her family had placed the burden of responsibility for their
problems upon the Aghori. "Now we have 'poured' the burden of these
problems on Baba," she said. "He will do it." She used the same term,
dālnā (to pour), as the people on the riverbank who spoke about the
dumping of pollution in the Ganga. As with the Ganga, the purifying
power of the Aghori was closely linked to their capacity to take on the
pollution of other people. Like the Ganga, the Kina Ram Ashram and
its sacred geography represented a kind of cosmic sink in which to pour

one's problems. A process of externalization and excretion transported the pollution of disease was from self to other.

This transportive approach did not require patients to identify closely with the symbols of their mortality to benefit from them. They did not have to identify with Aghor philosophy to obtain Aghor healing, just as they did not have to identify with the *dhuni-kund* healing sequence as a rite of their own cremation. So though most patients recognized that nondiscrimination was indeed a source of healing power, few sought this quality for themselves. The Aghori, not their patients, were surrogates for nondiscrimination.

However, these attitudes were neither universally definitive nor absolutely fixed. The transportive and transformative were no more exclusive for the bathers at Krim Kund than for the bathers in the Ganga. This chapter merely points to the predominance of a transportive approach to purification among nondevotee patients who pursued the sacred geographic modality of Aghor medicine. I also found important exceptions to this generalization. Later chapters show how the relative influence of these approaches reverses in Aghor disciples, most of whom were once nondevotee patients themselves.

CHAPTER 3

The Reformation

Eleven Aghori ascetics have succeeded Baba Kina Ram as the head of his lineage from 1771 to the present day (table 1). However, there is little available information about eight of them. Aghor was thought to have had a renaissance under the sixth head of the lineage, Baba Jainarayan Ram (1882–1927), who apparently reconsolidated the organization and improved upon its teachings and healing practices (Asthana 1994b). Unfortunately, a dispute after his death led Jainarayan's natal family members to break off from the lineage, taking most of its internal documents with them. The leadership became increasingly isolated over the next thirty years, with the membership declining and ashrams and shrines falling into disrepair. The Aghori published very little until their reformation.

The Kina Ram lineage underwent a major transformation between 1961 and 1978, a period leading up to the succession of Baba Rajeshwar Ram (Burhau Baba) by Awadhut Bhagwan Ram.[1] These two renunciates could not have been more different in their style of teaching, overall manner, and representation of Aghor to the rest of the world. Although most postreform disciples strongly maintained that these two babas shared the same underlying philosophy, their external differences had a profound effect on the membership, practices, and structure of the organization, just as they have had a profound effect on the practice of Aghor medicine today.

TABLE I. LINEAGE OF BABA KINA RAM
AND HIS SUCCESSORS

Name	Years of Leadership
Baba Kina Ram	Unknown–1771
Baba Bija Ram	1771–81
Baba Dautar Ram	1781–1846
Baba Gaibi Ram	1846–57
Baba Bhavani Ram	1857–82
Baba Jainarayan Ram	1882–1927
Baba Mathura Ram	1927–41
Baba Saryu Ram	1941–44
Baba Dalsingar Ram	1944–49
Baba Rajeshwar Ram	1949–78
Baba Siddhartha Gautama Ram	1978–present

NOTE: This lineage comprises the renunciates who sat at Krim Kund following Baba Kina Ram's arrival (date unknown). However, the Aghori consider the first head of the lineage before the establishment of Krim Kund to be Lord Dattatreya in the guise of Baba Kalu Ram.
SOURCE: Asthana 1994b.

BURHAU BABA

In many ways, Burhau Baba epitomized the popular stereotype of an Aghori.[2] He was a large, imposing man with a shaven head and severe expression who usually wore nothing but sandals. People typically described him in three phrases, often with one or more repetitions of *bahut*:

> *Bahut bahut mazbūt the.* ("He was very, very strong.")
> *Bahut bahut mote the.* ("He was very, very fat.")
> *Bahut bahut sharab pite the.* ("He drank very, very much.")

Burhau Baba was known for consuming supernatural quantities of country liquor, as well as marijuana from a *chillum* (clay pipe) that his disciples kept filled and ready. His manner was fierce, and he often gave his "blessings" through the medium of profanity and the business end of his staff to anyone who had the courage to come within his range.

Burhau Baba was a regular presence at the *shmashān* of Harischandra Ghat, where the Dom funerary attendants I interviewed continued to speak of his legendary strength. They told me that he would stand motionless for hours while wading chest deep in the river during the winter. He would visit the *shmashān* at all hours of the day and night, always

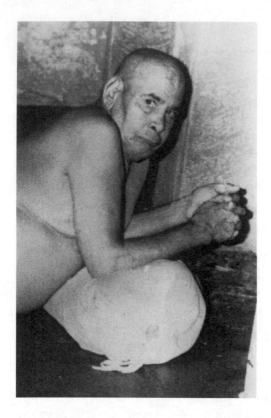

Figure 10. Baba Rajeshwar
Ram (Burhau Baba), date
unknown. Courtesy of the
Sonoma Yoga Ashram.
Photographer unknown.

returning to the ashram with an armload of wood for Baba Kina Ram's
dhuni. Baba Rajeshwar Ram enjoyed spending time with his Dom devotees, either in the *shmashān* or at the Kina Ram Ashram, where he often
held fish *bhojans* (sacred feasts) well into the night with the Dom raja at
his side.

Local men recalled Burhau Baba from their boyhood, telling stories
that sounded like urban legends of the "mean old man down the street."
Hari Baba said that in his boyhood, long before he joined the lineage
and became a baba himself, he once took *darshan* from Burhau Baba on
a whim while walking home from school. After the boy bowed to this
imposing figure, Burhau Baba looked at him sternly and said, "What are
you doing here? Go to school!" (Ram 1997: 3). Another local man,
Ramuji, recalled his boyhood when he used to play with other children
on the west side of Krim Kund, before the wall was built around it. One
time, when Ramuji was about ten or eleven years old, Burhau Baba
caught hold of him and made him sit down by the *dhuni*. He offered the

Brahmin boy some country liquor. The boy declined as politely as possible. Burhau Baba then exclaimed, "Well, then, what are you doing here, sister fucker?!"[3] He then chased the boy off the ashram grounds.

Without a doubt, Baba Rajeshwar Ram was a colorful figure. The Kina Rami were quick to point out, however, that as with most Aghori babas, there was more to Burhau Baba than met the eye. He was an educated man of Kshatriya origin who had traveled extensively throughout South Asia and fought for Indian independence before becoming an Aghori in his later years. Many believed that he had some method to his apparent madness, providing unforgettable lessons on material detachment. Burhau Baba was, if anything, a radical nonmaterialist.

Pagala Baba, a disciple of Baba Rajeshwar Ram and sometime co-caretaker of Baba Puran Ram's *samādhi* shrine, recalled how his guru redistributed money as quickly as it was given to him. Burhau Baba was a favorite customer of cycle rickshaw drivers, to whom he often paid a month's worth of wages for a single day of service. He often threw coins to groups of children only to chase them away with his staff when they tried to pick them up. Pagala Baba also recounted a well-known story about a wealthy couple who donated a fine shawl to Burhau Baba. He promptly threw the shawl into the *dhuni* fire and sent away the horrified couple, who did not realize that he had just made a sacrifice of their offering. Baba Pryadarshi Ram, one of the senior-most babas in the lineage today, affirmed this story, citing that Burhau Baba was notorious for suddenly tearing off the jewelry or *mala* necklaces of visitors and tossing them into the *dhuni* or the *kund*.

Along with the intensity with which he conducted his practices, Baba Rajeshwar Ram's radical nonmaterialism was considered a major indicator of his sincerity by both supporters and detractors. Just as people take Baba Kina Ram's self-sacrifice as proof of his sincerity, Baba Rajeshwar Ram's austerity and penchant for the redistribution and destruction of material resources left him above suspicion, with few people ascribing ulterior motives to his actions, such as they often cynically attribute to other renunciates.

As an "old-style" Aghori, Baba Rajeshwar Ram had the luxury of rejecting goods and money, for he was even more independent of them than most Indian renunciates were. Parry (1994) sums up this situation well, describing Aghori asceticism as the ideal solution to the dilemma of the religious renunciate, who must otherwise rely upon the gifts of householders while attempting to transcend the material world. Although even the most hard-core *kāpālika* (skull-bearing ascetic) was unlikely to fully realize this ideal, it nevertheless speaks to the relative freedom and sincerity with which Burhau Baba and his predecessors were able to pursue their spiritual practices.

Evidently, Burhau Baba had good reasons to be on his worst behavior. His verbal and physical abuses were bound to have a self-selective effect on visitors, ensuring a high degree of motivation among them, and minimizing time wasted on sycophantic charms and idle chitchat. The latter was a common complaint among Aghori ascetics, who remarked on the way that trivial interactions drained their time and energy when the days were otherwise filled with visitors seeking help for all manner of illnesses, family conflicts, wedding arrangements, crop planning, and school examinations.

> *Hari Baba:* Most of the time [Burhau Baba] had to put on that kind of façade to find a seclusion [because] people would just come to him for blessings, and this and that. Just look at [this busy day]. [We all laugh.] You don't get an edge!
>
> *Pryadarshi Baba:* The reason for that was this: the one who dared to come close to him [while] Baba is swinging the *daṇḍa* [staff], if he does not get the stick on him then he does not get the blessing. Some people are going and saying, "I will get two *daṇḍas*," but he is not even getting one. So the one who is the devotee, only he is getting the *daṇḍa* of Baba.

People commonly believe that the blessings of the guru can come in many forms and that the benefits of these blessings are often proportional to the intensity of their transmission. In keeping with this view, the old-style Aghori are not alone in conveying their blessings in the form of a beating. I learned this lesson the hard way after prostrating before a renunciate of the Naga lineage one day, only to have him "bless" me with a pair of steel tongs across my jaw.[4] I discovered that I was not alone. During the grand celebration of Kumbha Mela, police are needed to keep crowds of people from soliciting beatings by diving in front of the Nagas as they approach the Ganga to bathe. Little did I know my good fortune.[5]

This trial-by-fire approach to religious healing evokes a schema of reciprocating actions and reactions. This schema may seem familiar to an American reader, brought up under the theories of Newtonian mechanics and the meritocratic ethos of "You get out of it what you put into it." Within the domain of Indian religious traditions, however, the action-reaction schema finds its ideal prototype in the economics of ritual sacrifice. One offers something to get something, with the understanding that one must give even more to get even more out of exchanges between the human and the divine.

Action-reaction is present in the power dynamics of the *havan* and in the cremation rites of *antyeshṭi saṃskāra*. If the greatest sacrifice of the dead is to offer their bodies to the *havan* of the cremation pyre, then for the Aghori, the greatest sacrifice of the living is to identify fully with those corpses as representing one's own mortal destiny. Whether people approached Burhau Baba for healing or salvation, this "old-style" Aghori ensured that his visitors had ample opportunity to confront their mortality.

Spiritual teaching notwithstanding, controversy still remained among the Aghori about the use of intoxicants by Burhau Baba and his "old-style" disciples. The postreform Aghori divided into two camps on the topic of Burhau Baba's alleged drinking. Some conceded that he drank alcohol, but they maintained that the liquor did not affect him: that he would act drunk and crazy in one moment and be completely sober and lucid in the next. Others, such as Pryadarshi Baba, subscribed to the view that, like Burhau Baba's fierce persona, his drinking was simply an act for distancing himself from other people: "He did not drink anything. Neither did he get drunk from [alcohol]. In society, people come to *Aughar* people with big hopes and so many hopes [that] they irritate a lot. They don't give [Baba] time from morning to evening. If he drinks rainwater from a bottle, then people think that he is getting drunk. He hits his staff on the ground to get some leisure from these people. So he had to do this drama play, and they say he used to drink a lot."

Hari Baba offered additional reasons. He thought that drinking might have been a way for the Aghor guru to test his disciples. Alcohol allowed the guru to expose a disciple's real personality, after the drinking removed the person's inhibitions. "Sometimes people's personalities change when they get drunk," he said. "That personality is the real personality." Another possible reason was that in the act of drinking, the guru gave the Aghori a way to transcend yet another Brahminical aversion. "But once you've done this you can move on and forget about it," he said. Still, many reformed Kina Rami continued to use small amounts of alcohol as a traditional offering in certain rites. They also occasionally prescribe alcohol to reduce a disciple's initial anxiety when confronting a difficult challenge in his/her spiritual practice. Such challenges usually surround issues of death.

Pryadarshi Baba: The consumption of [alcohol] in the form of a game [is
used] to remove fear in the beginning. The one who is
coming and going [in the *shmashān*], his fear will be
removed in the first stage. Please give it up later. But
later [some] people are not able to give it up. Because of
not giving it up, it becomes a house of bad name. . . .

Hari Baba: So it is a medicine rather than [an indulgence]. If we take
too much, it will become a poison.

The controversy over Burhau Baba's relationship to alcohol was unresolved among the postreform Aghori, but everyone agreed that intoxicants were a poison to many of the disciples around him. "They would
offer a little bit of wine to the *dhuni*, and then drink the rest themselves,"
one devotee recalls. But Hari Baba cautioned that such indulgences are
not part of Aghor practice if they are done with attachment. "If it is an
addiction, it is not Aghor *sādhanā*," he said, asserting that most of the
people who engaged in these practices with Burhau Baba were alcoholics
rather than genuine Aghor practitioners.

My observations support this latter assertion. Bantu Mishra and I
spent many nights with Burhau Baba's "old-style" disciples at various
shrines and tucked-away locations around Banaras. I consumed large
quantities of intoxicants as *prasād* at these gatherings. Yet of the two
dozen or so self-described devotees that we sat with, only three seemed
more focused on Aghor philosophy than on ganja and alcohol. I saw this
pattern in action on New Year's Eve, when my fiancée and I celebrated
the Gregorian year 2000 with several of the old-style "devotees" at
Harischandra Ghat. We had come from a nice dinner with the Mishra
family, followed by chanting at the Kina Ram Ashram. As midnight
approached, I thought it appropriate to usher in the new millennium
while meditating in the *shmashān*. We went to the second level of a concrete platform overlooking a *dhuni* where Burhau Baba's disciples were
drinking low-grade whiskey and smoking a *chillum* while a family cremated a relative about fifty feet away from us. Intoxicated though these
devotees were, they were careful not to disturb our meditation. Afterward, they invited us to join them in celebration. We agreed.

Five men sat around the fire. Three were ascetics whom I knew as
longtime disciples from Burhau Baba's era. Two were local fishermen
whom I did not recognize. I was expecting a celebration and had come
prepared with a pint of Irish whiskey to supplement the "pouch" that
they had been drinking.[6] I knew one of the ascetics, Lal Baba, to be a
sincere man who was dedicated to his *sādhanā*. He took my offering as

an opportunity to do a *chakra pūjā*, an Aghor practice of offering alcohol to the *dhuni* out of a skull and then partaking of the *prasād* from the same container while passing it around in a circle. A small glass took the place of the traditional skull, from which Lal Baba poured a small amount of whiskey into the *dhuni*. One of the fishermen, fully drunk already, displayed his piety with much hyperbole during the rite. Yet his manner suddenly changed when the glass was passed to him. *"Jūṭhā!* This is *jūṭhā* [polluted leftovers] you are giving me!"[7] He was offended that we passed the glass to him without washing it first. He did not notice that we had been passing it among ourselves without washing it. Hari Baba later explained that drinking out of the same unwashed container (skull or not) was one of the most important features of the *chakra pūjā*, "but if that person was thinking of that after being drunk, then obviously he was not there for doing any Aghor *sādhanā* [spiritual practice]. He was there for getting drunk."

I discuss the consumption of alcohol and other antinomian practices in greater detail in subsequent chapters. I simply note here that such practices were supposed to be exercises for overcoming aversions that would impede the disciple from attaining a nondiscriminatory state of mind. When abused, however, these practices could cause people to sink into deeper states of attachment. For this latter reason, Burhau Baba's successor, Awadhut Bhagwan Ram, sought more socially acceptable alternatives for confronting human aversions.

SARKAR BABA

In the biographies of Awadhut Bhagwan Ram, or Sarkar Baba ("kingly father"), written by his postreform disciples, the reformer's life closely parallels that of Baba Kina Ram (cf. Ram 1997; Asthana 1994a, 1994b).[8] Like Baba Kina Ram, Sarkar Baba was born into a family of landowning Rajputs in rural Bihar. Even as a child, he had a reputation as a renunciate and healer. He left home at an early age and drew a significant following of devotees wherever he traveled. Like Baba Kina Ram, he was led to Krim Kund by a goddess, who appeared to him as a kind but mysterious old woman. The old woman directed him to bathe in the Ganga, where he cast aside his *lungī* as a symbol of worldly renunciation.[9] The woman then led him in a *pūjā* and pointed the way to the Kina Ram Ashram. Bhagwan Ram was fourteen years of age.

The young disciple's first meal of fish and rice in the ashram was a considerable challenge for someone who had been raised in a family of

Figure 11. Portrait of Awadhut Bhagwan Ram (Sarkar Baba) during his visit to Sonoma, California, 1992. This photograph is the most popular portrait of Sarkar Baba in India. Courtesy of the Sonoma Yoga Ashram. Photograph by Ari Marcopoulos.

Vaishnava (Vishnu-worshipping) vegetarians: "Even though he was hungry, he ate just a little of the rice and, when no one was looking, dumped the rest of the meal into the pond nearby. At the moment the food fell into the water, he knew instinctively that if he were to stay in this ashram and progress on the path of Aghor, he would have to give up discriminating between what was 'pure' and 'impure'" (Ram 1997: 15). He eventually overcame his aversions, consuming not only fish but alcohol. He also kept his guru's *chillum* perpetually filled with ganja, just as he kept the perpetual fire of the *dhuni* stoked with cremation wood.

Many local tales describe the younger Bhagwan Ram and his guru on the cremation grounds. Some of them are more believable than others. A few stories report that Sarkar Baba used to sit on corpses at Manikarnika Ghat and sometimes snatch meat off corpses before mourners beat him away. My Dom informants doubted such stories. They attested to the near impossibility of performing such acts in public without provoking a riot. They maintained that the Kina Ram Aghori have always respected the privacy and sanctity of cremation rites, just as they have expected respect for their own practices. Pryadarshi Baba and Hari Baba stated that to confront one's own fears, one had to perform cremation-ground practices alone in an isolated *shmashān*. Banaras, with its two main cremation ghats located in the heart of the city, was hardly the place for this kind of *sādhanā*. It is therefore unlikely that anyone ever witnessed Sarkar Baba, or any other Aghori, performing such acts at these locations.

Tall tales aside, everyone agreed that Sarkar Baba spent a lot of time in the *shmashān* and that he engaged in other kinds of difficult practices. Kamleshwar Baba said that Burhau Baba and his disciple spent long winter hours in the waters of Krim Kund and the Ganga, and they fasted for many days while sitting alone in wooded areas. A prominent Bengali disciple told of her first meeting with Sarkar Baba in the early 1970s. He showed up at her door wearing a long red *kurta,* and carrying only a staff and a small satchel. Skeptical of holy men, the woman and her husband reluctantly played the role of hosts. Planning for food restrictions and separate facilities, they were surprised by Sarkar Baba's easygoing nature and complete lack of dietary preferences. He ate one meal a day and was seen drinking only alcohol from a special container in his bag during the entire visit. Yet he never exhibited signs of drunkenness. His disposition remained even and calm throughout his visit. Sarkar Baba invited the husband to join him in a visit to an infamous *shmashān* at Tara Peeth just outside Calcutta. Charmed and intrigued by his unusual guest, the husband agreed to join him. He returned home an Aghor disciple the following morning.

Not long after his visit to Tara Peeth, Sarkar Baba stopped using intoxicants altogether. He banned them from his new ashram just across the river from Banaras. Until that time, he had been surrounded by many people of questionable devotion. Following the ban, many of them left the ashram and never returned. But Sarkar Baba gained many more devotees than he had lost. He sought to make Aghor more accessible to the general population and presented a kinder face to his visitors than that of his stick-wielding guru. As a result, he began attracting a large number of new devotees.

Many of these changes grew out of another kind of antinomian practice that had been associated with the Aghori since the day that Baba Kina Ram first put the mantra in Krim Kund: the healing of people with leprosy and other skin diseases. The Kushth Seva Ashram (Leprosy Service Ashram) in Parao began as a collection of straw huts on several acres of donated land. There, Sarkar Baba and his resident disciples manufactured and dispensed Ayurvedic medicines and cohabited with their inpatients.

Mr. Asthana, one of the founding organizers of the clinic, described these early days:

> Formerly, at the time of the beginning of the institution, the patients were residing in the huts. A very long hut was prepared. And the bamboo beds were placed [there while] treatment was going on in the clinic. In the beginning, for fifteen or twenty days, I worked as compounder [pharmacist] or doctor. There had been no doctor or compounder. I was doing the services of the patients with open hands, no gloves, no . . . fear of getting infection, et cetera.

Sarkar Baba modeled these behaviors himself, sitting with patients on their beds and touching them without fear or aversion. He held his closest disciples to the same standards. Asthanaji continued:

> In the evening, whatsoever is prepared in the kitchen, we take there our meal. So first, before taking our meal . . . the meal is sent to Baba Bhagwan Ramji or Baba Siddarth Gautam Ramji; then on the patients, they are being served; then the persons in *sādhanā*, et cetera . . . standing in the ashram, living in the ashram, they get their feed. It was our routine. And this routine was a very big power for the patients. And you can say it was a very big . . . idea to develop empathy [with] the patients.

This idea was big indeed, for this kind of empathy entailed a confrontation with people's vulnerability to a dreaded disease. It was an effective form of Aghor *sādhanā;* whereas most Hindus were willing to sit in the *shmashān* out of necessity, and some for spiritual gain, very few had the courage to sit on the cots of leprosy patients, much less eat with them or clean their wounds. The approach at the ashram was analogous to the penitent healing of leprosy in medieval Europe, only it went against a much stronger set of pollution and purity taboos (Ell 1994). In this manner, Sarkar Baba shifted Aghor practices and gave them a more worldly orientation; moving from the embrace of ritually polluted substances to that of ritually polluted people. At the same time, he accomplished these changes without making any large breaks with Aghor tradition. On the contrary, his reforms built upon precedents established at the founding of the lineage. Thus, if Baba Kina Ram could heal people with leprosy, then so could his successors. Eventually, Sarkar Baba's circle of disciple volunteers expanded to a core of physicians who ran a permanent outpatient clinic and separate living facilities for sixty inpatients. Despite the addition of professional staff, Sarkar Baba kept a strong hand in the treatment process, personally modifying most of the medications and offering his blessing as a key ingredient.

With his increasing reputation as a healer, Sarkar Baba attracted a large number of devotees throughout the country, many of whom came from the upper strata of Indian society. He took full advantage of this situation, marshaling further resources to establish Sri Sarveshwari Samooh, a secular organization that provided low-cost schools and free clinics in almost 150 ashrams throughout northern India. At the same time, he pursued further reforms in the areas of gender, marriage, and family for mainstream Indian society via this newfound influx of householder devotees.

Once again, Sarkar Baba found precedents for these reforms in the early days of the Kina Ram tradition, especially in linking goddess worship and the status of women in northern India. Although the Kina Rami are a Shaivite sect, they are distinguished from many other self-identified Aghori by their worship of the Goddess in many forms. With the exception of finding a trident planted beside a *dhuni* or a *shivalingam* (phallic representation of Shiva) resting upon a *samādhi* shrine, one is hard-pressed to find images or iconography outside the original ashram that reference anything but a goddess or a guru. Most Aghor *bhajans* (devotional songs) and prayers are dedicated to one of several goddesses. *Navarātri*, the "nine nights" of the goddess, which most Kina Rami celebrate twice a year, is the foremost religious festival. There is even a popular photograph of Sarkar Baba when he miraculously appeared as the goddess, complete with makeup and sari. The Kina Rami explain that they dwell on Shakti precisely because they identify with Shiva, for that is what Shiva himself does. Thus, by worshipping Shakti, the Aghori *becomes* Shiva. Shakti is the energizing principle that complements the otherwise inanimate essence of Shiva, a common theme in tantric traditions that takes from in the common saying "Without Shakti, Shiva becomes *shav* [a corpse]." Lakshmi, a college student and resident disciple of the Kina Ram ashram, described the situation in metaphysical terms: "Without the name Shakti, the Shiva is incomplete. So both are equal and both have equal rights and equal power." In the Kina Ram tradition, the place of the feminine is higher still, for though Shiva may worship Shakti as his divine consort, the Aghori claim that this kind of relationship is usually problematic for humans, who lack the strength to tame her as a lover. Instead, they encourage the devotee to see her as the Divine Mother, for a mother would never harm her own children. She is guardian, mentor, and nurturer to be respected in all her manifestations, especially the worldly ones.

Sarkar Baba interpreted this worship of the Divine Mother in highly practical terms, particularly by encouraging respect for women and girls within a family setting, albeit within the parameters of traditional sex roles. Asked to compare the status of women within Aghor with that in other Hindu religious traditions, another female resident replied, "Actually, here women are given a very appropriate regard. Sarkar Baba has given a very high level to women. For instance, he once said: 'I am very proud that this [organization] is in the name of women.'. . . and he used to give this education to women on how a woman should be kept . . . and how one should behave to her husband."

Although these latter comments may not seem progressive by European or North American standards, they are revolutionary for this part of northern India, where sex ratios are strongly skewed toward male children. The 1991 Census of India reports that in the state of Uttar Pradesh, the literacy rate of males (0.56) is more than twice that of females (0.25), and the National Family Health Survey of 1998–99 reports that 36 percent of adult women display signs of undernutrition.[10] Moreover, 22.4 percent of women reported having been physically mistreated since the age of fifteen, with 13.5 percent reporting physical abuse within the twelve months prior to the survey. At a more local level, many Banarsi residents state that men in the community may give offerings to the Goddess, only to beat and rape their wives after returning home drunk the same night. That Sarkar Baba would link devotion to the goddess with respect for women in the home is a significant improvement over the stance of many other sects that have focused more on orthopraxis in the temple than on ethical behavior in daily life.

Sarkar Baba elevated the status of his own mother from that of a mere widow to that of a renunciate within the Kina Ram lineage. He had refused the vows of renunciation until arrangements were made for the support of his parents. He also insisted that all his renunciate disciples continue to visit their families for as long as their mothers were alive.[11] He taught that husbands should honor their wives and sisters as the Divine Mother in her form as a teacher (Ram 1997). He also sought to eliminate dowry and created a simpler, less expensive marriage ceremony that would not overburden his disciples with debt. Within that ceremony, husband and wife made an oath that they would not bar the marriages of their own children according to caste (Ram 1997).

Despite these relatively progressive reforms, however, the worldly reorientation of Aghor posed significant challenges to its membership. Chief among them was the threat that Aghori would develop an attachment to money and power, the new intoxicants of this tradition. Sarkar Baba found himself in a dilemma common to many famous religious leaders, seeing his ascetic lifestyle challenged by the trappings of worldly affairs. Kina Rami who had been around during this transition insisted that such changes were merely superficial and that the essence of Aghor *sādhanā* had not changed. Mr. Asthana commented,

> As far as the *sādhanā* is concerned, there is no change. . . . The living, the talking, these things have been changed. But the *sādhanā* is at the same state as it had been. . . . The difference here was [that] in between the period of Baba Bhagwan Ramji and Baba Rajeshwar Ramji was Baba Rajeshwar Ram's time. . . . There had been the mentality that the saints living aloof from the society, free from all the accessories, luxurious materials. They were [seen] as a group of saints. But since my childhood, the education started taking a big field in the society. . . . Persons living in [the other] life, [who were] neglected away from the society, [who made] a poor living, they were being neglected. Glamorous persons having all luxuries with them were being regarded as the persons to follow, to hear their words, et cetera. So Baba Bhagwan Ramji changed the living of the ashram and saints, et cetera. He took all the luxurious accessories around him so that . . . "the educationists, all kinds of persons may reach up to me and get the knowledge of the real life."

Even the most skeptical observers attested to Sarkar Baba's apparent simplicity in the face of the worldly trappings around him. I observed a similar stance among his successors. Even the most skeptical outsiders reserved their criticisms for the newer generation of householder disciples and did not fault their ascetic teachers. Such criticisms often focused on a growing materialism and casteism within the lineage. Most such comments came from the Doms and fishermen who had spent a lot of time with Baba Rajeshwar Ram. Kalu Das, a Dom and Kina Ram disciple since early childhood, lamented that many of his fellow caste members had stopped coming to the Kina Ram Ashram after the death of Burhau Baba. He claimed that the higher-caste ashram residents had since given the Doms a much cooler reception and that they rarely invited them for *bhojans* of fish and rice anymore. Several Doms complained about having to sign a register when they entered the ashram and were angry that the old gate facing Harischandra Ghat had been sealed off and replaced with a new one "at the back."

The ashram residents explained that they were reluctant to host some of these Doms and fishermen because of their history of drinking and rude behavior. They noted that many of the Doms demanded special status, that they wanted the best seats at the *bhojans*, and that they wanted to be exempt from entering their names in the register even though everyone else had to sign. These explanations seemed reasonable; however, the new policies nevertheless set a different tone for communal relations. Commensality is an important rite for establishing and reestablishing social bonds and status in Indian communities. Consequently, the Aghori feast presented one of the few opportunities the Doms had to assert a higher status outside the *shmashān*. Although signing a guest register might seem a minor formality for some, it was a greater obstacle for illiterate disciples. Finally, these changes seemed especially poignant in the context of the changing ashram architecture. When the main gate shifted to the other side of the ashram, it literally turned its back on the old neighborhood beside Harischandra Ghat in favor of the newer and more affluent Ravindrapuri Extension. Whether the slight was intended or not, one could not help but draw a parallel between this move and the gentrification of the Aghori membership.

Almost seventeen years passed between the time that Baba Bhagwan Ram first established Sri Sarveshwari Samooh and the death of Baba Rajeshwar Ram. During that time, the two babas promulgated their respective styles of Aghor teaching, all the while maintaining a guru-disciple relationship that appeared to be complicated and difficult. Such was the case even in the early days, when the younger baba resided in the Kina Ram Ashram. One story describes how the young *chela* (disciple) locked all the doors and gates at the ashram and threw the keys into a well. When his guru redressed him for this misbehavior, he replied, "Look, all the locks are opened." And they had all opened on their own accord.[12] This story recounts one of Sarkar Baba's most famous miracles, but it also brings a metaphysical dimension to the tumultuous relationship between guru and disciple during their last few years of coresidence in the Kina Ram Ashram.

Their differences became more apparent after Sarkar Baba established his ashram across the river at Parao. Hari Baba described the elder guru's exclamation when he heard that intoxicants had been prohibited at the Parao ashram: "I raised you to keep my *chillum* lit, and now you ban it from your ashram?" Burhau Baba sometimes strolled across the bridge to make unannounced visits to the Parao ashram. When a devotee was able to call ahead or spot him on the bridge, Sarkar Baba would ask what kind of mood his guru was in and whether he had been drinking. A well-known story recalls the day that Burhau Baba came calling upon the ashram when the younger Baba was absent. Burhau Baba commanded all residents to assemble in a row and empty everything from their pockets. He then collected all their money, watches, and jewelry and distributed the items to a passing beggar. The story reinforces the elder

Figure 12. A rare photograph of Baba Siddhartha Gautama Ram
(Gautam Baba) performing *havan* at the *akhand dhuni* during Lolark
Chāth, 2000.

Aghori's attitude toward material possessions and his dramatic methods
of "encouraging" a similar attitude in anyone within range of his hand
or his staff.

In his last year of life, Burhau Baba circulated a flyer around the city
that read: "Beware of Bhagwan Ram. He is not my disciple!" But soon
thereafter, Burhau Baba offered his disciple the opportunity to succeed
him as head of the lineage. Hari Baba described the most accepted interpretation of these apparently conflicting acts: "Most people assumed,
when they saw the flyer, that Baba Rajeshwar Ram did not want his disciple to get too outwardly involved with the problems of society," albeit
with the disclaimer that "the actions of Gurus are incomprehensible"
(Ram 1997: 36–37). This explanation addressed a major metaphysical
tension between worldly and otherworldly approaches to the teaching
and practice of Aghor. Sarkar Baba declined the invitation to succeed his
guru, offering instead a young boy of unknown origins whom he had
adopted and raised to be the next designated head of the lineage, Baba
Siddhartha Gautama Ram. I suspect that Sarkar Baba understood that
his kingly role as the head of a large social-service organization precluded

him from simultaneously assuming a more priestly role as the head of the lineage. Ritual and temporal power were obviously interchangeable and intertwined among the postreform Aghori, and no one doubted that Sarkar Baba would be the power behind the throne for many years to come. Nevertheless, his refusal to head the lineage suggested that these roles should be as segregated as possible. This stance would also explain why Sarkar Baba originally designated a householder to head Sri Sarvesh-wari Samooh after his physical death.[13]

Having suffered from diabetes and chronic renal failure for many years, Sarkar Baba "took *samādhi*" in 1992 while in his midfifties.[14] Such an early demise is often considered inauspicious for an Indian saint, whose long life span is often held as proof of miraculous powers. Most Aghori turned this reasoning on its head, however, explaining the early death as a form of karmic transfer: Sarkar Baba had taken on so much sin and pollution from the people he healed that he eventually paid the price himself. In the guru's last years of life, someone once asked him to remove the pain of a suffering person, and he replied, "Sister, why do you want to get involved in that matter? Look at me. I used to roam around like a lion, carefree. Then I got involved in that profession . . . now see the condition of this body. If you pick up something from some-where, where are you going to put it?" (Ram 1997: 131).

With this explanation, the death of Sarkar Baba presented a sad twist to the transportive model of purification. Aghor is like the Ganga, but the river that was Sarkar Baba had its limits. Nevertheless, no one would deny that his power was great and his reforms far-reaching. Even his funeral was an opportunity for reform. By convention, most renunciates are buried in the ground in a yogic posture to create a *samādhi* shrine where people can come to worship the ascetic while he remains suspended in a state of enlightened hibernation. Instead, Sarkar Baba directed that his body be cremated so that his ashes could be spread across the many places and communities that he had touched. He further directed that this cremation take place in a small *shamshān* on the Parao side of the river so that people would have a less expensive option to the more famous Manikarnika and Harischandra Ghats, where the Doms were notorious for extorting large sums of money from mourning families.[15] The cremation also gave his disciples the opportunity to construct many *samādhi* shrines rather than one and to spread his ashes where he spread his teachings. On many levels, the cremation was an appropriate memo-rial for an Aghori.

CHAPTER 4

The Wrong Side of the River

You can make an ass of yourself, quite literally, by dying on the wrong side of the Ganga. The Kashi Kanda guarantees that those who die immediately across the river from Banaras will be reborn as donkeys, just as it promises spiritual liberation for all who die within the sacred interior of the city.[1] So while pilgrims and priests scramble for a few square feet along the ghats, not a single *sadhu* is willing to take up residence along the wide open spaces on the far shore of Mother Ganga. None, that is, except an Aghori.

On the "wrong side" of the river is where Awadhut Bhagwan Ram established an ashram and clinic to treat people with leprosy and other skin diseases using modified Ayurvedic medicines. Built in 1961, Kusht Seva Ashram (KSA) lies beside the Grand Trunk (GT) Road in the town of Parao, directly across the river from Banaras's northernmost bathing ghat. GT Road is a centuries-old trade route that has since become a perpetual traffic jam of honking trucks, cars, and autorickshaws moving between eastern Uttar Pradesh and the nearby state of Bihar. Parao is a noisy, sooty truck stop where mechanics, transport workers, and roadside vendors long ago displaced most of its local farming and fishing communities.

Parao would seem to be the worst possible location for a clinic or hospital. Yet Kusht Seva Ashram has become host to one of the most popular leprosy-treatment centers in the world. Indeed, the KSA clinic recently entered the *Guinness Book of World Records* for claiming to have treated over two hundred thousand people with leprosy since its founding (see www.guinnessworldrecords.com). While the *Guinness* book is certainly no substitute for census statistics, it is nevertheless a gold standard in the popular Indian imagination.

If the patients at Parao are anything like those at Krim Kund, then they must have practical reasons for pursuing this medicine, at least for *kushṭh* conditions. But these advantages are not immediately apparent. People do not choose the ashram medicines as a matter of convenience, for the average KSA treatment regimen is four times longer than the biomedical standard,[2] and many patients complain about the dietary restrictions that go along with KSA medicines. Nor is Aghor medicine more accessible or cheaper than biomedicine. Although the ashram is close to a major highway, it is also only two miles away from a major biomedical clinic that provides treatment free of cost. In contrast, a month's supply of KSA medicines represents several days of work for the tenant farmers and unskilled laborers who comprise most of the patient population.[3]

One must understand the social stigma of leprosy to understand the popularity of Aghor medicine in these circumstances. Many Indians consider leprosy (Hansen's disease, or HD) to be the most untouchable of human conditions. Thus, people travel great distances to avoid public discovery and the resulting social ostracism. The intense stigma also leads to the segregation of biomedical services for leprosy. Both these challenges impede effective communication between physicians and patients, which in turn impedes long-term adherence to treatment regimens. This lack of communication is especially problematic given the need to monitor and manage the more common side effects of biomedical treatment (Barrett 2005).

Blame is also a serious issue. Although biomedical models of etiology do not explicitly blame the patient, neither do they explain why one person and not another is afflicted with leprosy—a central feature of explanatory models in most medical systems (Kleinman 1988; 1978). Aghor medicine provides this kind of explanation using the metaphysics of traditional healing, but without the blame that comes from traditional notions of pollution and purity. Finally, the issue of efficacy is important in Aghor medicine. Simply put, people believe that the Aghori are powerful and that their medicine works. Yet this belief too is related to the stigma of leprosy insofar as the power of Aghor, like that of the Ganga, largely relies on its ability to assimilate the pollution of others.

A large mural on the wall beside the front gate of Kusht Seva Ashram depicts the boar-headed Varaha, one of the nine avatars of Vishnu. The common myth is that Varaha rescued the world by plunging into the ocean and raising it up with his tusks. But the Aghori residents of KSA tell a slightly different version in which Varaha plunged into the filth of humanity to rescue the world from itself. This latter story has special significance for the practice of Aghor medicine at Parao, for it was here that Awadhut Bhagwan Ram reformed the Aghor tradition. The cremation ground became a leprosy-treatment center, and the Aghori began to engage the world in social service to save people from themselves, disciples included. This was the reason I came to Banaras in the first place: to study the dynamics of stigma and healing for the most ritually polluting of human conditions, as well as those willing to embrace that pollution on the wrong side of the purest river in the world.

STIGMA AND SOCIALIZATION

I interviewed the resident patients of Kusht Seva Ashram in the late winter of 1999. At the time, thirty-one leprosy-diagnosed adults resided within the ashram, a typical census, according to the clinic physicians. All but one of these people identified with a Hindu religious tradition, and half were from twice-born castes. This number was a large proportion even for Banaras, which touted an unusually high number of Brahmins (20 percent) in its population (Freitag 1989). Most Banarsi Brahmins are poor, however, illustrating that caste is but one of several axes of social inequality in India. Upper caste notwithstanding, the resident patients of KSA were mostly tenant farmers, unskilled laborers, and housewives from poor and landless families in rural Uttar Pradesh and Bihar. Their economic situation reinforced the longtime association of leprosy and poverty in India (Buckingham 2002). One-third of the patients claimed some kind of formal education, but only five of them had reached the tenth grade or higher. None had a college education, and no woman claimed to have any education at all. The ratio of men to women among the resident patients was especially problematic. With twenty-six men and only five women, the five-to-one gender ratio at KSA was much greater than the two-to-one ratio of registered cases and the four-to-one ratio for permanent disabilities nationwide (Kumar et al. 2001; Noordeen 1994). These discrepancies were part of an unresolved puzzle that may well be explained by the diminished autonomy of women to make medical decisions and gain access to essential health resources (Bloom, Wypij, and das Gupta 2001; Beals 1976) as well as possible gender differences in manual labor practices (Barrett 1997).[4] However, the even lower representation of women at KSA was closely linked to issues of child care, for the ashram did not allow children to live on its grounds. I was therefore not surprised that the five female residents at KSA either had grown children or had none.

Given the centrality of family life in Indian society, I cannot imagine a more difficult challenge for these people than to live apart from their kin for extended periods. At most, the residents made two or three family visits each year, and only then, for a few days at a time. These visits usually tapered off over time, and several of the long-term residents had stopped visiting altogether. In addition, the resident patients were segregated within the ashram itself, hidden behind walls in a separate living area. They rarely made contact with the nonpatient visitors to the ashram, nor did they participate in regular ashram religious activities. Despite this isolation, people stayed at the ashram for years at a time. Indeed, the average length of stay for KSA residents was 5.2 years, well beyond the 3-year treatment period.

Whatever efficacy people attributed to the medicines of Kusht Seva Ashram, the inpatients clearly had a different reason for being there. The KSA inpatient facility was essentially a religiously sanctioned leprosy colony. As I soon learned, this religious element was very important, for it provided a well-known script of austerity for a tragic set of circumstances. Aside from labor migrations and village exogamy, family separations usually bore the mark of suspicion and blame for all involved. In contrast, living in an ashram was seen as an important religious duty, an auspicious act that might even raise the status of a family that would otherwise have difficulty concealing its relative's extremely inauspicious disease.

Here, the Ganga metaphor is highly appropriate, for leprosy is among the five major reasons for throwing the dead directly into the river.[5] Banarsis often speak of death as the great (social) equalizer, but they consider a person with leprosy to be so ritually polluted that his or her body is not a fitting sacrifice for the cremation fire. Thus, the pollution of leprosy mandates transportive purification, with the body still attached to the problem. Similarly, KSA patients' families dump both their afflictions and their afflicted upon the Aghori. Like Mother Ganga, the Aghori are even less discriminating than the funeral pyre. Yet as we shall soon see, much can be gained from this radical level of nondiscrimination.

THE SOCIAL AND PHYSICAL STIGMA OF LEPROSY

The social stigma of leprosy is far worse than the disease itself. Contrary to many popular beliefs, Hansen's disease is a mildly contagious condition that usually responds readily to treatment with antibiotics (Bryceson and Pfalzgraff 1990). In the minority of more prolonged and difficult cases, simple precautions and careful observation can prevent the onset of permanent disabilities (Srinivasan 1994). In contrast to these clinical realities, however, Indians often ascribe people with HD to the most untouchable categories of humanity (Frist 2000). Moreover, this untouchability often persists long after people have been "cured" of the disease, creating lifelong prospects of divorce, eviction, loss of employment, and ostracism from family and social networks (Kopparty, Karup, and Sivarum 1995).

The extreme discrepancies between the clinical and social realities of HD in India underscore a common distinction in medical anthropology between the pathophysiology of disease and the human experience of illness as suffering (Kleinman 1988).[6] As such, it is tempting to segregate the bacteria of Hansen's *disease* from the social burden of leprosy. Yet although this distinction may be useful for initial criticism, further examination reveals that, as with many other discredited medical conditions, the physical and social stigmata of HD are too interconnected to disentangle in a useful way. Thus, leprosy is best approached as an illness of discrimination inclusive of its physical condition.

One can see both a sharp contrast and an intimate connection between the clinical and social realities of leprosy in India. *Mycobacterium leprae* is among the least contagious of human pathogens. Researchers estimate that the bacterium produces symptoms in less than 10 percent of the human population, and only then after prolonged exposure and a five-year incubation period (Bryceson and Pfalzgraff 1990). Although some evidence suggests a hereditary component to this susceptibility, most spouses and children of those infected never contract the disease (Mira et al. 2004; Seghal 1994). *M. leprae* fares even worse outside of its human hosts. Indeed, it grows so poorly under most conditions, natural or artificial, that researchers have yet to prove its exact mode of transmission (Sasaki et al. 2001).[7]

In contrast to the bacterium, the social mark of leprosy in India is highly contagious. Consistent with Goffman's so-called courtesy stigma (1963), friends and relatives of people with HD risk severe social and economic losses for their affiliations. Consequently, many Indian families would rather banish their diagnosed relatives to a distant town or city than risk discrimination against the entire household (Kopparty, Karup, and Sivarum 1995). With very poor chances of employment, and little if any support from home, these exiles have few options for survival. Typically, they must find subsidized living in an isolated colony, or else live on the streets and beg in areas frequented by tourists and pilgrims. Both of these subsistence modes contribute, in turn, to the stereotypes from which their discrimination originated.

Among those susceptible to *M. leprae* infection, the disease is usually treatable with a combination of three antibiotics, commonly referred to as multi-drug therapy (MDT). This regimen can render most patients noninfectious in thirty days and noninfected in six to nine months (Ponnighaus 1995).[8] Yet for many people, the social stigma of leprosy can last a lifetime, regardless of whether they have been biomedically cured of the disease.

Some of the most prevalent myths about HD focus on its associated deformities and disabilities. Contrary to many popular beliefs, HD does not cause limbs to "rot off." Though a small percentage of patients can undergo internal loss of cartilage and bone at the face and digits, the vast majority of physical deformities result from accumulated trauma. Typically, the selective infection of peripheral nerves results in limb anesthesia, diminishing people's ability to rely upon touch and pain to prevent injuries to their hands and feet and to make the constant microadjustments necessary to prevent pressure ulcers. The resultant injuries and ulcers accumulate, and along with secondary infections, lead to progressive amputations not unlike those for people with diabetes (Brand and Yancey 1997; Bryceson and Pfalzgraff 1990; Jopling 1988).

Even in cases of permanent neuropathy, physical deformities and disabilities are preventable through basic measures like custom footwear and training in injury prevention. But that which is basic is not always easy. Because of the ever-present threat of injury to anesthetic limbs, people with HD neuropathies must be hyperaware of their bodies' relationship to their surrounding environments (Brand and Yancey 1997). Without the patient's constant visual inspection of an insensate hand, a cigarette or hot stove can result in a third-degree burn in less than a minute. More insidiously, without regular attention to footwear, or scheduled readjustments while sleeping, a pressure ulcer can work its way to the bone in a manner of weeks. Although the necessary preventive measures are straightforward, they are challenging to maintain under the best of conditions. They become formidable under the conditions of extreme poverty and demoralization that is common among people who are publicly branded as "lepers" in India.[9] The social and physical disabilities of HD are not only mutually engendering, but each actually impedes efforts to prevent the other.

THE DISEMBODIMENT OF LEPROSY

At Kusht Seva Ashram, I investigated whether the dynamics between the social and physical marks of leprosy discrimination could be interrupted within this more tolerant environment, and in a system informed by an ethos of radical nondiscrimination. I did not expect the Aghori to change the attitudes of Indian society as a whole, but I was keen to find out if Aghori healers had better rapport with their patients than did other health providers and if the explanatory models of Aghor medicine helped improve the self-concept of patients with leprosy. This avenue of inquiry actually produced mixed results, which are well illustrated in the following two cases.

Disavowal and Undertreatment

Sita was an energetic and outspoken woman in her early forties who belonged to a community of goldsmiths in a small town about seventy kilometers from Banaras. She was illiterate beyond the ability to sign her own name and cynically laughed at the slim chance that she or any other woman from her community could have a formal education. She had been living at Kusht Seva Ashram for many years and repeatedly spoke about the loneliness she felt from the years of separation from her natal family.

Sita was fourteen when she first noticed a gray patch on her upper arm. This spot caused great concern in her family, because any skin blemishes or spots would adversely affect her chances for marriage. Although she could still conceal the patch beneath her sari, no one knew whether the condition would spread. The senior males of Sita's family decided to send her to a doctor of "English medicine," who diagnosed the HD and prescribed a course of dapsone.[10] She was then sequestered at home while the family hastily arranged her marriage. With her condition kept secret, Sita was married within a month, after which she ceased taking her medication lest it be discovered.

Sita's condition remained unchanged until the birth of her first child, a daughter, four years later. She then began having numbness along her left arm and leg and contractions in her toes. With her condition no longer concealable, she feigned surprise when she was diagnosed a second time. To avoid being recognized at a regional leprosy clinic, she, along with her affines, went on long trips for treatment in the adjacent state of Bihar. Sita's daughter died of undisclosed causes at six months of age, and her husband died the following year. With no male children and no one to advocate for her within the family, Sita saw her already-marginal status decline further. With strong pressure from her mother-in-law, Sita took up residence at KSA. Years later, her natal and affinal families kept up the story that she was living the pious life of a widow in an ashram somewhere in Banaras.

Sita's story illustrates the tragic consequences of denial and concealment in the progression and spread of a discredited disease. Given the social consequences, it is understandable that people go to great lengths to conceal their condition. Unfortunately, such strategies usually result in delays between initial symptoms and diagnosis and foster nonadherence to medication regimens (Kopparty, Karum, and Sivarum 1995; Mull et al. 1989). Compounding this problem is the segregation of HD-treatment services in India (Arole et al. 2002).[11] Under these conditions, the most public sign of early-stage HD is someone's appearance near a leprosy-treatment worker or clinic. To prevent such associations, people often travel great distances to nonlocal clinics or avoid treatment altogether (Arole et al. 2002; Dharmshaktu 1992).

In my interviews with KSA patients, the majority (60 percent) reported delays between initial symptoms and their first visit to a licensed professional healer. Most interviewees described these delays in the context of concealment strategies, as in Sita's history, or some form of denial ("I did not want to know"). Others reported that not only were they ignorant of early signs of HD, but their health providers were as well. The latter issue reflects discrimination of another sort: the segregation of leprosy-treatment services also results in a segregation of clinical knowledge.

Goffman (1963), in his reformulation of deviance as stigma, includes a taxonomy of strategies for disavowing the social mark: (1) sheltering—segregation within protective social environments; (2) passing—concealing or camouflaging the mark; and (3) covering—minimizing tensions during social interactions. Yet these disavowal strategies provide only limited benefits to the discredited and can even reinforce the stigma of a condition over time (Goffman 1963; Jones, Scott, and Markus 1984). This situation is even worse when the stigmatized condition is an infectious disease, and the disavowal results in delayed testing or incomplete adherence to treatment (Alonzo and Reynolds 1995; Rubel and Garro 1992).[12]

Such dynamics forge a direct link between social stigma and the epidemiology of Hansen's disease in India. Unfortunately, however, this link has yet to be adequately measured. In accordance with World Bank guidelines, India's National Leprosy Elimination Program (NLEP) bases statistics solely on the passive detection of registered cases in WHO-approved treatment centers (Ponnighaus 1995). Among such centers that I observed in the Varanasi district, staff members assumed that registered patients who fail to return after six months have sought treatment elsewhere, and they drop these patients from the books. Significantly, 74 percent of the KSA inpatients had initially sought biomedical treatment for their condition elsewhere.[13] Yet because all these patients had now shifted to an unrecognized mode of treatment, they were not represented in national or WHO statistics. It was not just patients and families who were concealing the problem of leprosy.

Dissociation and Self-Neglect

Sadness and resignation were pervasive emotions among the KSA residents. Laxman was no exception in this regard. In his mid-twenties, he had a ninth-grade education and an acre of land, which would have made him an attractive marriage prospect in many parts of rural Bihar were it not for contracted fingers and wounds on his toes and feet. Ten years before I spoke with him, he had begun having difficulties holding on to farm implements and repeatedly injured himself while working in the fields. Initially misdiagnosed, his condition worsened until he started MDT six months later. Unlike Sita, however, Laxman was never able to conceal his condition. Soon after his diagnosis, his neighbors spotted a local leprosy-treatment worker visiting his home. In no time, word spread among prospective in-laws, and Laxman's family gave up trying to arrange his marriage after two aborted attempts. Laxman related these latter events as if they marked the end of his life.

Laxman continued MDT on a sporadic basis, and I suspected he was eventually cured. Although he was tolerated in his family and village, no one spoke with him and he kept to himself. In accordance with ritual pollution taboos, he ate his meals from separate pots and *thalis* (rimmed plates) and sat alone during village celebrations. Laxman stated, "In our society, people hate anyone with this disease." Yet he insisted that the problem did not lie with his village but with himself.

I was struck not only by the content of Laxman's story but also by the manner in which he related it. Laxman kept his hands to his sides throughout most of the interview. He related his loss of manual dexterity and subsequent injuries without making a single gesture. This gesture-free narrative was repeated by nearly all the KSA residents with whom I spoke. They kept their affected limbs beneath garments whenever possible and assumed positions and postures that minimized any remaining exposure. Even within the isolated confines of the ashram, the mimetic disavowal of leprosy seemed to persist as a deeply ingrained habit.

The KSA residents also expressed linguistic dispossession from their affected limbs. In their illness narratives, they dropped the possessive pronoun when narrating the succession of injuries to, and problems with, their hands and feet. Thus, in accounts of a cut or burn in regional Bhojpuri, *hamāre hāth* (my hand) simply became *hāth* ([the] hand). In Standard Hindi, someone would say, "Doctor pair ka ilāj kya" (The doctor treated [the] foot) instead of *mera pair* (my foot). A few even went so far as to say *yah angulī* (that finger) without looking or gesturing toward the digit. It was as if the appendages that remained had already been amputated, and those that were amputated had left no signs of previous attachment.

These habits of word and gesture were particularly disconcerting given that many KSA residents continued to suffer from limb anesthesia, necessitating constant visual inspection and a hyperawareness of affected limbs to prevent further injuries. Though the residents of KSA may have been all too aware of their situation on the whole, these data indicate that they were actively dissociating themselves from their physical disabilities on a moment-by-moment basis. If so, this dissociation would have significant consequences for the further progression of their physical condition, even in the absence of infection.

With this background, it is interesting to note that leprologists from the U.S. Hansen's Disease Center in Carville, Louisiana, relate anecdotal observations of some patients' disdain for and neglect of affected limbs (Yoder 1998). Although situated in very different cultural contexts, many Carville patients describe themes of isolation and shame very similar to those of the KSA residents (Gussow 1989). When I conducted life-history interviews in Carville in 1997, two patients presented their narratives without making gestures or using personal pronouns for disabled limbs.

Murphy (1990) described a similar process of dissociation during the progression of his paralysis and cancer. He examined the "silencing" of

his body, beginning with a loss of proprioception and ending with emotional detachment. In his book, he refers to his limbs as "the arm" or
"the leg," his body as a "faulty life support system," and his remaining
self as "Donovan's Brain." Murphy and others examined issues of stigmatization among people with paralysis, characterizing them in terms of
liminality arising from lost social roles associated with sexuality and
physical independence (1988). Within the same time frame, Murphy
ignored parts of his own body to the point that he became nearly septic
from bone-deep pressure ulcers (1990).

For stigmatized neurological conditions with anesthesia, the combined
loss of physical sensation and social identity creates a strong potential
for bodily neglect, thereby perpetuating feedback between physical
pathology and the social pathology of its discrimination. Moreover, the
internalization of stigma is likely to be deeper in people who acquire
such conditions in adulthood, given that disability prejudices are often
learned early through socially ascribed prototypes of health and beauty
(Ablon 1995; Jones, Scott, and Markus 1984). Thus, when confronting
the physical parts by which they once identified themselves, parts that
had since become misshapen and senseless, it is not surprising that some
of these people would dissociate themselves from that which they have
long known to be alien, and that which marks their alienation from the
world around them—a process constituting a disembodiment of leprosy.

FROM POLLUTION TO HEALING

I was disappointed to find that Aghori medicine had done little to change
the attitudes of the KSA resident patients. On the contrary, the prolonged isolation from family, as well as segregation from the social and
religious activities of the broader ashram community, seemed only to
reinforce the already-diminished self-concept of these people.

Granted, the Aghori provided their residents with medicines that were
both free of cost and free of blame. They also created a protected living
environment with a veneer of social legitimacy. Nevertheless, by sheltering the stigma of leprosy behind ashram walls on the wrong side of the
river, the Aghori ultimately reinforced the social attitudes that brought
disability to an otherwise treatable condition. These attitudes, in turn,
were further internalized by KSA inpatients to the point that they exac-
erbated the progress of the disease. Waxler (1981) discusses how people
"learn to become lepers" by being socialized into the discriminatory
models around them. In the case of Sita and Laxman, these models were

not only deeply internalized, they were ultimately inscribed onto flesh per the original definition of stigma: a permanent mark, cut or burned upon the skin of people to publicly brand them as members of a socially discredited group.

In contrast to their resident patients, the Kina Ram Aghori appeared to benefit a great deal from having a major program for leprosy treatment. In chapter 3, we saw how leprosy treatment became a central prototype for the reformation of Aghor. Before this development, the Aghori were part of a socially marginalized sect whose members and practices were largely isolated within the cremation grounds. Twenty years after establishing the Kusht Seva Ashram and clinic, they had accumulated 150 ashrams and service centers, receiving thousands of members from the middle-class Indian society, as well as millionaires, politicians, and even an Indian prime minister.[14] Apparently, leprosy did much more to destigmatize Aghor than the other way around.

Yet these dynamics were only part of the picture. I had been volunteering as a part-time nurse in a street clinic for leprosy patients in the city, where I gained an appreciation of the range of people with this condition. I came to know the street-dwelling beggars on the main bathing ghats at Dashashwamedha, the Bengali squatter community near the Sankat Mochan Temple, and the colony residents in the nearby town of Asapur. I noted their different backgrounds and how these differences resulted in radically different life trajectories after they were diagnosed with the disease. I saw even greater contrasts among the outpatient visitors at Banaras Hindu University and the Seva Sadan hospital, the two major biomedical treatment centers in the city. Though all patients faced the threat of social ostracism, and all shared a willingness to try anything and everything to fix the problem, some were clearly better able to seek medical help and to do so while concealing the disease. Not surprisingly, these hospital outpatients seemed most able to manage the physical and social stigma of leprosy. I expected the same to be true of the many outpatient visitors to Kusht Seva Ashram.

Unfortunately, collecting outpatient data at the KSA clinic proved very difficult. Most outpatient visitors were still actively concealing their condition, and were therefore reticent to share personal information with anyone, least of all with a foreign researcher. I had little if any opportunity to establish rapport and therefore had to rely on the physicians and staff to vouch for me. This strategy was helpful in approaching return visitors, but many more were visiting the clinic for the first time. Subsequently, my efforts resulted in only twelve outpatient interviews, and a

lot of time watching clinical dynamics. These latter observations, however, proved especially helpful.

In South Asia's highly pluralistic medical cultures, Nichter and Nordstrom (1989) identified the Sri Lankan concept of "medicine answering," a term used to describe healers who effectively communicate with
their patients and are able to meet their broader needs for overall well-
being, regardless of the treatment modality. Although not articulated as
such, this concept could be readily applied to the more highly regarded
medical providers in Banaras. Moreover, I would argue that the KSA
clinic appeared to approach this ideal of medicine answering more closely
than did most other providers I observed in this region.

The physical layout of the KSA clinic reminded me of the better-
managed clinics in rural South India. Patients entered the ashram from
an entrance near the main gate, just beside the mural of Varaha. A hundred meters down a tree-lined path, and right next to the inpatient com-
pound, visitors approached a large cottage building with two sets of open
and closed porches. The latter served as a waiting room, flanked on
either side by a pharmacy and (unusually) a records department. Unlike
most Indian outpatient providers, the KSA clinic kept detailed records
on its patients. Beyond the waiting area was a spacious room with abun-
dant natural lighting and a few outer rooms for (rare) private consul-
tations. Most doctor-patient interactions took place in the center of the
main room around a large square table: doctors sat on either side of the
table, and an assistant stood nearby when not running errands.

The table in the center of the room is a ubiquitous feature of Indian
clinics, regardless of the type of medicine practiced. People huddle around
it, waiting for an opportunity to talk with the physician, and pass the
time listening in on other people's problems. In most clinics, the patient
sits orthogonal to the physician, who gives a cursory pulse reading or
auscultation with a stethoscope while barely pretending to listen to the
clinical history. The physician then writes a long shopping list of medications and vitamin supplements, and hands the patient the prescription with a highly authoritative and terse set of instructions. Under these
conditions, the patient is too intimidated to ask questions, nor is he or
she encouraged to do so. I have observed these interactions again and
again: in clinics both private and public, in northern and southern India,
and with different kinds of healing systems—allopathic (biomedical),
homeopathic, and Ayurvedic. These interactions were the baseline
dynamics of professional healing in India. They reinforced a long-held
assertion among those who study medical pluralism in India that the

quality of provider-patient relations is usually independent of the kind of medicine practiced (Nichter and Nordstrom 1989; Kakar 1982; Minocha 1980).

The patient-healer dynamics at the KSA clinic were exceptional in this regard. Although I would not characterize its physicians as especially warm and friendly, they appeared to have good rapport with their patients. The doctors actually faced their patients and looked them in the eye while talking. The patients spoke more freely than I had seen in other clinics, and the physicians encouraged them by giving frequent cues that they were listening. At the conclusion of the consultation, the KSA doctors usually asked their patients if they had questions. I had seen such inquiries only twice in the two dozen or so clinics that I had visited during my fieldwork.

Granted, these people were aware of my presence. But their interactions were more practiced and natural than they would have been if they had been performed for my benefit. Moreover, I could see the comfort with which returning patients initiated questions and conversations with their doctors. Finally, the fact that the doctors could effectively vouch for me spoke to the trust that the patients had in their healers. These physicians, Aghor disciples themselves, appeared to have learned the practice of medicine answering. Thus, it is not surprising that they would have so many patients.

In addition to having a good "tableside" manner, the physician-disciples of KSA strongly adhered to an etiological model of leprosy that displaced the blame, both implicit and explicit, of previous sins. The classic text of Ayurvedic medicine, the Caraka Saṃhitā, gives many reasons for the affliction of leprosy. For example, the condition may stem from the sins of previous lives, such as killing a Brahmin or cow, or from sex with a menstruating woman or prostitute (CS II.7: 1). Yet the text also points to dietary incompatibilities, such as the consumption of fish with milk, as the cause of a *kushṭh* condition such as leprosy. The chief medical officer of the KSA clinic, Dr. K. P. Singh (also known as Dr. Sahib), was adamant about this point. A middle-aged man with a friendly manner and a white coat, Dr. Sahib contrasted the Aghor approach to that of traditional Ayurveda. He affirmed the Ayurvedic emphasis on bodily constitution over that of pathogens but did not subscribe to the "old ideas" that leprosy was caused by "bad deeds." "Fooding and eating is the main cause for these things," he said.

The KSA emphasis on dietary etiology contrasted with the models of blame that other physicians in Banaras, regardless of medical persuasion, promoted in explaining leprosy. In addition to physicians who cited past misdeeds to explain differential susceptibility, several promoted more implicit models of self-neglect or evoked random chance to explain leprosy. On the surface, chance would seem to absolve the patient of personal responsibility, but it instead left open a metaphysical niche that physicians inevitably filled with a more common answer: *bhāgya* (fate) and its associated models of karma.

In exploring the role of karma in popular explanations of suffering, Sharma (1973) observes that although karma is never the first explanation given for a misfortune, it is also the last explanation to be abandoned. This phenomenon makes sense in light of two important themes. The first is psychological indeterminacy about the actions of previous lives. The second is the tendency to shift in and out of karmic frames of reference so as to maximize agency and minimize personal responsibility (Daniel 1983). When people combine karmic explanations with other explanatory traditions, they almost always give the former as the ultimate cause and the latter as the proximate cause of misfortune. Only when people cannot find a proximate cause for a misfortune, or when nothing can be done about it, do they explicitly evoke karma (Babb 1983; Keyes 1983). So even when people with leprosy are not explicitly blamed for their condition, the blame is implicit in the absence of an explanation for why the disease occurred, especially when the blame impedes the treatment.

Most residents and inpatients with whom I spoke cited the dietary explanation, even if it was not their first or primary model. Raju, a young tailor with leukoderma who lived with his wife and daughter in Banaras, once believed that his condition was caused by Brahminicide. "Actually . . . it is a custom here that [leukoderma] is *Brahm rog* [a Brahmin disease]. It [is] the blame you get for killing a Brahmin." He quickly disclaimed this idea as an old belief. In the modern world, according to Raju, leukoderma is "all from eating and drinking [dietary habits], meaning from eating and drinking it starts in the liver."

Raju was more explicit about causes than most patients were, however. As with other explanatory models, people commonly cited their beliefs using the third person—"the doctors say" or "Baba says"—as if to defer responsibility until the final therapeutic outcome was certain. This stance is typical of Indian religious-healing traditions: people place their faith in the ideology and prescriptions of the guru or deity for a while, with the understanding that they need not maintain their commitment if the problem is resolved within a reasonable period (Kakar 1982;

Obeyesekere 1981). Thus, although everyone acknowledged the Aghori model of dietary incompatibility, their commitment to the model also appeared to be tied to the outcome of the treatment. They were optimistic for the time being, opting to place their problems in the hands of the Aghori, and doing their best to follow the treatment regimen, should the treatment eventually work.

As with the bathers at Krim Kund, the power of the Aghori was the most common theme among the resident and outpatients of the Kusht Seva Ashram. This power was typically validated with the performance of miracles. Raju, for instance, spoke of how Sarkar Baba brought a young boy back to life during his travels in Switzerland. "This [ashram] is therefore a sacred place," he said. "Concerning only me, I have seen only this Guruji. I mean Baba [Sambav] Ram [the current baba in residence at KSA]. The landlord of this place at the present time is considered to be a big blessing." As with the saints and sacred geography of Banaras, the healing miracles of the Aghori were closely tied to Kusht Seva Ashram: one was a proxy for the other.

Once again, people cited the metonymic relationship between the Aghori, the Ganga, and the *shmashān* when speaking of their healing powers. Rohit, a Banarsi metalworker in his thirties, spoke hopefully about the power of the Aghori to cure his skin condition: "The synonym of the word *Ganga* is Aghor. So that which is Aghor . . . that [is how] God happens. There are Ishwars [lords]. They are one Aghoreshwar. He is one in the world. A human has worshipped him, I mean, in all forms. . . . Therefore, we can get everything by doing the *tapasyā* [austerities] of only one. I mean, Aghor means guru *tapasyā*; guru *sadhāna*."

Shivani made a more explicit connection between the Ganga and the *shmashān*. A student in her early twenties, she was worried about the consequences of early-stage leukoderma for her marriage but had great faith in the curative powers of the Aghori, which she explained as follows: "Actually Baba and these [other people] are Aghoris. They sit only at the *shmashān*. Their [relationship is] just there. Because . . . Baba had done *sadhāna* only sitting at Ganga. And Kina Ram, he used to sit only at the Ganga. He used to call the Ganga. Sitting at the *shmashān,* visiting with Kaluram Baba . . . was those people's [routine], and eating fried fish. It was their daily routine. [Baba Kina Ram] was the avatar of Shiva."

Notably, Shivani referred to Lord Shiva in the feminine, an obvious reference to the Divine Mother, especially given the Mother's manifestation as both Ganga Ma and Svaha of the cremation fire. Patients, even those who knew little about the Aghori, commonly cited the maternal source of Aghor healing. Srikant, an elderly farmer with visible leprosy deformities, had traveled from central Bihar to see the Ganga and Kusht Seva Ashram, referring to the latter as a kind of *shmashān* on the sacred river and describing how both could purify a person of anything, just like "one's mother."

The eating of fish also has an important connection to Aghor medicine. Having been raised near the Kina Ram Ashram, Shivani knew that the Aghori made a point of eating fish as the *prasād* of the river. Informing this practice is the belief that Mother Ganga embraces the excreta of humanity, including the corpses rejected for cremation. Fish eat everything within the Ganga, and the Aghori eat the fish with the conscious intention of assimilating—physically as well as symbolically—everything and anything rejected by society.

Although most patients did not have the benefit of Shivani's background, nearly everyone from Banaras understood there to be some connection between the healing powers of the Aghori, the Ganga, and (sometimes) the *shmashān* and their common ability to transcend limitations. Newcomers who came from outside Banaras learned this from more experienced patients or from the people who referred them to the clinic. It could therefore be argued that the nondiscriminatory nature of Aghor was ultimately responsible for Kusht Seva Ashram's becoming home to one of the most popular leprosy-treatment centers in India. First, the popularity of Kusht Seva Ashram resulted from a common perception that the Aghori were powerful healers. Second, this power was closely linked to the Aghori's transcendence over pollution and purity taboos. Third, one could find evidence for this transcendence in the Aghori's voluntary and public embrace of the feared and discarded. And finally, because the *shmashān* was once the ultimate site of human aversions, the place where the Aghori tested their mettle, the leprosy clinic became the new cremation ground.

The ritual pollution of leprosy and other diseases is extremely disempowering for the afflicted as well as for their kin and close associates. Yet this pollution can be as intensely empowering for those who voluntarily embrace it. The former situation is a product of misfortune, of *bhāgya,* with all the karmic baggage that it entails. The latter situation, however, is an austerity: Aghor *tapasyā,* Aghor *sadhanā.* Devotees and nondevotees alike see this voluntary embrace of pollution as the driving force of Aghor medicine. The Aghori gain much more status for their healing of leprosy than the resident patients can ever hope to achieve, but they channel that power into medicines that they distribute to thousands of people each year. They also channel their power into schools, public works projects, and the social education of those who seek the Aghori for spiritual guidance—people who are usually former patients of Aghor medicine. I explore the dynamics of this power (Aghor *shaktī*), its transformations and exchanges, in the next chapter, looking at how the medicines of Aghor can be a medium for the exchange of power between patients and healers.

CHAPTER 5

Dawā and *Duwā*

The one who [ingests one of our medications] knows that
it cures by the blessing of Babaji. And he knows that this is
not only *dawā* [medicine]; it is *duwā* [blessing] as well. And
they get cured as well. The one believes in this place—[for
example,] "This is the medicine of Babaji and I will be cured
for sure." And then he gets cured.

Sangita

This statement by Sangita, the chief manufacturer of herbal medications
sold at the Kina Ram Ashram, echoed many others by disciples who had
worked in healing occupations under the auspices of Aghor. All attributed the efficacy of their therapeutic interventions to the blessing of the
guru. Similarly, many patients who sought out the Aghori for healing
spoke repeatedly of the *dawā* and *duwā* of the ashram medicines, with
a particular emphasis on the latter. *Dawā* and *duwā* relate the pluralism
of Indian medicine to the pragmatism of Indian patients, who often
stress the power of the healer over the intrinsic properties of a specific
medical system or therapy. These terms also have particular significance
for the patient-disciple who takes a transformational approach to the
healing process.

THE MEDICINE IS THE MEDIUM

To better understand the *dawā* and *duwā* of Aghor medicine, we must
examine how these therapies are practiced in the context of medical pluralism. Given India's countless communities, languages, and religious
traditions, it is difficult to make generalizations about the country. For
this reason, I tell my American students that the answer to almost any
question about India is yes, even when the question does not require
a yes or no answer. Perhaps the safest generalization is that India has a

limitless capacity to assimilate the cultures that it encounters, and to recombine them in every conceivable permutation. Mother India is akin to Mother Ganga in this regard.

The same goes for India's healing traditions, which we can roughly divide into the categories of "professional" and "ritual." The government of India officially recognizes three professional medical systems in addition to biomedicine (also known as allopathic or "English" medicine). Ayurveda and Unani rest on the metaphysical foundations of Hindu and Islamic tradition, respectively. Yet these healing traditions have become increasingly Westernized with the formation of government-sponsored colleges, official licensure, and the mass-marketing of medicines by pharmaceutical companies (Jeffery 1988; Leslie 1973). At the same time, the so-called western systems of medicine have at least partly adapted their practices to the so-called traditional systems (Nichter 1992a, 1992b; Madan 1980). Consequently, the stethoscope is almost as common among the so-called Indian systems as extended pulse reading is in the so-called Western systems, and nearly everyone prescribes antibiotics and herbal remedies.

Ritual healing systems are even more pluralistic, to the point that distinguishing the more mainstream priest or Vedic astrologer from the tantric *oja* or possession medium can sometimes be difficult. I once had a consultation with a Sufi astrologer, an Unani hakim, and a French allopathic physician, all of whom were spirits inhabiting the body of a young man who claimed no special knowledge in any of these subjects. Although an extreme example, the Sufi consultation exemplified my Western disorientation with respect to the multiple voices of the living healers I encountered.

Whatever their representation, ritual practitioners can have a profound impact on the health of Indian communities. Many of these practitioners are major referral sources for other physicians and healers in their communities. An astrologer, for instance, might recommend one medical system over another because of certain planetary influences, whereas a religious leader might vouch for the integrity of one physician over another (Glucklich 1997). In addition, ritual healers typically provide their patients with a level of explanation that is often unavailable in professional systems. Whereas a CT scan or pulse reading can tell patients *how* an affliction occurred, a ritual specialist can tell them *why* it occurred and why it afflicted someone (and not someone else) at a particular moment in his or her life. Kleinman (1988) suggests that such explanations are key elements of explanatory models that address human illness at the level of experience. The problem, however, is that the number of explanatory models of healing is almost as vast as the number of people in India. Nearly every patient adopts multiple-use strategies, mixing and matching healing systems according to a variety of needs and circumstances. How, then, are we to make sense of it all? The question is of both theoretical and practical importance, encompassing issues of ideology and materialism, matters of structure and agency, and the health decisions of a billion people.

Theories for understanding the complex health-seeking patterns of Indian communities generally fall into one of two categories of explanation. The first are socioeconomic explanations for patients' differential utilization of health-care services and variable adherence to certain therapies over time. These explanations often, but not always, draw on larger quantitative studies. They tend to focus on the social distribution of health-care resources and the structural inequalities affecting people's geographic and financial access to such resources. Such theories have been especially useful in examining gender-based health disparities, rural-urban differences, and health-care utilization by India's poorest communities (Kumar 2004; Thind 2004; Buckshee 1997; Beals 1976). They do not, however, explain differences in health-seeking decisions when access to alternate systems is equally adequate or poor for everyone in a given community, as is often the case in the greater Varanasi area.

The second category of explanations is ideological in nature. These explanations emphasize the agency of patients as decision makers and the role of health beliefs in treatment choices, with treatment adherence being one of these choices. Study methods usually, but not always, involve qualitative analysis of patient narratives. The best known of these approaches is the aforementioned explanatory-models framework, which emphasizes the role of etiological beliefs and the quest for meaning in health-seeking decisions (Atre et al. 2004; Banerjee and Banerjee 1995; Pool 1987). Explanatory models have highlighted the role of ethnomedicine in alleviating illness as human suffering (Garro 1993) and the position of physiological beliefs within broader metaphysical frameworks (Zimmerman 1987). These studies can be problematic, however, given the ethnographic maxim that people do not always say what they believe or do what they say.

Neither approach alone is sufficient to explain the pluralism and pragmatism of Aghori patients or their healers. When I was at the ashram, both patients and healers made practical decisions that often had more to do with the opportunities and limits around them than with particular models of medicinal action. Yet this pragmatism did not exclude the importance of personal belief in these decisions. For instance, both groups explicitly emphasized the importance of the *duwā* in the *dawā* of Aghor medicine, regardless of the type of medicine. Somewhere across the domains of structure and agency, certain cultural models must exist that inform and channel this pragmatic flexibility.

I argue that a cultural model of medicine as *prasād* explains the *dawā* and *duwā* of Aghor medicine in light of the practical concerns of patients and healers, and the therapeutic interactions between them. As we saw in the *pujas* and *havans* of previous chapters, the primary function of *prasād* is to serve as a medium of exchange between the human and the divine. Similarly, Aghor medicine serves as a medium of exchange between the pollution of patients and the power of their healers. Particular medicines and therapies are important only insofar as they propagate these exchanges. This theory helps explain broader patterns of medical pluralism in Indian society. It also has relevance for the Aghori themselves, given their models for the metaphysics of digestion, transformative purification, and the *shaktī* of Aghor.

CULTURAL MODELS OF FOOD EXCHANGE

Prasād is a prototype for the transmission of positive and negative characteristics (pollution, power, et cetera) via the medium of ingested substances. In the cyclical schema of ritual sacrifice, we recall that *prasād* involves a three-stage process in which (1) the worshipper offers an encoded substance—such as food, flowers, incense, or flame—to a deity or saint; (2) the deity/saint imbibes the subtle attributes of the offering; and (3) the worshipper partakes of the physical leftovers. In the first phase of the cycle, the offering is laden with the qualities of the worshipper, which, if acceptable, are transmitted to, and assimilated by, the divine. In the second phase, the qualities of the divine are transmitted to the worshipper via the leftovers. This exchange is usually a good deal for the worshipper, but it can be problematic for the divine, especially when the offering is not made by the right person, with the right intention, or with proper attention to ritual details.

This schema can also apply to the ritual dynamics of food exchange between people of different qualities or status. For example, there is a popular parable about a young and dedicated religious disciple who was invited to dine at the house of a well-to-do family. On the advice of his guru, he graciously accepted the invitation. That night, he received the utmost hospitality, with his hosts serving a vegetarian feast upon a lavish Western-style table. During the meal, the young ascetic impulsively and inexplicably stole a silver spoon, placing it in the folds of his shawl when no one was looking.

The young disciple was not fully aware of his actions until he had nearly returned to his guru's abode. The realization of his deed shocked and distressed him. Until that evening, he had been diligent in his spiritual practice, emulating the piety of his guru in every waking moment. What then could have possessed him to steal the spoon? The disciple immediately sought the guidance of his guru, prostrating before him in heartfelt confession.

The guru listened to the story with a sympathetic and knowing smile. "There is very good reason for all this," he said. "When receiving food from another, a spiritually sensitive person such as yourself will absorb some of the qualities of the person who serves you. Someone in that kitchen must have been a thief, and you took on that larcenous quality when you ate the meal. The effect wore off as you came closer to me," he said. The young disciple was relieved to hear that the effect was temporary. Soon thereafter, he learned that the daughter who served the disciple that night was indeed a thief.

This parable illustrates the shared metaphysics of commensality and ritual sacrifice. I have seen these sacrificial dynamics many times as the dinner guest of Indian families. In contrast with the American custom of dining and talking with my hosts, Indian hospitality often restricted my discourse to exchanges with my fellow guests. We ate and talked with one another while our hosts hovered over us, staring and smiling, when they weren't running around ladling food and pushing sweets upon us. On a cognitive level, I knew that these meals were two-way exchanges. I knew that I was affirming the status of my hosts by receiving their hospitality, a well-documented custom in the ethnographic literature (Raheja 1988; Parry 1986; Marriott 1976; Babb 1975). Thinking about cultural differences, however, is not the same as internalizing them. I often had as much trouble digesting the effusive generosity of my hosts as I did eating the endless piles of food on my leaf plate.

My breakthrough came during a particularly auspicious feast. I was traveling with Hari Baba and some Western disciples in eastern Madhya Pradesh and Bengal. Together with Pryadarshi Baba, we were invited to dine at the home of a well-to-do Malayali family. There, we were served

a lavish feast of three fish curries, a half-dozen vegetarian dishes, and numerous trays of sweets and chai—all wonderful, delicious, and excessive.
The family literally ran around the house, barking orders to one another
in an effort to execute this complex affair. Because of space constraints,
the babas were shunted to another room, leaving the rest of us alone
while we guiltily stretched our stomachs to the bursting point.

Our only solace was the belief that this arrangement would allow the
family some quality time with the babas. However, this was not the case.
Upon completing our gastronomic endeavor, we reunited with the babas
in the adjacent room, where we found the two of them sitting alone,
reading newspapers to each other while Krishna played on the television.
They paid little attention to our hosts other than to offer the occasional
grunt of approval as the family poured the chai. I asked Hari Baba if they
were able to spend some time with our hosts.

> *Hari Baba:* No.
>   *Ron:* Any conversation at all?
> *Hari Baba:* Not really. They were too busy.

I was appalled. No amount of reading prepared me for what seemed
to be an extremely asymmetrical social exchange. Not until our hosts led
us to the upper balcony did I begin to realize what the family had gained
from our presence. Neighbors were milling about on the streets below,
sitting on rooftops, and peering through windows. They were looking
at us, smiling and pointing, and talking excitedly among themselves. The
balcony was a stage, and we were making a curtain call with the Malayali family beside us. The dinner turned out to be a major event, a street
play starring two babas and a supporting cast of Westerners. Pryadarshi
Baba was especially famous in this neighborhood, but his ascetic lifestyle
was such that he rarely dined in family homes. Yet not only did he deem
to receive hospitality from this family, he brought along another baba
and an entourage of Western "VIPs."

The message was clear. This family was of such status that holy men
and other important people were willing to visit their home and, more
importantly, consume their food. We willingly partook of the family's
hospitality, assimilated their qualities through the medium of food and
service, and then marked the event for all the world to see. That the
Aghori could assimilate almost anything was of little consequence, because
few holy men or Westerners lived in this town; we represented these pop-
ulations by default. In exchange for food and drink, we publicly affirmed
the ritual status of an Indian family. Wonderful though the hospitality

was, it became apparent to us that the family had gained far more from the exchange than we had.

In his classic article, Marriott (1976) examines the social dynamics of food exchange among six South Indian caste groups. Building upon Mauss's (1990/1953) structural-functionalist model of competitive exchange rituals (such as potlatches and "Big Man" feasts), Marriott develops a matrix of exchange relationships that demonstrates how people of different status seek to minimize certain transactions while maximizing others. In contrast to Western notions of individuality and dualism, these transactions occur across a continuum of *dividual* actors through the exchange of coded substances. Cooked food is one of the most heavily encoded of these substances. It is therefore among the most important media for people to share, albeit differentially, in body and spirit.

While setting the stage for more fluid and dynamic notions of caste and kin (cf. Daniel 1984), Marriott's transactional theory follows Dumont's *Homo Hierarchicus* (1966), in which social inequalities are justified because they cancel each other out within a hierarchy of the whole. Other studies highlight the unresolved inequalities in these exchanges, noting the ambivalence of high status groups, such as Brahmin priests, when they must rely upon the "gifts" of economically dominant but ritually inferior communities (Raheja 1988; Parry 1986). For this reason, as Parry (1994) points out, the old-style Aghori acts a scavenger—as a means of maintaining his or her asceticism without having to rely upon the generosity of householders.

Granted, the Aghori do not recognize intrinsic categories of ritual or social hierarchy. They do express a strong preference, however, for having their meals prepared and served by people of good character and a proper frame of mind whenever possible. I have seen Hari Baba and Pryadarshi Baba eat all manner of food without hesitation, but I have also seen each complain vociferously when disciples did not prepare a meal with the proper attention and intention *(bhāv)* that it required. Nondiscrimination was never an excuse for a lack of discipline.

The same schema can be applied to the *dawā* and *duwā* of Aghor medicine. Aghori healers and patients may differ in their underlying philosophies and modes of purification, yet they share a foundational schema for the exchange of coded substances in which medicine, like food, functions as a kind of *prasād*. Once encoded, medicine becomes a medium for transmitting power from healer to patient, with all the opportunities and hazards that this transmission entails.

ENCODING THE *DUWĀ* IN THE *DAWĀ*

The medicines of Aghor span the range of India's professional and ritual healing traditions, biomedicine included. Patients and healers often insist that the unique qualities of Aghor medicines do not lie in a particular mode of treatment but rather in the blessings they convey: the *duwā* in the *dawā*. When I asked which was most effective, people usually emphasized the *duwā* over the *dawā*, but not without first struggling with the way that I had framed the question. In my phrasing, I had carelessly assumed that *dawā aur duwā dono* (both medicine and blessing) meant that medicine and blessing were distinct entities that one could evaluate separately. They were not. Although the blessings of Aghor could be encoded into any kind of medicine, the medicines themselves were not arbitrary. The blessing was not *contained within* the medicines. It *became* the medicines via the selection of ingredients, the preparation of compounds, and the "preparation" of the people who made and distributed them.

The *duwā* began with the inspiration for a particular combination of ingredients, medicines, or other therapies. Pryadarshi Baba taught me this lesson while pointing out the medicinal qualities of local flora during his late-afternoon walks in rural Chhattisgarh. Having a reputation for being the most attentive of Sarkar Baba's disciples, Pryadarshi Baba learned a great deal about the properties and uses of many plants. Yet the most important of these lessons was that if one achieved an Aghor-like state of exceptional stillness, the plants would reveal their medicinal purpose to him (see also Ram 1997). Direct knowledge of plant medicine was a dividend of Aghor in its purest sense. Divine inspiration was key to the development of herbal medications at Aghori ashrams. In discussing the early days at the KSA clinic, Mr. Asthana claimed that Sarkar Baba's decision to establish an Ayurvedic base of treatment primarily stemmed from practical considerations such as the cost and availability of materials, rather than from a specific ethnomedical theory. Yet this practicality was also linked to spirituality by the inspiration with which he modified Ayurvedic formulae with locally grown materials.

The Aghori were very clear about the fact that their medicines were not genuinely Ayurvedic. Sarkar Baba had modified all twelve of the most popular medications produced at their ashrams according to his inspiration (table 2). The Aghori were proud of this fact. A former physician of the KSA clinic stated, "[Sarkar Baba] used to also give suggestions in every medicine—[for example,] 'This is the medicine. It has to be adjusted

TABLE 2. TWELVE TOP-SELLING MEDICATIONS
MANUFACTURED BY THE KINA RAM ASHRAM

Name	Common Indications
Chyavan Prash	Fatigue, anemia, respiratory infections, impotence
Arhor Batī	Loss of appetite, arthritis
Awadhut Prameh Chūrṇ	Diabetes
Gēsor Chūrṇ	Digestive problems
Shatsakār Chūrṇ	Constipation, loss of vitality
Trifla Chūrṇ	Constipation, anorexia
Sindūrī Chūrṇ	General skin disorders
Kārha no. 3	Leukoderma (vitiligo)
Bāl Kādhā	Rheumatoid arthritis
Sudāmāvaleh	Cracked feet
Amogh Manjan	Tooth powder
Sri Siddharth Tēl	Hair oil

SOURCE: Dr. H. N. Uppadhaya, Kina Ram Clinic, 2000.

in this way.' Through this adjusting, Baba kept putting his *duwā* and *ashirwad* [blessing] in it. Very good results kept on coming supernaturally [because] all the medicines are not [that] pure."

One cannot easily separate the *duwā* from the *dawā* when the ingredients are divinely inspired and when this inspiration entails the ubiquitous theme of transubstantiation. In many popular Hindu traditions, the divine are not merely *represented* by statues and paintings of deities, shivalingams, or other religious features; they are those features themselves. They become what they inhabit, just as the wine of the sacrament becomes the blood of Christ for Catholic Christians. When Kina Ram charged Krim Kund with its healing powers, god and goddess became the mantra, the mantra became the grains, and everything became the *kund*.

Transubstantiation works for people as well. During the Ram Lila celebrations in Banaras, actors take to the streets as demons and deities in a locally written version of the epic Ramayana. The actors do not merely portray the divine. They become the divine figures, and thousands come to seek their presence no differently than if the deities took the form of statues sitting atop a temple altar (Lutgendorf 1989). Likewise, the television becomes a shrine when broadcasters present the Ramayana, Mahabharata, Krishna, and other religious plays. The actors who star in these shows are permanently typecast, however. They are not able to play any other kind of role thereafter, for the public will not tolerate their portrayal of mundane characters just as they will not tolerate their participation in the worldly vices of other Indian celebrities (Lutgendorf 1995).

The Aghori consider Sarkar Baba to be a manifestation of Lord Shiva. By extension, so are his disciples, albeit to a lesser extent. The ashram physicians claimed that Sarkar Baba, rather than education or experience, was the primary reason for their clinical successes. Such was the case for Dr. V. P. Singh, the chief medical officer of KSA in the days of Sarkar Baba, when the ashram physicians sometimes saw more than a hundred patients a day. Dr. Singh had since become famous for his treatment of leprosy, but he insisted that he knew little if anything about *kushṭh* diseases when he first met his guru. He merely allowed himself to be the instrument of Sarkar Baba, and the healing arose from there. "With Baba, I saw that his *duwā* was doing the thing [for] any patients. I used to keep on my work and *sevā*. In my mind [was the idea that] 'Everything is getting cured with Baba's *ashirwad.*'"

Of course, issues of legitimacy arise. One could argue that Sarkar Baba was the instrument of Dr. Singh and that by submitting his professional practice to ritual authority, the doctor could gain a distinct advantage in the intensely competitive medical marketplace. Just as the Kshatrya king relies upon the Brahmin priest to justify his worldly power, so the physician can rely on the holy man to justify his preeminence as a healer. Dr. Singh was a recent graduate with little experience and no reputation when he came to work for Sarkar Baba. Ten years later, he was famous.

Power dynamics notwithstanding, personal belief and personal advantage need not be exclusive of one another. Although I sometimes questioned the motives of professional healers who "volunteered" their time in Aghori clinics, I could easily identify the most dedicated among them. They were the ones who had the reputation without the wealth. They worked in the ashrams or held government jobs during the day and did not return to private clinics in the afternoons and evenings. They lived by modest means, in modest homes or in the ashrams. They were not unlike the Aghori babas, insofar as their asceticism was a mark of dedication. Under these conditions, professional healers like Dr. Singh were probably sincere instruments of their gurus. Many of their patients certainly believed them to be so.

Submission to the guru entails a certain frame of mind, which in turn informs the preparation and administration of medicines. The Aghori use the term *bhāv*, which translates as "intention" or "attitude," to describe this metaphysical link between attitude and action. As with the preparation of food, the Aghori strongly believe that a disciple must have the proper *bhāv* when preparing medicines. Sangita described this belief: "When I do not feel good, then I do not make the medicine. When I will like to make it, then I [will] make it; whether the medicine is finished and the patient is not being given [it]. But when I feel [ready] to do [it], then I will make the medicine. [Otherwise] I do not even touch [it]. The same thing with food . . . : When my mind will be still, then I will make [medicine]. Otherwise, I will not make [medicine]."

Through the principle of *bhāv,* Sangita's discussion of her guru's *duwā* extended to her own *duwā* insofar as the efficacy of the medications at least partly depended on her state of mind as she prepared them. She also cited the importance of *bhāv* in ensuring that the ashram pharmacy maintained higher standards of quality than those of other pharmacies making the same or similar medications: "The same medicines obtained from the outside are not as good. This is because there is so much [blessing] and feeling in this place. Ayurvedic medicines work much better when they are fresh. They are not as effective when they are old and dry. I make the medicines with that feeling and that is why they work."

Even with fresh ingredients, the manufacturing of medications can be complicated, requiring strict attention to detail. The preparation of *chyavan prash* is a good example. A specialty of the Kina Ram and Kusht Seva Ashrams, *chyavan prash* is one of the most popular Ayurvedic preparations in India. It is a thick brown paste, sweet and sour, and is a bit of an acquired taste. One could argue that *chyavan prash* is the cod liver oil of Ayurvedic medicine, the cure-all for whatever ails you, and a promoter of vitality and overall health if taken in heaping spoonfuls twice a day. I found it the most palatable of the Ayurvedic medicines that I tried.[1]

The *chyavan prash* produced by the Kina Rami had exactly fifty-two ingredients. I can attest to the difficulty and complexity of its manufacture because I once assisted a group of disciples in all the additions, extractions, and recombinations necessary to produce the final product. The process was tedious and exhausting, requiring twelve hours of constant attention. Not surprisingly, given the production demands and the importance of the product, the people who produced *chyavan prash* at the Kina Ram Ashram were the same ones entrusted with the preparation of offerings to the *akhand dhuni.* As with Aghor *prasād,* so too with Aghor medicine.

These themes of intention and attention have a practical dimension as well. Achieving quality control for herbal medications is very difficult. In contrast to biomedicines, which typically have only one or two kinds

Figure 13. Dr. H. N. Uppadhaya making Ayurvedic
medicine *(chyavan prash)* in
the kitchen of Aghor Guru
Seva Peeth Ashram, 2001.

of clinically active molecules, even the simplest herbal preparations can
overwhelm a chromatographer. Lacking the technical means of feasible
oversight, herbal manufacturers must trust in the integrity and compe-
tence of their employees. The public, in turn, must trust the manufacturers. Thus, for the patients of Aghor medicine, trusting the *duwā* was
a step toward trusting the *dawā;* it ensured the quality of their medicines
via the quality of the people who produced them.

The same model could be applied to physicians. Regardless of the
medical system, only a few people in any society have sufficient knowledge to evaluate the technical practice of one doctor over another. Most
patients must trust in the training, the reputation, or whatever positive or
negative cues the doctor provides during a therapeutic interaction. When
any of these better-known qualities are questionable, then, by extension,
lesser-known quantities may also come into question. Likewise, when a
patient trusts in the *duwā* of the doctor, then he or she can extend that
trust to the physician's therapies, prescriptions, and advice. The technical
details of the latter are not as relevant.

A cultural schema that casts medicine as a medium of exchange squares the plurality of Indian medical systems with the pragmatism of the people who must choose among them. If the primary function of the medicine is to transmit power from healer to patient, then the patient can employ a multiple-use strategy while being selective about the overall qualities of the healer. So when I asked patients about the etiology of their condition, they typically responded with the local equivalent of "How should I know? I'm not a doctor." But when I asked them why they chose Aghor, or some other medical system, they usually said that someone had told them that the Aghori were good healers, had helped other people with similar conditions, or had a lot of knowledge and power.

Of course, the Aghori had the greatest faith in the underlying knowledge and power of their own tradition. Discriminating only in the *duwā*, they were the most pluralistic of patients in taking their own medicines. Sarkar Baba was a prime exemplar of this attitude. I once asked Dr. Vindeshwari Singh of the KSA clinic what kinds of medicines the guru took. He shrugged his shoulders and let out a big sigh. "What can I say? He took them all."

Sarkar Baba suffered from diabetes, hypertension, and chronic renal failure. He simultaneously pursued Ayurvedic, homeopathic, and biomedical regimens for these conditions. Each regimen required that he take certain quantities of multiple medications at different times throughout the day. Yet, although he was fond of his doctors, Sarkar Baba had his own rhythm and manner of doing things. One disciple described the early days of his treatment: "One day he was visited by a medical doctor who gave him some tablets, then a homeopathic doctor came and gave him some small white pills and some liquid in a vial, then an Ayurvedic doctor came and gave him some powder and pills. After everyone left, Baba took all the pills, powders and liquids that were his supply for a week, put them in his bowl and swallowed them all in a gulp" (quoted in Ram 1997: 81).

This seemingly indiscriminate polypharmacy also applied to his prescriptions for patients. Sarkar Baba was known to offer anything within his reach to treat a patient: an herbal remedy, a sweet, or his own blood-pressure medications. All became Aghor medicine by an act of blessing. He was very particular about the latter, just as he was particular about his own medical counsel.

Hari Baba and Pryadarshi Baba attended to their guru while he received biomedical treatment in the United States. Both emphasized the importance of the relationship that Sarkar Baba had with his American physician, pointing out that their guru approved of him more because of his character than because of his technical reputation. The guru sought his attending physician for the briefest of personal interactions whenever he felt in need of assistance, therapy, or advice. Third parties would not do, including the residents, fellows, and other attending physicians on call. Having blessed his own physician, he considered this personal interaction to be a necessary condition for further biomedical treatment. One might argue that the physician became an instrument of Sarkar Baba's self-treatment and the healing power of Aghor.

AGHOR *SHAKTĪ*

Among patients of Aghor medicine, one of the major distinctions between disciples and nondisciples was their degree of faith in the power of Aghor. This power was represented by a cultural model of *shaktī* as a manifestation of the feminine divine. *Shaktī* is a fundamental principle of dynamism, (pro)creativity, and "heat" energy, or power. She is also a goddess. Shakti Ma manifests as *shaktī* energy just as Ganga Ma manifests as the river. On a higher level, all the divine mothers are essentially one. Thus, Shakti Ma and Ganga Ma are particular manifestations of a greater divinity that encompasses all goddesses, women, and dynamic processes. That greater divinity of all that is feminine is also known as Shakti. One can therefore imagine *shaktī* on at least three successive levels: as energy or power; as a particular goddess; or as all the goddesses rolled into one (cf. White 2003; Kurtz 1992).

In whatever form or scale that *shaktī* manifests, the Aghori reportedly had a lot of her. The Aghori were not shy about this point. Kamleshwar Baba strongly asserted that Aghor had the power to transform one's fate or karma. Lakshmi, a young college student and resident devotee of the ashram, asserted that "whatever God has written, only the Aghori can defy that." Rohit, a retired schoolteacher and patient-disciple, spoke with similar confidence: "One hundred [people] are not one hundred [people] for them. . . . And by *sādhanā* they can even tame one hundred dead bodies. They get the [dead bodies] to [work for them]. They . . . make everything suitable to them. They . . . take everything in their fist. Nothing is impossible for them."

Given such claims, we should not be surprised that so many nondisciples were willing to brave the skulls at the gate, prostrate themselves before Aghori ascetics, and eat the ashes from a *dhuni* fueled by leftover wood from a cremation pyre. Aghor *shaktī* is the power of those who live where no one else dares to tread. It is Shakti Ma in her ferocious and bloody form, dancing in the cremation grounds while holding a bladed weapon and a severed head. Srikant, an elderly Brahmin village leader with leukoderma, claimed that the *shaktī* of the Kina Ram Ashram was so great that people came only as a last resort. But India has no shortage of desperate people. Every year, thousands of people seek the Aghori for solutions to major social problems that no one else can solve, or for treatment of socially stigmatized illnesses that no one else can cure—conditions signifying that pollution and purity taboos had already been violated.

Most disciples had been in similar predicaments when they first approached the Aghori. They came seeking cures for chronic diseases or solutions to intractable problems. Significantly, the popular devotional literature of the Kina Ram Aghori presents more stories of miracles than treatises on metaphysical philosophy. Many of the stories describe Sarkar Baba's clairvoyance, his telepathy and foresight. They describe how, shortly after visiting him, people found their social and monetary problems spontaneously resolved. They tell of his ability to heal people of any and all manner of conditions. In the case of a small dog that was killed by a rickshaw, they even tell of his ability to resurrect the dead (Ram 1997).

Every disciple I knew had a story about how Sarkar Baba had performed a concrete miracle in his or her life. A retired professor described how Baba had ensured his safe passage on a long and difficult journey at a time when he was alone and penniless. An Ayurvedic physician once saw him cure a leprosy patient with a single sweet. Former residents said that they dared not misbehave on ashram grounds, for Sarkar Baba was aware of everything that happened around him. Disciples testified that he could instantly move from one part of the ashram to another; he could be in two places at once. He could also change his shape and appearance. Once, he even changed into a woman, an earthly manifestation of Shakti Ma. Sarkar Baba's powers, his *siddhis,* were godlike.

Members of the Mishra family told me about a time when Bantu was diagnosed with appendicitis. Just as he was about to have surgery, Sarkar Baba phoned to say that the diagnosis was wrong. He told his family to ask for a second opinion. As it turned out, Bantu's condition had spontaneously resolved. This and other miracles were particularly relevant for the Mishras. They were instrumental in bringing this family of orthodox Brahmins onto the spiritual path of Aghor and authenticating their decision to do so in the years to come.

The person who first brought the family into contact with Sarkar Baba was Bantu's father, Bharata Mishra. Bharata was a very spiritual man. He was generously charitable with the little money he earned, and he spent his off-time visiting many temples and holy men. One day, he took *darshan* with Sarkar Baba during one of his daily pilgrimages. Bharata was instantly taken by the peace and power of this ascetic. He eventually persuaded his brothers to visit the baba as well, but not until Sarkar Baba solved a major personal and financial crisis in the Mishras' natal village did the extended family begin to visit him regularly. Eventually, nearly all the Mishras became Aghor disciples.

Testimonies of miracles were of central importance to new Aghor disciples, most of whom had once been patients in some form or another. These testimonies usually occurred just before or after audiences with the guru, which were typically mixed gatherings of the faithful and the hopeful. They were also self-selective affairs. Those who did not resolve their problems eventually looked elsewhere. Those who did, however, returned again and again to tell their stories to the others around them. This process helped maintain a climate of collective optimism and expectation of the supernatural around Sarkar Baba and other Aghor ascetics. Under these conditions, return visitors eventually embraced the tradition as a way to obtain some Aghor *shaktī* for themselves.

THE FIRE OF DIGESTION

Cultural models of "medicine as *prasād*" and "power as *shaktī*" can both be found in the domain of alimentation, where spirit and substance are internalized and then transformed by the heat of digestion. Digestion is a central theme of Ayurvedic theory, serving as the crucible for mental and physical well-being. It is also central to Aghor philosophy, in which the omnivorous ascetic is the major prototype of nondiscrimination. Both systems link digestion to the element of fire. This link is especially relevant for the disciple-patient of Aghor medicine, for whom the fires of digestion entail a transformative approach to the healing process.

An Ayurvedic physician and self-identified Aghori, Svoboda (1993b) discusses the broader implications of digestion in Ayurveda:[2]

> Everything that enters a human being must be turned into a form that the human organism can utilize. Food, water, air, sunlight, touch, odours, tastes, sights and sounds and even thoughts and emotions from the outer world enter the inner world and alter it, forcing it to adapt. How well an

organism responds to these challenges and adapts to new conditions, how well it "digests" its experiences, is an expression of its innate equilibrium, its immunity to imbalance, its degree of coherence relative to external chaos. (50).

The concepts of *rasa* and *jaṭharāgni* are important to this digestive model. Derived from the Sanskrit word "to go," *rasa* has been alternately translated as an essence (Svoboda 1993), savor (Zimmerman 1987), or nutritive juice (Wujastyk 1998). All these interpretations emphasize the importance of underlying qualities *(guṇas)* in food and medicine and the energy necessary to transform the oppositions between these qualities into a state of balance.[3] This energy is *jaṭharāgni,* the fire of digestion. It is a manifestation of Agni, the Vedic fire deity. Dr. Dixit, an Ayurvedic physician at Banaras Hindu University, told me about the importance of Agni in the Ayurvedic model of digestion:

> Digestion is a major theme in Ayurvedic medicine. Appetite is also needed to be corrected—Agni—because in our Ayurvedic literature, Agni is very important. If the Agni is getting corrected, all the problems of the body are getting corrected. . . . [If there is] any problem in the body, the Agni is getting disturbed. The best physician is the one who is correcting the problem of the Agni. If the Agni is getting corrected, several problems are getting corrected. By the Agni, the *vata* can be corrected. The *kapha* can be corrected. Several diseases are there that can be corrected. Ayurvedic physicians are in the habit of treating the Agni primarily.

Agni is also the presiding deity of the *dhuni.* The Aghori sometimes refer to the *akhand dhuni* of Baba Kina Ram as the *Agni kund,* which literally means "well of fire." Here, the *akhand dhuni* not only represents the cremation pyre but also the digestive principle by which the "food" of one's worldly life is transformed into another mode of existence. For the Aghori, the fires of cremation and digestion are essentially the same. A young resident of the Kina Ram Ashram summarized this idea while describing Kina Ram's *dhuni:*

> It seems that everything that is here is a corpse. Meaning, just before you it [the *dhuni*] is burning. . . . It is burning, and we are dumping food in it. Here the cremation is happening. This is all corpse. Meaning, it has nothing to do with life. We do not use it as we should. That is the main thing. The energy that we are getting from it [stomach]; the energy which we are getting from that [*dhuni*] that is in the form of fire. My whole body is running from the energy it gets from it. [switching to English] Like we eat food. You can understand that it is the cremation ground wood. Here is *dhuni* [pointing to his stomach]—continuously burning. It is gone. This is *dhuni.*

With but a few exceptions, the Agni of the cremation pyre does not discriminate among the corpses that it consumes. Likewise, the *jaṭharāgni* of the Aghori should be undiscriminating in the substances that it digests. It burns bright enough to transform anything that it encounters. Mishraji, an elderly Brahmin disciple of Baba Rajeshwar Ram, spoke with Sujata about the assimilating effect of Agni in Aghor:

> *Mishraji:* If you put cream in [the fire], or you pour milk in it, or you pour buttermilk in it, what will happen to it? It will burn. Now, you put excrement in it, then what will happen?
>
> *Sujata:* It will burn.
>
> *Mishraji:* Any Aghor is like Agni. The Aghor sect is an Agni sect.

Shakti and Agni are closely intertwined in Aghor tradition. Shakti lives in Agni as its heat and activity. Shakti also lives beside Agni as Svaha, his divine consort. When celebrants make offerings in the *dhuni* or cremation pyre, they utter the name of Svaha aloud so that she will pass them along to Agni. Svaha is the Shakti of all fires just as Ganga Ma is the Shakti of all rivers. Both are as indiscriminate as they are powerful.

Anything and everything—whether milk or excrement, medicine or meat—is potentially digestible in Aghor. The *jaṭharāgni* of the Aghori can break down and transform anything it receives. Given the choice, the Aghori will consume those offerings that are given with the best of intentions, but they do not have to do so. The Aghori can take the best of the offerings and convert the rest into something better than before. Because of this power, the Aghori healer need not worry about contamination from his or her patients. Nor does the patient-cum-disciple have to worry about the mortal implications of what is being transmitted with the medicine.

As we have seen, many nondisciple patients at Krim Kund described their approach to healing as a process of dumping *(dālnā)* problems on to the Aghori. This approach is predominantly influenced by a transportive schema of purification in which the Aghori function much like the Ganga, relieving humanity of pollution and sin by taking these matters on themselves. The promise of Aghor *shaktī* brings nondisciple patients through the gates and even gets them through the rituals, but most patients lack the motivation to internalize the symbols and meanings of these ritual actions. They can bathe in the *kund* and take *darshan* in the *dhuni* without having to consider their own inevitable cremation. They can take advantage of the nondiscrimination of their healers without having to give up their own prejudices.

Not so with Aghor disciples, for whom the fire of digestion entails a transformative schema of purification by which symbol and substance are deeply internalized. Others may dump or pour their problems on the Aghori so as to push them away. The Aghori, however, must confront their problems by ingesting them, breaking them down, and transforming them into something useful, something that is part of themselves. Thus, the primary ritual prototype of Aghor medicine, the *kund-dhuni* healing sequence, not only enacts the basic elements of cremation; it challenges the participant to consume the *prasād* of his or her ultimate sacrifice. The ultimate medicine of Aghor is the *prasād* of one's own mortality. In the next chapter, we will explore the idea that this medicine holds the key to attaining a state of discrimination.

CHAPTER 6

Death and Nondiscrimination

Aghorānnā paro mantro nasti tattvam guroh param.

Shiva Mahimnah Stotram, v. 35

One afternoon, I was sitting with the Mishra family in the *shmashān* at Harischandra Ghat when the second-eldest son of the patriarch, Ramchandra, asked what I thought to be a fairly basic question:

> *Ramchandra:* How many people do you think there are in the world?
> *Ron:* Maybe six and a half billion.
> *Ramchandra:* No, no. More. Many more. *All* the people who have lived in the world. [pause] Think of all the people who have lived in the world. All these people, and none are the same. You and me, and even my brothers . . . there may be some small like-nesses, but we are cut differently. Imagine the mechanism that can do this.

He then discussed how he had studied various arguments for the existence of God when he was attending university. Of all the arguments and evidence that he had considered, this miracle of human diversity struck Ramchandra as the most compelling proof for the existence of God. We were quiet for a long time afterward.

I was moved, partly by the content of Ramchandra's statements, but even more by the context in which he was making them. Ramchandra's father, Lakshman Mishra, had died that morning, and we had come to the *shmashān* to cremate his body. Ramchandra and I were among thirty friends and family who had joined the procession to Harischandra Ghat. We had taken turns carrying the bier (litter) on our shoulders while chanting "Ram Nam Satya Hai," "God's name is truth." I had mixed feelings at the time. On one hand, I felt a sense of obligation. Lakshmanji was the father of my key informant and future guru, the grandfather of my fictive brother, and a sometime patient whom, despite my better intuition, I had not visited the previous evening because of reports that his condition had improved. On the other hand, I also felt a certain sense of excitement. This funeral was a unique ethnographic opportunity—a chance to share some of the emotions and dynamics surrounding the process of death and grieving in a family whose members were Brahmins by birth and Aghor disciples by choice.

The situation became more complicated when we arrived at the *shmashān*. The ritual mechanics were pretty much the same as those I had seen during previous visits: we washed the body in the river, negotiated for the wood, placed the body on the pyre, and made our final offerings of incense and ghee. We then retreated to the sidelines while Lakshmanji's eldest son, Balavanji, cremated his father under the guidance of a Dom attendant.

I had observed these rites a hundred times among strangers but could not fully process the feelings that I was now experiencing for people whom I had come to know and love. I felt the solidarity of a strong extended family coming together for a single purpose. I felt the pain of an old wound that caused one granddaughter to break her customary silence and cry aloud before returning home with the rest of the women. I felt the quiet sadness of Lakshmanji's sons that rose and fell like waves beneath their stoic poses. The most stoic of them all, Balavanji—with shaven head, white shawl, and a staff in his hand—squatted alone beside the pyre. He was the dutiful son who had stayed back in the village to care for the family farm while his brothers went to college in the city. He now stood apart from his brothers once again to perform another duty, waiting for the right moment to crack open the thousand-petaled chakra at the top of his father's skull to release his soul from this round of worldly existence. Afterward, Balavan Mishra would become the family patriarch.

Ramchandraji talked with me about human diversity and the existence of God shortly after his father's soul was released. As he spoke, his gaze frequently shifted to his father's burning body. My gaze shifted as well, as I tried in vain to cognitively process the feeling that somehow integrated what I was hearing with what I was seeing. At one such moment, the Dom attendant broke off the corpse's legs and placed them atop the chest. In strictly visual terms, this was like a scene out of a horror film. Yet emotional though he was, Ramchandra did not flinch or cry, nor did he turn away from this graphic destruction of his father's body. Instead, he meditated upon the uniqueness of all human bodies and the cosmic power behind their creation.

This experience exemplified what my informants had been trying to tell me throughout my fieldwork: that Aghor is not a specific religion or set of practices, but rather a state of mind. It is a state of nondiscrimination in which there is no hatred, no fear, and no aversion to anyone or anything. I recalled the sense of *shantī aur shaktī dono* (both peace and power) that some resident informants at the ashram had described to me. I felt something like it at this moment, though I could fathom only enough of Ramchandra's experience to appreciate its further depth.

Contemplating divinity in the face of decomposition is the ideal Aghor *sādhanā*. Its purpose is to overcome fears and aversions that impede the process of spiritual liberation. The Aghori believe that the greatest human fear is that of death; all other aversions are but diminutive examples of this mortality anxiety. Consequently, they developed spiritual exercises for confronting death. Some of these exercises have brought them considerable notoriety: meditating atop corpses in the cremation grounds, consuming human waste and, occasionally, human flesh. The renunciates of the Kina Ram lineage replaced most of these extreme practices with more socially acceptable alternatives, such as service work with the indigent poor and the healing of stigmatized diseases. They admit, however, that some of their adherents perform the old-style practices from time to time. In either case, mortality confrontation still lies at the heart of Aghor *sādhanā,* and nearly all the disciples I knew had spent at least some time meditating in the cremation grounds.

One of my major objectives in this ethnography is to clarify some common misconceptions about the Aghori. The antinomian practices (hereafter "the practices") of the Aghori lie at the heart of these misconceptions. Taking up my earlier argument that discrimination is an illness in itself, I suggest that Aghor *sādhanā* represents a powerful therapy for this condition. But Aghor *sādhanā* can be one of the most difficult medicines to take, especially when disciples must balance their ideals of nondiscrimination with the realities of living in contemporary Indian society.

THE FOUNDATION

Old style or new, every Aghori spiritual practice is founded upon a mantra and a guru-disciple relationship. Both these elements are common in Indian religious traditions. The mantra can be any sequence of sounds, words, or phrases that aim to focus the disciple in meditation. Most often, mantras take the form of short prayers or a series of seed syllables known as *bijas*. The most common prayer mantra is the Gayatri Mantra, a hymn from the Ṛg Veda to the goddess of mantras and songs (RV 3: 36). Many people chant the Gayatri Mantra at dawn while offering water to Surya, the sun god, as part of their ritual ablutions in the Ganga.

Bija mantras are a sequence of seed syllables that many people believe to be the root of all sacred language. *Aum* is considered to be the ultimate *bija*, the source from which all others emanated when the universe emerged (Woodroffe 1994/1922). All *bijas* are considered to be a fundamental part of the greater cosmos, from which each sound manifests a particular deity or principle. *Krīm* is the *bija* of Kali; its sound manifests the principles of fiery dynamism and severance from worldly attachments. These principles contain worldly power as well, for *Krīm* was the *bija* with which Baba Kina Ram charged the *kund*.

Bija mantras are fundamentally linked to the microcosm of the human body. According to the classical schools of Samkya and Yoga, the physical body is merely one of five interrelated "sheaths," ranging from gross (physical) to subtle (ethereal). Within the subtle body, currents flow along certain channels *(nadis)*, the major intersections of which are known as chakras. Different traditions dispute the exact number and location of the chakras, but many associate them with certain *bija* sounds (Woodroffe 1994/1922; Tirtha 1980). Interestingly, when the Aghori chant *Krīm* aloud, they are taught to focus on the Manipura Chakra, the chakra associated with digestion.

Esoteric teachings notwithstanding, the Aghori believe that a disciple needs little if any background information to reap the benefits of a mantra. The mantra can influence the disciple even if he or she knows nothing about it other than its sound and its practice. This precept is so common among Indian religious traditions that Staal (1990) has described *bija* mantras and their associated rituals as "rules without meaning." Staal's assertion is part of a larger argument that rituals in general, and Vedic rituals in particular, communicate nothing more than orthopraxy. Unvoiced *bija* mantras are a prime example of this principle. Lacking explicit definition, these mantras are prelinguistic and meaningless, for they do not convey a specific message.

However, Staal does not discount the possibility that mantras can be individually meaningful. Unvoiced mantras are an important constituent of mystical experience, which rests on the epistemological premise that one can obtain specific knowledge by direct experience, without resorting to empirical or rational inquiry (cf. Staal 1990; King 1988). Aghor mantras, like those of other liberation traditions, are devices for apprehending truths that cannot be adequately described by ordinary language. Indeed, as meditative tools, *bija* mantras actually help to negate ordinary language and the day-to-day thoughts they convey, serving to clear the mind and make it receptive to another kind of experience. The mystical nature of this experience disqualifies any proof or disproof of its reality by logical or empirical means. Insofar as meaning has a truth value, the truth of the mantra (or lack thereof) cannot be humanly communicated even by the guru. Far be it for the scholar to attempt such communication.

Nonetheless, I disagree with Staal's disconnection of ritual action from meaning. Mysticism aside, the ritual use of the mantra conveys important social messages. The orthopraxy to which Staal refers is the fidelity with which a disciple performs a specific set of instructions that he or she receives from a religious teacher or sacred text. The disciple therefore affirms his or her relationship with the teacher or text by faithfully performing these instructions. When someone practices a mantra given by a guru, the *practice* of the mantra conveys the message "I am the disciple of my guru" regardless of any other meanings or experiences it may carry. In this manner, the orthopraxy of ritual action entails certain kinds of social relationships.

Mantras can also convey a sense of collective identity within broad sets of social relationships. Until this point in the book, I have used the terms *devotee* and *disciple* interchangeably to describe members of the Kina Ram Aghor lineage. However, the Aghori make a distinction between the two: the disciple has taken a secret mantra from an Aghori ascetic in a special ritual known as *dīkshā*, whereas the devotee has not necessarily done so. The *dīkshā* is a private rite in which an Aghori teacher gives the candidate a mantra and instructs him or her on its use. Ideally, this occasion is the only time that the mantra is spoken aloud. Thereafter, the mantra becomes a silent secret between guru and disciple, as well as the primary marker of their special relationship. The disciple may have other kinds of teachers, even other spiritual teachers, but she or he is expected to have but one *dīkshā* guru in a lifetime. Likewise, the *dīkshā* guru has only one such guru, and so on. In this manner, the ritual conveyance of secret mantras establishes a primary chain of formal relationships that comprises the religious lineage. So when an Aghor disciple practices the mantra received by *dīkshā*, he or she affirms membership in the Kina Ram Aghor lineage. The spiritual ancestors of the guru become his or her ancestors as well, and the disciples of those ancestors become his or her guru brothers *(guru bhāīs)* and guru sisters *(guru bahans)*. So in addition to all its other meanings, the mantra entails a special kind of kinship.

However personal the mantra may be, Aghor disciples share a common set of rules governing its formal practice in *japa* meditation. Aghori *japa* begins with a cyclical breathing exercise *(prāṇāyama)* and proceeds to a series of voiced preparatory chants. The disciple then mentally offers flowers *(manasic pūjā)* to at least one of three goddesses—Kali, Lakshmi, or Sarasvati—that represent the three most essential aspects of the Divine Mother, Sri Sarveshwari. The disciple also makes mental offerings to her or his *dīkshā* guru *(Sri Guru)*, Awadhut Bhagwan Ram *(Parama Guru)*, and Lord Datattreya *(Ādi Guru)*. After these preparatory rites, the disciple silently recites his or her mantra in factors of 108 repetitions, an auspicious number in many Indian religious traditions. The disciple counts these repetitions with a necklace *(mala)* of a corresponding number of beads, usually made of wood or seeds from the *rudraksha* tree ("the eye of Rudra").

For *japa* meditation, the disciple commits to practicing a certain number of *malas* each day from the beginning of one full moon *(pūrṇima)* to the next. At the end of each lunar cycle, the disciple participates in a *havan* ceremony in which he or she offers the accumulated mantras into the *dhuni* fire. Hari Baba likens this ritual to making a deposit in the bank, for each successful offering is thought to confer long-term benefits for the disciple. It is also thought to confer collective benefits. However personal the experience of the mantra may be, the rites of *havan* can be highly social in their action and purpose, especially when the participants share a common *dīkshā* guru.

In addition to following the formal rules of *japa* meditation, the disciple is encouraged to informally practice the mantra throughout the day. Hari Baba likens the mantra to a good friend with whom one should spend time whenever possible. Consequently, Aghor disciples recite their mantra(s) to enjoy a quiet moment, prepare for a challenging encounter, or simply pass the time. These recitations often take place during spontaneous moments, free from the ritual rules of *japa* meditation. The only requirements at these times are that the disciple avoid negative thoughts during the recitation itself and that he or she not recite the mantra aloud. The Aghori believe that voicing the mantra dissipates its *shaktī*. The disciple also runs the risk of being heard by someone else.

The only aspect of the mantra practice that disciples do not share is the mantra itself. No Aghor disciple ever knows the mantra of another.

Only the *dīkshā* guru knows whether or not any of his or her disciples have the same mantra. Pryadarshi Baba once told a parable about a disciple who received a mantra from his guru, "Aum Namo Shivaya" ("Om, in the name of Lord Shiva"). The disciple diligently practiced his mantra until he heard a man chanting "Aum Namo Shivaya" while bathing in the Ganga. The disciple berated his guru for having given him such a common prayer. In response, his guru sent him to find the best possible price for a particular stone. The disciple first approached a government official, who offered to pay him ten rupees for its use as a paperweight. He then found a blacksmith, who, noting the unusual hardness of the stone, offered to pay him one hundred rupees so that he could fashion it into a cutting tool. Finally, the disciple came upon a gemologist, who instantly recognized it as a rare and valuable stone and offered to pay ten thousand rupees for it. The disciple recounted these findings to his guru. The guru then explained that his mantra was like the stone: it may be common to many, but only a few understand its full value.

In the spirit of this parable, Aghor disciples practice their mantras in the hopes that they will someday come to realize the full value of their *sādhanā* (practice). Of course, to make a lifetime commitment to their mantras, disciples must have a great deal of trust in the guru and in the spiritual rewards of Aghor *sādhanā*. They must trust in the *shaktī* of the guru, believing that the act of conveying the mantra ensures its intrinsic value, regardless of its particular form. Aghor mantras are homologous to Aghor medicines in this regard.

Vivek Sar is a primary text for Aghor *sādhanā*. Attributed to Baba Kina Ram, the text is similar to the Yoga Sutras of Patañjali in that it comprises aphorisms for eight stages leading to a state of spiritual liberation while still living in the material world *(jīvanmukti)*.[1] But whereas Patañjali begins with a list of instructions for right and wrong conduct, Baba Kina Ram begins with only one: "Worship at the Lotus Feet of the Guru."[2] Submission to the guru is a common theme in Indian religious traditions, and the Aghori are no exception in this regard (cf. Flood 1998; Brooks 1990). Aghor babas often tell new disciples that if their own guru was sitting across from Lord Shiva himself, they would first bow to the guru. Pausing long enough to ensure that the puzzle sinks in, the babas then explain that (per the unstated principle of transubstantiation) the guru is but another manifestation of Shiva. In bowing to their guru first, the disciples would simply be choosing a more familiar form of Shiva— the guru form—over another. In Aghor, as in many Indian religious traditions, the guru is God.

The academic literature has mainly taken a psychoanalytic approach to the guru-disciple relationship and to the nature of submission in Indian religious traditions. Kakar (1999) treats the guru-disciple relationship as a traditional form of the psychotherapeutic relationship. He argues that the guru, like the psychotherapist, "heals" the disciple through the relationship itself, by serving as an object of identification. In contrast to the classic transference cure, in which patients reveal unconscious conflicts by projecting them onto the therapist, identification focuses on positive personality attributes, whether projected or not. By identifying with the ideal aspects of the guru, the disciple is inspired to improve upon his or her personality, in a process called "health via identification" (Oremland cited in Kakar 1982: 277). By extension, one could view the deification of the guru, and the subsequent identification with that deity, as an attempt to deify the self. This proposition resonates with one of Sarkar Baba's most popular sayings: "The guru does not create a disciple. The guru creates another guru."

Psychoanalysts sometimes create other analysts, partly by means of the therapeutic process. Yet none would accept divine status along the way. Deification might seem to be a powerful proxy for individuation, but it presents at least two important dilemmas for psychoanalysis. The first concerns the Indian Oedipus and the question of whether and how individuation is possible within India's joint families. Some scholars argue that the reciprocal ties of the Indian family preclude children's individuation from their parents (Kurtz 1992) or redirect individuation into a familial form of self (Roland 1990). Others take a more culturally relativistic approach. Obeyesekere (1999) suggests that identification by submission leads to a Hindu-specific form of individuation in which the son duplicates his father rather than replacing him. Kakar (1999) asserts that individuation among Hindus must be understood in Hindu terms, as a process of internal self-awareness in which gurus and gods serve as transitional objects that disciples can dispose of once they have served their purpose. But this disposability may work better in theory than in practice because, unlike the temporary psychotherapeutic relationship, the guru-disciple relationship is supposed to last a lifetime or more. Thus, if the guru is God, then the guru will always be a god from which individuation is impossible.

The second dilemma concerns the more general phenomenon of submission in Indian religious traditions. The concept builds on the Freudian argument that the mystical search for an "oceanic feeling" of cosmic union is actually an attempted regression toward an infantile stage of development that does not differentiate between ego and mother (Freud 1961). One argument holds that total submission to a deified guru is simply an anthropomorphized version of this regression. Applying a similar argument to Indian goddess traditions, Kurtz (1991) asserts that many Indians have an affinity for submission to the Goddess because they experienced the traumatic interruption of an indulgent mother-child dyad at around the age of five, when their parenting, by custom, was delegated to the extended family.[3]

Although this argument seems ethnocentric, it is difficult to discount completely. The Aghori compare the guru-disciple relationship to that of parent and child. Likewise, they refer to the guru as *baba* ("father"), and the word they use for disciple, *shishya,* means "child." One could interpret the fatherly role as that of guiding the child to his or her "mother," the Divine Mother in this case.[4] From here, transposing the roles of father and mother is relatively easy, bringing additional meaning to Sarkar Baba's miraculous appearance as the Goddess. Perhaps even more telling is the Aghori's explicit comparison of their spiritual objective to the nondiscrimination of infants and small children. The Freudian case has rested on less evidence than this.

Yet the problem with extending the regression argument to guru deification is that it rests on a mistaken premise about the elements that the disciple and guru bring to their relationship. As both a psychoanalyst and a disciple of an Indian religious tradition, Vigne (1997) has drawn important distinctions between these two domains. In contrast to the psychotherapeutic relationship—in which the patient does most of the talking and the therapist does most of the listening—the Indian teaching relationship calls for the disciple to actively listen to and observe the guru. Whereas the patient learns to express all manner of thoughts and emotions in therapy, the disciple is on his or her best behavior in the presence of the guru, consciously projecting the most positive elements of his or her personality. The therapist maintains a nonjudgmental stance during a session, but the guru has no such restrictions. The guru may respond with sharp criticism or detached neutrality, as he or she deems appropriate. The guru may be a mirror to the disciple, but this mirror need not offer the kind of passive reflection that the psychotherapist is trained to provide. The guru may be more like a parent than a therapist in this regard, but this parental role is geared more toward the needs of an older child than toward those of an infant. The guru may have unconditional love for the disciple, but the expression of this love can be highly contingent.

In this context, transference and identification become the selective processes that Kakar (1999) describes. Disciples transfer the ideal aspects of themselves to their gurus as deities. Gurus modify the image as they see fit, and the disciples identify with the ideal aspects of the reflection. Each disciple becomes more like the ideal personality, the guru-deity, yet retains the basic elements of his or her personality, which he or she never projected onto the guru in the first place. This does not exclude the possibility of *unio mystica* in the guru-disciple relationship. But the submission need not entail a complete merger of ego and guru along the way. The Indian teaching tradition emphasizes superego development, not infantile regression, even though it leaves the questions of individuation and enlightenment unanswered.

Clearly, the guru-disciple relationship can be a complicated affair. If I could generalize about my observations during the many hours I spent sitting at the feet of Aghori babas, I would say that the gurus' interactions with individual disciples are more varied than are the disciples' interactions with one another. There is a regular pattern in the ways that Aghor disciples behave toward one another in the presence of a baba. Within the traditional bounds of polite interaction, they typically treat each other as (1) kin (real or fictive, but not just old friends), (2) occasional friends (but not acquaintances), (3) or new friends (but rarely guests), or (4) they deftly avoid each other altogether (a situation that may be inclusive of kin). Though exceptions and nuances to these interactions certainly exist, these are the dominant patterns.

In contrast, the interactions between Aghor babas and their disciples are difficult to characterize. Their relationships often go through a honeymoon period of variable duration after *dīkshā,* during which time the guru is kind, generous, and forgiving. But once the disciple becomes "established" in the initial stages of his or her practice, anything goes. The babas may be attentive or ignore their disciples altogether. Sarkar Baba stopped talking to one of his senior disciples for more than a year. Yet this disciple eventually became a fully recognized renunciate, the head of the Parao Ashram and Sri Sarveshwari Samooh, the service organization that oversees most of the clinics and schools of the lineage. But it is also possible that Sarkar Baba had been communicating indirectly with this disciple all the while. With multiple disciples in the audience, Aghor babas often use public discussions *(satsangs)* as to teach lessons to one or more disciples while ostensibly communicating with other people. In this manner, an Aghor guru can transmit different messages to different disciples within a single conversation. Moreover, these indirect conversations need not take place through another disciple or devotee. They can happen while the guru talks with a patient, a guest, or a complete stranger. A visitor can be an especially good muse for this kind of meta-instruction, especially when a basic question prompts the guru to offer an unpredictable answers or affirm a seemingly counter-intuitive statement.

Aghor disciples become increasingly aware of these dynamics after they have been around a while. Consequently, they learn to become active listeners. They also learn that submission to the guru has a practical component, for they cannot predict when a suggestion or command will contain a key lesson for their spiritual development. Once, while caring for Sarkar Baba during his visit to the United States, Pryadarshi Baba and Hari Baba began massaging the feet of their guru while he slept.[5] Sarkar Baba suddenly awoke and began chastising them. "What are you doing? Go and wash the dishes!" The younger Hariji was about to tell his guru that they had just finished washing the dishes when he saw his elder guru brother return to the kitchen. Without hesitation or comment, Pryadarshiji rewashed each and every dish. Sarkar Baba may have been unaware that the dishes had already been washed. But a slight possibility existed that he did know and that the additional dish washing contained an important lesson. Either way, the dishes certainly contained an important lesson in spiritual pedagogy. The media of Aghor teachings can be as varied as those of Aghor medicines.

Even in the postreform tradition, the Aghor guru can be harsh at certain times and with certain people—if, for example, the disciple is not living up to his or her potential, appears to be too complacent or egotistical, or is ready to move to the next level of practice. In those instances, the guru may scold or berate the disciple in private. In other instances, the guru may adopt more public forms of humiliation to break down the disciple's ego or provide a metalesson for other disciples. The guru may have the disciple work with a particularly difficult devotee or visitor as a learning exercise or test. This technique is reminiscent of the popular fables of Birbal, the chief advisor in the Mughal court of King Akbar. In these stories, the king often tests Birbal by allowing other people to put him in difficult situations. He then observes the clever manner in which Birbal overcomes them. Unlike the games at the Court of Akbar, however, the challenges of the *"shmashān"* (read broadly) are rarely overcome by the intellect alone. The Aghor guru usually operates at a much deeper level in guiding the disciple on the path to nondiscrimination.

The Aghori claim that nondiscrimination is a simple goal. Achieving that goal, however, can be difficult. A seeker must face core fears and aversions and overcome years of socialization. If the disciple is a householder, he or she must gain independence from many aspects of the surrounding culture while retaining enough structure to manage family, occupation, and community status. Krishna described a similar ideal of balance to Arjuna upon the battlefield of the Bhagavad Gita: the ideal of living in the world while not being of it. The task of the guru can be even more difficult. The guru must guide the disciple according to his or her needs and capabilities in the situation at hand. The guru must also inspire growth in the disciple without throwing him or her too far off kilter. Consequently, dyadic interactions between Aghor gurus and disciples are as varied as the individuals themselves. The gurus' challenges to disciples are just as varied; they may take the form of general "suggestions" for daily living or specific instructions for ritual actions. The pedagogy can be conventional or unconventional, as can the lessons themselves. It is in the context of unconventional lessons that the Aghori sometimes perform unusual ritual practices.

THE LEFT-HAND PATH

In my fieldwork, collecting data on the old-style Aghori practices was highly problematic. An inverse relationship seemed to exist between the willingness of people to talk about such practices and the reliability of their knowledge. Just outside the Kina Ram lineage, I encountered non-disciples (middle-aged men, mostly) who claimed secret knowledge about *shav sādhanā* (corpse meditation), cannibalism, and other antinomian rites. With a smile and a wink, these men alluded to their secrets without prompting. But their subsequent narratives were either inconsistent or well within the range of popular knowledge. I was dubious about their stories.

Among the few old-style disciples who continued to practice antinomian rites along the peripheral domains of the Kina Ram lineage, most rites involved the consumption of alcohol and marijuana. With rare exceptions, such as Lal Baba and a young Naga I knew at Manikarnika, their motives were suspect even when their ritual actions were not. Like the fishermen who drank whiskey at the *shmashān* but refused to share the same cup, these old-style practitioners seemed more interested in intoxication and social discourse than in achieving a state of nondiscrimination.

The time that Bantu and I spent with them was not entirely wasted, however. We learned much about the old days of Baba Rajeshwar Ram during our initial moments of sobriety before we all slid into a stupor. These sessions mainly resulted in hangovers and hours of incomprehensible recordings. They helped me appreciate why Sarkar Baba reformed the lineage.

I figured that my best sources of information on the practices would be the officially recognized Aghori babas within the Kina Ram lineage. After all, the insights of Baba Kina Ram's successors on these matters would be salient to the members of the lineage and, by extension, for my operationalized definition of Aghor tradition. Unfortunately, however, I was following in the footsteps of previous researchers who had come bearing microphones and notebooks in search of exotic tales. Many of my predecessors had made the Kina Rami distrustful of scholars and journalists. Those who were in the best position to speak about the practices were reticent to do so.

I decided to tread cautiously and take my time. I did not ask the babas about the practices until my second year of fieldwork, after I had spent time living and working with the community, and after they had developed a sense of who I was and what I was doing. Although I did not take *dīkshā* until my final months of fieldwork, the Aghori nevertheless regarded me as Hari Baba's (Western) disciple throughout my time in the field. They therefore assumed that I had a spiritual agenda that extended beyond my academic research, which was indeed the case. They understood that my research focus was the *dawā* and *duwā* of Aghor, not unusual ritual practices per se. Many believed that this work would help clarify popular misconceptions about Aghor. Moreover, I had already been around enough to know that some of these rites were still practiced. By speaking with me about these practices, the babas could help me place them in an appropriate cultural context. For these reasons, I was able to discuss the details of these rites with the living ascetic who was considered to be the most knowledgeable about Aghori rituals. Pryadarshi Baba shared his insights on the antinomian practices with the understanding that I would represent them fairly. Hari Baba served as our interpreter as well as a frequent discussant.

Pryadarshi Baba was emphatic that the extremely heterodox practices of the old-style Aghori occurred rarely if ever in the postreform tradition, because they had other, equally valid but more socially acceptable approaches to attaining a state of nondiscrimination. He likened these alternatives to algebraic equations:

Figure 14. Hari Baba (left) and Pryadarshi Baba (right) on a cycle rickshaw in Banaras, 2000. Photograph by Howard Morris.

One equation could be very short and quick. That may get you the same result. The other equation may take a little longer time, but it is simple and easy, and steady and . . . you get there. It takes longer. But today [if] you are confronting the fear, and just going for it, it's a little quicker way. But it is equally dangerous. You may be caught in the equation, some little square root or something. You may spend time . . . all of your time trying to figure that one out. So both are valid.

In earlier conversations, Hari Baba used the more traditional terms *dakshinamarg* (right-hand path) and *vamamarg* (left-hand path) to describe these two approaches. The left hand is considered inauspicious in Indian society, as it is in many others (Hertz 1960).[6] Whereas the right hand is used for ritual exchanges and eating, the left hand alone has the inauspicious duty of cleaning one's anus after defecation. Extending the left-hand metaphor to spiritual development, *vamamarg* refers to traditions that use inauspicious methods to attain a spiritual goal. Hari Baba stressed, however, that *dakshinamarg* and *vamamarg* traditions shared the same goal, in keeping with the popular saying that "the paths may be many, but the goal is one." His was the nondualist assertion that a

single teleology underlies apparent differences in Indian religious traditions just as a single underlying mystery can be manifested in many different gods and goddesses.

Hari Baba then pointed out that *vamamarg* and *dakshinamarg* are
complementary to one another; they are like two banks of a river that
work together to channel the water in a certain direction. The disciple
might use one or the other path, or a certain combination of both, at
different stages of his or her development. Moreover, the disciple need
not be an Aghori to combine left-hand approaches with right-hand ones.
Many famous seekers have undergone a *vamamarg* stage, usually just
before achieving a major breakthrough. The Goddess did not appear
before the Bengali saint Ramakrishna until just after he renounced his
Brahmin status and ate rice off the temple floor. Banaras's famous poet
Tulsi Das had a similar experience before becoming inspired to write a
Hindi version of the epic Ramayana. The Aghori claim that the Buddha
underwent a similar stage prior to his enlightenment.

However apocryphal, these stories and claims illustrate an important
point: although disciples may use the *vamamarg* at certain stages, this
approach is not appropriate for every stage of spiritual development.
Hari Baba and Pryadarshi Baba affirmed that antinomian practices are
too dangerous for beginners because they are potentially destabilizing
and often corrupting. The alcoholics who flocked to Baba Rajeshwar
Ram were a prime example of this danger. In addition, the babas said
that these practices were not appropriate for the more advanced seekers
who had already moved beyond their basic fears and aversions. The guru
is the best judge of whether or when to travel along the *vamamarg*. The
decision depends on the teaching style of the guru, the needs of the disciple, and the relationship between them.

Left-hand practices are meant to be temporary exercises, not permanent ways of living. They are supposed to be practiced in moderation,
no more than is needed to overcome a particular obstacle to nondiscrimination. For instance, when I spoke with Pryadarshi Baba about the
practice of consuming one's own feces, he measured an inch between his
thumb and forefinger as if holding up an imaginary piece of *bhang*.
"That is not to fill your belly with," he said. We all broke into laughter
while he continued: "You may want to take a little to get over aversion
. . . just to get over [it]." Pryadarshi Baba spoke about coprophagy in
the context of *agrna*, (nonaversion). Next to Aghor, *agrna* is a common
synonym of nondiscrimination among the Kina Rami. When practicing
coprophagy, disciples should not be averse to a product of their own

bodies, especially when it is something they ate in the first place. Then again, practitioners need not make a feast out of their feces once they have understood the lesson.

Coprophagy is supposed to be practiced without ceremony. But the handling of most traditionally polluted substances occurs within the ritual framework of the *havan,* in which substances are sacrificed to the *dhuni* fire. For instance, a celebrant may offer menstrual fluid, along with particular mantras, to the Goddess because of the intense *shakti* associated with this substance. The offerings are made by squeezing a used menstrual cloth into the fire.

> *Pryadarshi Baba:* It's a cloth that has . . . you know, like you take a tampon . . . a cloth that has been soaked in it or something. You take a little piece of that cloth and make offerings with it.
>
> *Ron:* Into the *havan* . . .
>
> *Pryadarshi Baba* [nodding]: Just like there are different kinds of offerings for different deities. . . . It's not something that you go and ask some woman to give to you. In olden days . . . women would use [these] cloths and then discard them . . . but then you would go and pick one up and . . . [long pause].
>
> *Ron:* Scavenge?
>
> *Pryadarshi Baba:* Scavenge.

Pryadarshi Baba likened the scavenging of menstrual cloths to that of cremation shrouds in the *shmashan.* The simile reminded me of Parry's (1994) point about the Aghori's ability and willingness to scavenge anything from anywhere in order to achieve the ascetic ideal of worldly independence. For the male disciples at least, the requisite scavenging involves a significant transgression of a deeply internalized taboo. The disciple must carefully search through filthy places for an intensely polluting and dangerous substance—one that has the *shakti* to cause leprosy just as it has the *shakti* to create life. A menstrual offering to the Goddess concentrates large amounts of *shakti* at three levels. The offering is laden with the *shakti* of reproductive potential. The recipient of the sacrifice is Shakti herself. But perhaps less obvious is the *shakti* of someone willing to prepare and make the offering. All three speak to power. The third speaks to power by way of independence.

Menstrual offerings are not for consumption. "You don't take it in . . . like ghee," Pryadarshi Baba said, laughing once again. However, other culturally forbidden substances may be ingested in a ritual manner. The chakra *puja* usually provides the framework for such practices in the Aghor tradition. As we have seen, the chakra *puja* is a modified *havan* in which a celebrant offers a substance, such as alcohol or meat, from a bowl into the fire of the *dhuni*. The rest of the participants then share the remaining *prasād* while passing the bowl around in a circle (the chakra). Traditionally, the bowl is a human skullcap, preferably from a particular caste of oil pressers. No one could tell me why the Aghori once preferred the skulls of oil pressers. I suspect that the Aghori previously had reciprocal ritual ties to one or more of these communities, just as they still have long-standing ritual ties with the Dom community today. Among the few (old-style) Aghori I knew who had skulls, none claimed this origin. Most of the skulls in Banaras came from anonymous corpses that had washed up along the northern banks of the Ganga. In any case, the skull is not an essential feature of the chakra *puja*. A cup or glass can serve the same purpose.

The chakra *puja* has two essential objectives, both of which entail transcendence over ritual pollution taboos. The first is to convert polluted substances into sacred substances through the schema of ritual sacrifice. Assuming that the ritual offering (the "sacrifice") is accepted in the divine realm, the substance becomes *prasād*, transformationally purified by the divinities of fire and oblation, Agni and Svaha, respectively. Technically, no real transgressions take place in this rite. The *havan* deities are like Mother Ganga in that they can accept any and all offerings, provided that the offerings are made with the proper intention. Nor do celebrants transgress taboos by consuming a substance that has already been purified. Yet even when a substance becomes a divine blessing, it is difficult to consume when one has spent a lifetime avoiding it. Therein lies the irony of the practice. The disciple must confront his or her aversion, even after the ritually polluted has become ritually pure. This irony reinforces the Aghori teaching that categories of pollution and purity exist only within the mind of the discriminator.

The second major objective of the chakra *puja* is to eliminate social distinctions among participants. Sharing the offered substance from the same bowl is a step toward this goal. The traditional rules of food exchange forbid the consumption of leftover food or drink unless the second person is intimately connected to, and of lesser status than, the first: a wife follows her husband, a child follows his mother, or a disciple follows a guru. Sharing leftovers within the chakra *puja* underscores the irony of the practice. The only real leftovers are those of the gods—the *prasād*—which are pure by definition. But socialization runs deep. In passing the same bowl around in a circle, again and again, people who still hold on to the rules of food exchange are likely to feel that they are eating the leftovers of everyone else. Thus, even when food taboos still exist in the minds of some participants, awareness of the taboos serves to make them intimate equals of everyone else. As Pryadarshi Baba said, "We are all one. We are all drinking from the same cup, and we are not worried about the saliva of the other person and any of those little things that we have."

Indian social hierarchies are as linear as the ritual hierarchies that inform them (Babb 1975). People are above or below one another. Occasionally, they may be "forward" or "backward" of one another. But they are never side by side. Some groups may be interdependent, as Dumont (1966) emphasizes in the *varṇa* system of caste. Nevertheless, this interdependence is neither symmetrical nor chiral. There are no ties of reciprocity linking those at the very top and bottom that are as close as (roughly) adjacent groups in the ritual hierarchy. The chakra *puja* changes this structure by imposing a horizontal circle where a vertical line once stood, a circle that has no beginning or end. It also makes every participant a witness to the ritual deeds of everyone else. After all, a person cannot easily claim status over someone else when sharing the other's saliva and eating leftover meat from the same bowl.

The chakra *puja* has been the ritual framework within which the Aghori have historically practiced ritual cannibalism. The babas affirmed this fact, as did many other Aghori with whom I spoke. But beyond describing some of the ritual details, no postreform Aghori had ever discussed a specific incident with me. The closest I came to the ingestion of human flesh was when an old-style disciple offered me *mahaprasād,* ash taken directly from the partially cremated remains of an unclaimed corpse. He made the offer spontaneously, outside of any ritual context. More significantly, he probably did not have the permission of his guru to do so. It was as furtive as a teenager sneaking a cigarette from his parents.

Adolescent though it was, the *mahaprasād* incident gave me an appreciation for some of the logistics required to get away with ritual cannibalism in India. Contrary to popular stories, no family would tolerate an Aghori's stealing flesh from a dead relative during a cremation rite. Corpses are immediately cremated after death, and families stay close to the body from the moment of demise to the final toss of the ashes. For this reason, a covert theft is also unfeasible. Murder is completely out of the question, colonial accounts notwithstanding: nonviolence is as important as nondiscrimination to Aghor practice. Even a staff-wielding renunciate like Baba Rajeshwar Ram was not known to have ever harmed anyone.

Eliminating these methods leaves only two other possibilities. First, a family might make a willing and private donation. I knew of no families who would do so, but I could not discount the possibility. The other possibility is that the Aghori would "fish" the river for an uncremated remnant, an unclaimed body, or a body unworthy of the pyre. The fishing option seems logistically more feasible than the other options, but it also seems more gastronomically challenging—which is why it might present the ideal opportunity for an old-style Aghori. Interestingly, when our conversations turned to scavenging, several Aghori made a point of telling me that they were very good swimmers.

However obtained, the flesh is prepared for the chakra *puja* by cutting it into bite-sized pieces. From here on, no one besides the participants need know the specific nature of the rite. A close bystander might see a group of people sharing some meat around a fire but would not be able to ascertain its origin or species. By these methods, the Aghori could easily have kept cannibalism a secret outside the chakra. Such practices were like mantras in this regard. The only practical way to observe them is to do them. I ate many things with the Aghori while I was in the field, but human flesh was never on the menu.

Secrecy notwithstanding, I found that the Aghori were almost as reticent to completely deny cannibalism as to admit it. Cannibalism was a recurring theme of daily conversations and a recurring joke at meal times. Many Aghori were quick to denounce claims of present-day cannibalism, dismissing them as tabloid journalism or the ramblings of crazy renunciates. Yet the Aghori also maintained their authority about such matters, even if they were no longer cannibals themselves. Though the postreform Aghori clearly did not want the stigma of cannibalism, they did not want to give up this association entirely either. Whether cannibalism was myth or reality, history or current practice, the *possibility* of it seemed to play an important role in the lives of the Aghori.

Given this context, I was surprised that Pryadarshi Baba denied the consumption of human flesh had anything to do with *shmashān sādhanā,* the meditative practices that the Aghori performed in the cremation ground. Though cannibalism involved the flesh of the dead, it was not an effort to confront death per se. Pryadarshi Baba asserted that cannibalism is simply an exercise for overcoming an aversion. Human flesh is like any other meat or piece of food. It is just another substance. No big deal.

The *shmashān sādhanā* confront major fears, particularly those of ghosts, malevolent spirits, wild animals, and most importantly, death. These *sādhanā* involve several kinds of ritual meditations in the *shmashān*. Some involve more elaborate practices such as meditation while sitting atop a corpse, *shav sādhanā*. The logistics of such practices are even more difficult than those for cannibalism, and I seriously doubt that the Aghori engage in them anymore. Other forms of *shmashān sādhanā* are more basic, involving nothing more than *japa* meditation. Although the logistics are much simpler, these more basic forms of *shmashān sādhanā* present their own difficult challenges. As Pryadarshi Baba said:

> The main thing about *shmashān sādhanā* is [that] you practice some mantra [of] a certain deity . . . for a certain number of repetitions. It could be one hundred thousand, fifty-one thousand, whatever. . . . The main thing is to be able to sit in the *shmashān* when there is silence all around. It is easy to sit in the *shmashān* when there are people . . . milling around [who] are interested in [what is going on]. . . . But to find a *shmashān* where there is total silence, and loneliness, and to be able to sit, to do the *japa,* is very difficult because [of] the fear factor.

Until then, I had spent time only in the *shmashāns* of Banaras, mostly in the cremation ghats of Harischandra and Manikarnika. These places were anything but remote. They were the two most central and sacred foci of the city's inner crescent. Both were busy with cremations, ascetics, feral dogs, drug dealers, tourists, and passersby. Each had its own hypnotic rhythms and hidden nooks for stealing a quiet moment, but neither was completely silent or lonely. These sites hardly fit the criteria that Pryadarshi Baba described; I felt foolish for having spent so much time in these places. Pryadarshi Baba seemed to know this, for his narrative addressed not only the foolish foreigner but so many other Indian devotees who went to the *shmashān* on their own accord, contemplating their mortality and getting in touch with the "deathplaces" as the birthplaces of their spiritual tradition. Pryadarshi Baba did not seem to be critical of such ad hoc practices. He simply emphasized that they were not true *shmashān sādhanā*. The latter required specific directions from the guru, and those directions underscored the importance of orthopraxis: performing the appropriate mantra at the appropriate time and place.

Pryadarshi Baba continued to emphasize the importance of place when I pressed him on the possibility of equivalent alternatives to *shmashān sādhanā*. Was working with dying patients equivalent? I saw a lot of death in my six years of clinical experience as a registered nurse. I participated in brain-death protocols on a neurointensive care unit, held the hands of family members while their loved ones died, and gave medications to ease the passing. I cleaned the corpses of fluids and feces, pulled their tubes, and tried to make them presentable after the fact. Consequently, I felt a bit smug that death did not hold the same novelty for me that I supposed it did for the rubbernecked tourists who gawked at the cremation ghats as if they were car crashes. And what should we make of other people's firsthand experiences with the dying process? What of the terminal-cancer patient who must confront the certainty of imminent death? Surely this confrontation is at least somewhat equivalent to that of *shmashān sādhanā*, yes?

Pryadarshi Baba affirmed the importance of such experiences but maintained that the *shmashān sādhanā* were nevertheless distinctive in their proper performance. "There is definitely an importance of place," he said. "Because the place itself evokes a different kind of fear. [A different] intensity." He explained that the prescribed mantras for *shmashān sādhanā* are meant to have different effects on the mind of the practitioner. Moreover, these effects can change as the practice proceeds for several days or more. "Some mantras you have to do for like twenty-one times for seven days in a row. From that, each time you go through different experiences; some could be very fearful; some could be very pleasant, very attractive, very hypnotizing. You go through these different strata of experience."

During these altered states, spirits appear in different forms to distract the disciple from his or her practice. A spirit may take the form of a seductive woman or a terrifying animal. In each case, the spirit attempts to distract the disciple from his or her *sādhanā*. If it does so, the disciple is done for. "[The spirit] could come as a wild animal like a leopard. . . . It could come in a very concrete form. It could even come right near you and lick you . . . but as soon as you move, and you show any fear and move, then you are gone. There are many many many stories of people who got . . . scared in the cremation grounds, and they never recouped."

The babas emphasized that the *shmashān sādhanā* can be dangerous. If the disciple is not ready, or if he or she strays from the prescribed practice, then the rite may result in permanent psychological damage. "So that is why these [practices] are [not for everybody]," he said. "It is a great responsibility for the guru to have someone to do that." In the realm of left-hand practices, the guru is as essential for the disciple's worldly survival as for his or her spiritual development.

I could not presume to understand the psychospiritual hazards to which Pryadarshi Baba alluded. I could imagine, however, some of the challenges of *shmashān sādhanā* if one performed them as he described. *Shmashāns* are considered inauspicious places; they are loaded with ritual pollution. Consequently, they are usually in isolated places on the outskirts of human settlements. The disciple who spends a night in the *shmashān* has no other company but the remains of the dead and the animals that scavenge them: feral dogs, jackals, snakes, and rats, as well as the occasional lion or tiger in some remote places. These animals typically avoid direct contact with humans, but neither do they stray far from their best food sources. They are also instinctively aware of their relative strengths in numbers when a human is sitting alone at night, and they can smell fear and vulnerability.

A pack of feral dogs once charged me as I walked along the ghats with a friend at three in the morning. The dogs were small, a mangy pack of street mutts like those in Indian cities everywhere. We pitied them during the day, cynically assigning them the breed of "Banarsi hairless." But our feelings turned to fear on this night, as fifteen or twenty of them barked animatedly and ran in our direction. We froze, and the pack ran past us. It turned out that they were chasing a smaller number of dogs behind us, territorial intruders that we had previously failed to notice. That incident was disconcerting enough. I tried to imagine how I would feel if I sat alone, at eye level with a similar number that had developed a taste for human remains.

In addition to facing these practical fears, the disciple must have a deep belief in the power of the mantra and the teachings of the guru. The guru says that the mantra will function as a beacon, and the disciple recites it with this belief. The disciple is already in an aroused state when he or she begins the *sādhanā*. The stress response prepares the body for fight or flight, but the disciple neither fights nor flees. Instead, he or she transmits a spiritual call to attract the worst fears imaginable. After several hours of recitation, the expected fears manifest themselves in the altered consciousness of the disciple, who attempts to transcend them in the belief that to do otherwise will result in permanent psychological damage. Under these conditions, insanity caused by the malpractice of *shmashān sādhanā* could certainly qualify as a culture-bound syndrome. Yet even if such syndromes reflect the power of culturally specific suggestions, they are nevertheless associated with real pathologies and even death in some societies. Examples include the so-called Voodoo deaths of the Afro-Caribbean traditions (Samuels 1997) and the nightmares accompanying sudden unexplained nocturnal death syndrome among the Hmong of Southeast Asia (Adler 1994). Spirits notwithstanding, disciples would seem to have good reasons for approaching the *shmashān sādhanā* with a great deal of caution and respect.

   Despite apparent differences, the *shmashān sādhanā* have a common function; they all challenge the disciple to embrace certain fears and aversions and eventually to overcome them as a means of achieving a state of nondiscrimination. Of these challenges, the Aghori believe that overcoming fear of death is the most important. Correspondingly, they assert that the *shmashān sādhanā* can be the most challenging and dangerous of the left-hand practices. As with cannibalism, coprophagy, and all the rest, the status of these practices in the postreform tradition remains publicly ambiguous. Insofar as the left-hand practices persist at all, they are mantralike secrets between guru and disciple. Yet although the practices themselves remain a mystery, they serve as major prototypes for Aghori rituals today. Disciples might not offer menstrual fluids in the *dhuni,* but Aghori women worship at the fire regardless of menstrual status. Human flesh and feces might be off the menu, but the fish that feed on these substances are an important form of *prasād.* The specific rites of *shmashān sādhanā* may be difficult and dangerous, but Aghor disciples continue to make visits on their own. At the ritual center of all these practices lies the cremation pyre of Baba Kina Ram's *dhuni,* a perpetually burning reminder of human mortality. Whether by practice or by proxy, the *vamamarg* remains an integral part of the Aghor tradition.

AGHOR AS MEDICINE

Parry (1994) argues that that even the most heterodox elements of Aghor tradition are rooted in mainstream Indian philosophy. They are the logical extension of a liberation theology striving to transcend worldly attachments. The most mainstream of all are the *Advaita* (nondualist) schools of Vedanta (see Zimmer 1951). These schools maintain that a single unified reality underlies all creation: *Brahman* (not to be confused with *Brahmin*). Enlightenment comes when the seeker eventually realizes this truth, at which point the seeker and the universe merge into one. The merger is encapsulated in a simple and very popular formula: *Atma Ram,* the Soul (is) God.[7]

Aghor philosophy is very similar to *Advaita* Vedanta in this regard. To transcend discrimination is to recognize the unity of all things, that the soul and the divine are essentially one and the same. On this point, the Aghori acknowledge their affinity with *Advaita*. They even claim that Shankara, the most famous of *Advaita* sages, was once an Aghori himself. This affinity has some history, for people associated the Aghori Lord Dattatreya with Vedanta teachings for several centuries, during the time of the *kāpālikas* (Rigopoulos 1998).

The gurus and disciples of Aghor believe their state to be primordial and universal. They believe that all human beings are natural-born Aghori. Hari Baba has said on several occasions that human babies of all societies are without discrimination, that they will play as much in their own filth as with the toys around them. Children become progressively discriminating as they grow older and learn the culturally specific attachments and aversions of their parents. Children become increasingly aware of their mortality as they bump their heads and fall to the ground. They come to fear their mortality and then palliate this fear by finding ways to deny it altogether. In this sense, Aghor *sādhanā* is a process of unlearning deeply internalized cultural models. When this *sādhanā* takes the form of *shmashān sādhanā,* the Aghori faces death as a very young child, simultaneously meditating on the totality of life at its two extremes. This ideal example serves as a prototype for other Aghor practices, both left and right, in ritual and in daily life. Ramchandraji engaged in this *sādhanā* while contemplating the mysteries of human creation during his father's cremation. His meditations may not have held the same dangers as *shmashān sādhanā* proper, but they had the same overall objective. Then again, Ramchandraji was probably not a stranger to the *shmashān*. Although orthodox in many ways, he had faced these kinds of spiritual challenges before.

Although I will never fully understand Ramchandraji's experience, my time spent with the Aghori helped me peel back a few layers of this hermeneutic onion. From here, I will attempt a feasible explanation for the link between death and nondiscrimination in Aghor tradition: that anxieties about human mortality motivate cultural models of discrimination against human morbidity. This discrimination can be seen as an illness in and of itself. By confronting human mortality, Aghor *sādhanā* is the ultimate form of Aghor medicine—a therapy for the illness of discrimination. This argument synthesizes contributions from biocultural medical anthropology, cognitive anthropology, and social psychology.

Yet more importantly, it builds upon the Aghori's own theory of the nature of human prejudice. The argument rests on the following three propositions.

Proposition 1: Disease discrimination is itself an illness. The biocultural dynamics of leprosy stigma that I describe in chapter 4 illustrate this proposition. In the Indian context, the social stigma of leprosy far exceeds the physical challenges posed by the infection alone. Because of the severity of the social condition, however, leprosy discrimination feeds back to the physical condition by contributing to delayed detection, undertreatment, self-neglect, and in extreme cases, deliberately self-destructive behaviors. These behaviors exacerbate the spread and course of the disease while continuing to reinforce the cultural models of discrimination from which they originate. In this manner, the social stigma of leprosy is intimately tied to its physical stigma. Leprosy discrimination is an illness inclusive of its marked condition.

The social stigma of leprosy is by no means universal. Cultural and historical factors strongly influence people's attitudes toward this disease (cf. White 2002; Gussow 1989; Waxler 1981). Nevertheless, the severity of leprosy stigma in certain parts of the world has made the disease a major prototype for other socially discredited conditions, such as HIV/AIDS and tuberculosis (Barrett 2005). As in the Indian example, social discrimination has contributed to the epidemiologies and trajectories of these diseases. The same dynamics are evident in noninfectious conditions, such as the association between racism and hypertension (Dressler 1993), and the long-term impact of social isolation on mortality in the United States (Seeman et al. 1987; Berkman and Syme 1979). The biocultural dynamics of disease discrimination may be neither universal nor inevitable, but they are certainly a recurring theme in the unnatural history of human health and sickness. The Aghori are definitely on to something.

Proposition 2: The source of the illness lies with the discriminator, not the discriminated. Placing disease discrimination within the illness category entails questions of etiology: What are the sources, the causes, and the engines that drive this illness? To address these questions, one must first distinguish the marking process from the mark itself. Historically, making such a distinction has been difficult. In the first half of the twentieth century, sociology focused upon the mark as a problem of "deviance" from socially established norms, an undesired personal attribute that contrasted with a shared belief about how people should appear and act under given circumstances (Pfohl 1985). Deviance itself

was a problem in need of solutions, for which sociologists had examined
the roles of poverty, education, family structure, and heredity without
considering the other side of the equation: how and why do certain societies become intolerant of certain human differences (Pfuhl and Henry
1993)?

The focus on the social pathology of deviance began to shift in the
decades following World War II. This shift partly grew out of the reve-
lations of the Holocaust in Europe, an emerging civil rights movement
in the United States, and numerous countries' struggles for independence
from colonial powers around the world. Within this historical context,
the American social sciences began to shift the locus of attention from the
deviance of the discredited to that of their discreditors, focusing on the
processes by which negative labels are constructed and assigned to particular human attributes in particular sociocultural contexts. This social-
constructivist movement, which traced its intellectual pedigree from
Marx to Manheim, sought to understand the ways in which these categories were constructed into objective realities and then internalized into
first-order cognition (Berger and Luckman 1966).

Howard Becker (1963) and Erving Goffman (1963) were early pro-
ponents of this social-constructivist approach, although they used different labels. Whereas Becker continued to define the new problem in
terms of the old label, *deviance,* Goffman relabeled the entire phenomenon in terms of *stigma,* the Greek term for a permanent mark of discredit, but redefined it as the social disgrace itself. Goffman's *Stigma*
(1963) provided a useful lexicon for describing the problem of discrimination as well as some mechanisms for its disavowal and perpetuation.
This work led to studies ranging from interactionist psychology at the
microsocial level (Jones et al. 1984) to macrolevel studies of social justice (cf. Ainley and Crosby 1986). It also influenced numerous studies
of the stigmatization of disease conditions (Farmer 1992; Inhorn 1986;
Ablon 1981; Becker 1981) and of the legitimation and delegitimation of
sick roles (Kleinman 1992; Ware 1992; Freidson 1979). The concept of
stigma proved to be productive for the social sciences; it was especially
useful in medical anthropology.

Nonetheless, the reformulation of deviance as stigma presents a
problem: labeling the issue (social discrimination) in terms of its mark
(stigma) focuses attention on an objectified attribute (such as a disease
or a disability) at the locus of the stigmatized rather than the beliefs and
behaviors of their stigmatizers.[8] Though we certainly need to understand
the effects of this process—the suffering caused by social discrimination—

we should devote at least equal energy to understanding how and why the process works: what leads people to discriminate against one another (see Weiss, Rama Krishna, and Somma 2006). This effort requires a more holistic approach, one that also considers the dynamics of discrimination at the locus of the discriminator. The Aghori are social constructivists in this regard. Not only do they treat people that no one else would dare touch, but they challenge the overall notion of untouchability in the community at large.

Proposition 3: Mortality anxiety motivates morbidity discrimination. The Aghori believe not only that the greatest of human fears is that of death but also that death lies at the heart of all other fears and aversions. This belief resonates with the work of Ernest Becker (1973), who argues that mortality anxiety and its repression are the primary sources of human neuroses as well as the primary engines of human social institutions. Becker begins with the premise that human beings are the only known animals that are consciously aware of their inevitable mortality, even when the threat of death is not imminent. He then draws upon Kierkegaard's (1989[1849]) existential analysis of the "sickness" that lies between the natural and supernatural aspects of humanity and Rank's (1941) psychoanalytic proposition that deeply internalized anxieties are related to a human fear of biological processes, particularly those of decay. Incorporating these ideas, Becker argues that a conflict exists between the ubiquitous instinct for survival and the uniquely human awareness of death and that this conflict results in a fundamental repression. The repression may lead to neuroses in some cases, but it also serves as a necessary and "vital lie" for all humanity, one that drives collective traditions of social allegiance and heroism.

Aghor philosophy agrees with Becker's basic premise about the nature of the lie, but it does not accept that this repressed fear is a necessary element of the human condition. Repression may lead to great works and great civilizations, but all are worthless if the lie brings social discrimination along with public works, human hatred along with human heroes, as the Aghori believe. Indeed, one of the major critiques of the functionalist enterprise is that it makes utilitarian arguments to justify conditions of human inequality. Dumont (1966) makes an argument for the social function of pollution taboos in the Indian caste system. He argues that the opposition between ritual purity and pollution delineates specialized social categories whose interdependence sustains Indian society as a cohesive whole, creating a state of social equilibrium much like the Durkheimian model of organic solidarity. Douglas (1966) follows a similar argument in her cross-cultural analysis of pollution taboos. She argues that pollution taboos help maintain specific social boundaries and punish those who transgress them. Ritual pollution is also closely linked to blame. Both serve as defensive models against the risks of social disorder.

Some have accused Dumont and Douglas of overgeneralization (Fuller 1996; Searle-Chatterjee 1994), but the Aghori would not dispute the utility of such systems. That Banaras has existed for at least twenty-nine centuries is testament enough to the efficacy of social hierarchy in Indian society. The exception comes with the implication that pollution and blame are necessary ingredients for a lasting solidarity and that individual agents can do little to resist such institutions. This implication raises the strongest criticisms of functionalism in the Western academy (see Giddens 1977). The Aghori share these criticisms, for their ideology and practices emphasize resistance to established hierarchies and optimism about the possibility of a world without them.

The Aghori proposition that human hatred stems from the fear of death has a parallel in social psychology. Lerner (1980) makes a similar argument that discrimination is a coping strategy for anxiety about human tragedy. He conducted experiments in which subjects viewed depictions of simulated suffering, documenting the tendency of observers to believe that the victims deserved what happened to them, especially when the tragedy appeared to be random and severe. Based on these data, Lerner hypothesizes that blaming people for their misfortune serves to maintain the perception of a "just world." According to this just world hypothesis, discrimination is a coping mechanism for reducing the stress of perceived vulnerability to an unwanted condition. Through this mechanism, the blamers can reduce their perceived vulnerability to the same misfortune by abiding to certain rules or belonging to certain human categories. If someone empathizes with the apparently random tragedy of another, that person must also recognize his or her own vulnerability to the same circumstance. "If I am no different than this person, then this could happen to me as well." In this manner, empathy leads to anxiety. Alternatively, this anxiety can be reduced by attributing a just cause to the tragedy—by blaming it on an infraction or associating it with a certain category of *other* people. In this manner, people with leprosy, infertility, and other tragic conditions are categorized as sinners, and the willfully impoverished members of society of castes, classes, and clans other than those of their discriminators.

Integrating Lerner's just world hypothesis with Becker's denials of death, I argue that disease discrimination is strongly motivated by a desire to maintain the perception of human perpetuity in the face of inevitable human decay. After all, a "just world" is an ordered world, and death is the ultimate threat to that order. Moreover, the threat of death need not be restricted to biological mortality alone. Humans face many lesser and more immediate deaths in their daily lives, such as the social death of ostracism and the economic death of poverty. Some forms of human morbidity also threaten mortality by their partial removal of features with which people identify their lives. In its extreme form, leprosy may represent such a condition, given its potential for physical deformation and strong association with poverty. Leprosy infection may not represent the fantasy of total maximal illness that Skinsnes (1964) describes, but rather one of maximal decay through many other kinds of human loss: all the little deaths that circumstance entails. This decay explains why the Aghori would use leprosy treatment as the prototypical proxy for *shmashān sādhanā*. The question that remains is whether and to what degree such practices may actually work.

Conclusion

This book began with the proposition that the medico-religious practices of the Kina Ram Aghori comprise a unique healing system, which I refer to as Aghor medicine. This system has two major aspects. The first aspect is the medicines of Aghor: an eclectic combination of modified herbal medications, biomedicines, and ritual healing practices. Within a cultural model of *dawā aur duwā*, these medicines are a medium for the transmission of healing power, Aghor *shaktī*, from the Aghori to the patient. This *shaktī*, in turn, is closely associated with human mortality. Indeed, the prototypical healing rite for all these medicines—the *dhuni-kund* bathing sequence at the Kina Ram Ashram—follows the same overall schema as the *antyeshti saṃskāra*, the final sacrifice of human cremation.

The second major aspect of Aghor medicine is the role of Aghor philosophy and practices as culturally specific medicine for the illness of discrimination. When discrimination is directed against people with certain diseases and disabilities, then the illness can directly affect the physical conditions that it discredits. This link is well illustrated by the intimate relationship between the social and physical stigmata of leprosy in India. The Aghori attempt to treat this illness at its origins: the fears and aversions of the discriminators. Because the Aghori believe that the ultimate human fear is that of death, many of their spiritual practices are intended to help the disciple confront his or her mortality. Although much of the old-style *shmashān sādhanā* have given way to more socially acceptable practices, the symbolism of the *shmashān* is central to this aspect of Aghor as medicine just as it is essential for the medicines of Aghor.

Whether, or to what extent, confrontations with mortality diminish discrimination among Aghor disciples remains unclear. We have seen how non-Aghori patients use a transportive schema of purification to dump ritually polluted afflictions onto their Aghori healers while minimizing contact with the symbols of death that pervade the therapeutic process. In contrast, Aghor disciples take a more transformative approach to their "purification." As with other Indian rites of purification, however, these two approaches to Aghor medicine are not an all-or-nothing affair. Both are evident among Aghori in the *shmashān* just as both are evident among bathers in the Ganga. The question is a matter of emphasis and outcome. It is also a matter of social practicality. How do Aghor disciples of the postreform tradition negotiate these different approaches and move toward a state of nondiscrimination while struggling for status and survival in the social hierarchies of Indian communities?

The Mishra family has negotiated these challenges from the extremes of several social axes: as high-caste Brahmins and noncaste Aghori; as rural farmers and urban professionals; and as Indian nationals and citizens of an increasingly Westernized world. Nowhere are these axes more evident than in the youngest son of the Mishra family patriarch. Harihar Mishra grew up on the family farm, attended university in Banaras, and established a successful business in the United States, only to renounce everything and become the last officially recognized Aghori ascetic under the reformed teachings of Awadhut Bhagwan Ram. The transformation of Harihar Mishra to Baba Harihar Ram (Hari Baba) followed changes within the Mishra family that illustrate the broader challenges that postreform Aghori face today.

ASCETICS AND HOUSEHOLDERS

By most Indian standards, Lakshman Mishra died a good death. He lived to more than ninety, a rare feat even among the more affluent members of Indian society.[1] He was prolific, having left behind a joint family of four sons and a daughter, sixteen grandchildren, and fourteen great-grandchildren. He was somewhat prosperous, having developed a modest homestead into nearly sixty acres of productive crops and more than a score of cattle. His was the first Brahmin family to settle in the village of Morahua and one of the first to send its sons to college in the city of Banaras. Having accomplished these things, Lakshman Mishra was prepared to die. Throughout the year before his death, he requested the blessing of visiting priests and Aghori (including his ascetic son) so that he could die soon. He moved into the joint household of two sons in Banaras so that he could die within the sacred boundaries of Kashi. He then died just as he had hoped, within the appropriate time and place, and just as the babas had foretold. He died surrounded by his immediate family. He was relatively alert and expressed little distress or discomfort until the last two days of his life. His body was blessed at the Kina Ram Ashram and cremated at Harischandra Ghat with more than thirty friends and family in attendance. Everyone agreed that his was a good death.[2]

One important exception to the Indian ideal of a good death was the survival of Lakshman Mishra's wife, Nandini, who was ten years his junior. In many parts of India, it is a disgrace for a woman to outlive her husband, a view that is reflected in the shame of widowhood and the vulnerability of elderly women (Lamb 2000; Cohen 1998). The Mishras, however, were as proud of Nandini's longevity as they were of her husband's. Widowhood was neither uncommon nor a source of shame among the Aghori I knew. In fact, the Aghori considered the care of one's widowed mother to be an important form of devotion to Shakti. Thus, Nandini Mishra continued to enjoy her senior status within the family, to whom she freely asserted her opinions on a variety of daily matters.

The lack of stigma attending Nandini's widowhood was but one of several areas in which the Mishra family distinguished itself from the discriminatory traditions around them. As we have seen, the status of women is especially poor in this part of northern India; it is evident in literacy rates, economic participation, and access to health care (Buckshee 1997; Rajeshwari 1996; Dasgupta 1987). It is also reflected in birth ratios that strongly favor male over female children (Griffiths and Hinde 2000). Yet when most Indian families were praying for sons, Lakshmanji's son, Bharata, was visiting the homes of newborn girls and touching their feet to receive the blessings of Shakti. A local story tells of one family that had several girls in succession and asked Bharata to stop visiting lest these "blessings" bring more girls. For Bharata, as for most Aghori, the Goddess was no abstraction. She was present within every female from infant to widow, and he strongly believed that all should be treated accordingly.

Bharata Mishra introduced the rest of his family to Sarkar Baba and the Aghor tradition. Balavan Mishra joined not long thereafter. His was one of the most dramatic conversions within the family. As the eldest son, Balavan was the acting manager of and heir to the family farm. He was a former wrestler and was known for his temper as well as his strength. Balavan described himself as an angry man before he met Sarkar Baba, with set ideas about social hierarchy and the Brahmin's place at its head. All this changed after his initiation into the Aghor tradition. He discarded the thread signifying his twice-born status and never looked back. Today, Balavan Mishra is one of his family's most steadfast Aghor disciples.

Balavan's impressive transformation and Bharata's charisma helped bring most of the remaining family members into the Kina Ram lineage. The converts eventually included Harihar Mishra, who would eventually be a Mishra no more, once he "took *langota*" and became Baba Harihar Ram. Harihar was among the last in the family to become a disciple. The youngest of the four brothers, he obtained a general science degree at Banaras Hindu University and was accepted into the MBA program at the University California, Berkeley, where he supported himself as a Hindi language tutor. He quit the program before graduation to start a travel business in Northern California and soon became financially successful. Hari fully enjoyed the material fruits that the West had to offer. Yet he remained the dutiful son, which included making regular visits to his family in India. During one of these visits, he accompanied his elder brother to sit with Sarkar Baba. His future guru was initially welcoming but quickly dismissed him in their first meetings. Sarkar Baba felt that Hari needed to continue his worldly pursuits for a while, but his time would eventually come. As Hari Baba recalls the process, their relationship developed gradually but grew very deep over the years (see Ram 1997).

Sarkar Baba's health declined during those years. He had developed adult-onset diabetes, which led to chronic renal failure and the need for dialysis and a kidney transplant. In his last years, Sarkar Baba traveled to New York for treatment, and Hari left his California business to care for his guru. They lived together in the city along with two other disciples, Pryadarshi and Anil, for a little over a year. During this time, Bharata Mishra contracted hepatitis and died in Banaras. His death was a tremendous blow to family members. They struggled to find meaning in the inauspicious and premature death of someone so pious. Sarkar Baba explained that Bharata was meant to die ten years before but that he had kept his disciple alive so that the latter could complete his duties on earth. Some of the Mishras had trouble accepting this explanation, and some time passed before they regained faith in their guru.

Harihar Mishra was very close to Bharata. He took it upon himself to look after his elder brother's wife and three children. Harihar's status as an educated and economically successful Brahmin living in the United States had made him a prime marriage prospect. The family pressure to marry was high, and hundreds of offers poured in whenever he returned to India. He declined them all. Having already distanced himself from his business in California, he moved further in the direction of renunciation. He made several such requests to his guru. After giving Harihar time to contemplate his decision, Sarkar Baba finally initiated him as a renunciate *(sannyāsī)*. As is the case for taking a mantra, the details of this initiation are a secret between gurus and their disciples. The initiation rite is simply referred to as "taking *langota*," calls for the initiate to wear a strip of cloth wrapped tightly around the groin to symbolize his celibacy. Per the Kina Ram tradition, Harihar kept his first name but exchanged his Brahmin surname for Ram: a name of God commonly used as a family name in lower-caste communities. In this manner, Harihar Mishra became Baba Harihar Ram, better known as Hari Baba.

Despite his official renunciation of the world, Hari Baba continued to maintain close ties with his family in Banaras. He did so partly because of his guru's edict that he continue to visit his natal home for as long as his mother lived. He also depended on his relatives as trusted assistants for social-service projects in India. Sarkar Baba had tasked him to teach Aghor in the West, for which Hari Baba established an ashram in Sonoma, California. But the need for *sevā* was much greater in India, where U.S. dollars could go a long way toward helping many people. Because he spent most of his time in the United States, however, Hari Baba could not take the time to establish a network of competent and reliable people to oversee his service projects. Nor could he take the uncollegial step of siphoning talent from other Aghori ashrams. As a result, Hari Baba had no choice but to use the talents of his own family, whom he could trust to accomplish challenging tasks while he was out of the country. The Sonoma Ashram began to sponsor a free school for indigent children in Banaras. Little Stars School was run by Hari Baba's niece, Tara, with logistical support from his nephew, Bantu, his brothers, and their families. More recently, his family oversaw the construction of a small ashram-based orphanage and clinic in the south of the city. Neither of these projects could have proceeded without the trusted assistance of key family members. Worldly *sevā* requires worldly connections.

Hari Baba's reliance on his family was reciprocated following the death of Sarkar Baba, after which family members presented all major decisions for his blessing and advice. They sought him to help with marriage arrangements, resolve intrafamily disputes, and improve community relations. Whenever he visited his natal village, hundreds of people consulted him on health problems and other practical matters. They asked him which crops to plant and when. They asked about the best locations to dig their wells. They asked about the health of their family members and their livestock. They asked him what to name their babies and to whom they should marry their children. Hari Baba did his best to answer these requests, holding court on the front porch of the house where he lived and played as a child. It was as if he were the youngest son of a Catholic family who had left home to become a priest, only to return and give counsel to his old neighborhood. But Aghori ascetics have more authority and responsibilities than Catholic priests do, and they rarely return to their natal homes.

I spent my first month of fieldwork accompanying Hari Baba and several Western disciples during their annual visit to India. We paid a visit to Hari Baba's natal home in Morahua, where I met Lakshman Mishra for the first time. He was sitting on a cot in the courtyard, casting a stoic pose that I later came to associate with his eldest son. He seemed taller than any of his sons, however, an impression given by his gaunt appearance. He had the look of a man in chronic pain who had endured his afflictions long enough to have given up complaining about them. I watched as Hari Baba approached. The meeting was almost a classic scene of present-day India: the successful son returning from afar to pay respects to his father in their village home. But here the roles were reversed, with the father bending down to touch the seam of his son's robe. The act was surreal but traditional, a gesture of respect to a holy man who had renounced his family attachments along with everything else in the world. It was also involved a tricky juxtaposition of religious and consanguinal affiliations, made rare by the fact that most full-fledged ascetics never return home.

The baba and the patriarch sat as equals on a mat, an exception to protocol that the Aghori grant to other religious and political authorities. Lakshmanji told Hari Baba that he was ready to die, having taken the *darshan* of his youngest son-cum-renunciate. His words were a request as much as a statement, and Hari Baba gave his blessing. This meeting proved to be their last. The two men mostly sat in silence, surrounded by a dozen male relatives with whom they shared a certain stoicism combined with a misty-eyed intensity. I saw these same sentiments during Lakshmanji's cremation later that year. But at this moment, Nandini

Mishra was much more expressive. She tearfully touched Hari Baba's feet, after which he held her—both attempting to strike a balance between the ideal of worldly detachment and the affectionate bond between mother and son. After a few more exchanges and a large meal, Hari Baba quickly took his leave from the house under the auspices of showing the mango grove to his disciples. On the way to the mango grove, I asked Hari Baba if it was difficult for a renunciate to come home to his family. "Yes, very difficult," he said. "It's very conflicting for an Aghori. That is why I took us for a walk right away. I needed to get away from that place for a little while."

Although unusual in some respects, Hari Baba's ongoing family relationship exemplified a common challenge faced by renunciates of the postreform lineage. Aghori babas are relatively self-sufficient in meeting their personal needs, but they must rely on householders and immerse themselves in the daily affairs of the world to fulfill their service obligations to human society. Having renounced the world by some of the most radical methods imaginable, the Aghori's newfound emphasis on *sevā* has brought them back into the realm of material affairs and the challenge of being in the world but not of it. Renunciates and householders alike face this challenge: both must find ways to internally detach themselves from the social and economic activities around them even as they participate in these same activities. In many ways, this separation is more difficult for Aghori householders, who must negotiate the multiple axes of material and social status to ensure the welfare of their families. Such negotiations require a great deal of creativity and compromise.

SANSKRITIZATION AND NONDISCRIMINATION

Whereas Aghori renunciates deal with the competing requirements of *sevā* and asceticism, their householder disciples attempt to meet minimum community expectations of ritual orthodoxy while striving toward the Aghori ideal of nondiscrimination. These challenges are closely linked: renunciates have to rely on householders for assistance in social-service projects, and householders have to maintain their community status if they are to continue making effective contributions. Unfortunately, doing so often entails participation in orthodox rituals, adherence to Sanskritic rules, and membership in hierarchical institutions that run counter to the egalitarian ethos of the Aghori.[3] These expectations have intensified in recent years with the influx of upper-caste Indian families into the lineage who are most likely to feel the pressures of Indian orthodoxy.

The Mishras felt these tensions as soon as they began associating with Sarkar Baba. Balavanji recounted that people whom he had known all his life started making disparaging remarks behind his back about his spending time with the Aghori. Discarding his sacred thread caused even more controversy, especially because his was one of the few Brahmin families in the village. Such tensions diminished over the years, however, owing in part to the strength and reputation of the Mishras and in part to Sarkar Baba, who gradually won over other village families with his charisma and healing abilities.

Not all of the Mishra men discarded their threads, however, and a few remained staunchly vegetarian. Everyone continued to observe most of the *saṃskāra* rituals in the manner expected of Brahmins, but they made some compromises for marriage ceremonies. When the Mishras made marital alliances with other families within the Kina Ram lineage, they adhered to the Aghori ideal of a simple wedding without dowry. When their children married outside the sect, however, they acceded to the traditional expectations of a large fancy wedding and a generous dowry. This dual approach was a common strategy among postreform Aghori families, and the babas were usually tolerant of these traditional activities when the families could not avoid them. Parents often arranged marriages according to the traditional rules of caste endogamy and, in some cases, hypergamy. Pryadarshi Baba even offered no-interest dowry loans to poor families. He reasoned that he could better end the practice of dowry by offering education and employment to women than by allowing them to fall deeper into poverty. Social reform was a gradual and tricky process.

Whenever possible, devotee families tried to have the best of both worlds by combining elements of Aghori and Brahminical rites. Lakshmanji's funeral was a good example of this approach. Immediately following his death within the sacred boundaries of Kashi, his middle sons contacted Hari Baba in the United States to receive blessing for cremation at Harischandra Ghat. As we have seen, Sarkar Baba had asked to be cremated across the river in Parao to establish a cheap and simple alternative to the auspicious (Sanskritic), Dom-controlled *shmashāns* of Banaras. The Mishras, however, had at least two good reasons—neither of which had anything to do with their Brahmin status—for using the more traditional site. The first reason was historical, reflecting the long-standing relationship between the Aghori and the sacred geography of Harischandra Ghat that had begun when Baba Kina Ram first reunited with his guru in Banaras. The second reason was more practical: Harischandra Ghat was the closest *shmashān* for family members carrying their father's bier on foot. After all, the Aghori way was to take the simplest and most direct path.

Hari Baba gave the blessing, but he also instructed family members to take their father to the Kina Ram *dhuni* first. Thereafter, they could do whatever they thought best. The ashram was en route to Harischandra Ghat, where I joined the family in the procession to the *shmashān*. From that point forward, the funeral proceeded in Brahminical fashion, from cremation through twelve days of ritual mourning and the *shrāddha* ceremony in which rice *pindas* were offered to ensure the transition of the deceased. Following this ritual, the Mishras hosted a large *bhojan* (feast) in the village. They hired a dozen cooks, and together with the extended family and some close friends (including an anthropologist for amusement), we made preparations throughout the night: making *ras gulla,* playing cards, and chewing a great deal of *pān.* The next day we took turns serving guests as they shuttled in according to their social standing: high status to low, elder to younger, male to female. We spent the better part of that day serving food and running in and out of a giant tent that had been erected in front of the house for the occasion, while the next group sat outside in cots, chewing *pān* and gossiping. The occasion was a grand ceremony of reincorporation in which more than nine hundred people celebrated the Mishras' return to the community following a liminal period of ritual mourning and death pollution. By consuming the Mishras' meal, the community reaffirmed the family's status and the succession of a new patriarch.

Only after fully completing the rites of the *antyeshṭi saṃskāra* did the Mishras hold a second feast at the Kina Ram Ashram. The Aghori *bhojan* traditionally calls for fish and rice, but the Mishras served vegetarian *puris* (fried stuffed flatbreads) instead to accommodate all the dietary preferences of the two hundred guests who attended. The food was nevertheless offered to the Kina Ram *dhuni* first, thereby making it *prasād* of the *mahashmashān.* In this manner, the funeral rites of Lakshman Mishra began and ended with a blessing from the Kina Ram *dhuni.* The family preserved the Sanskritic rites in their entirety but bracketed them with Aghori rituals. This family of Brahmin Aghori succeeded in observing both traditions with little conflict or compromise.

The postreform Aghori were tolerant of combined rites, provided that the ceremonies preserved the ideals of nondiscrimination. But they had general concerns that further compromises with orthodox traditions might open the floodgate of social discrimination within the Aghor community. These concerns arose with disputes between the old-style Dom Aghori and the newer generation of upper-caste and upper-class disciples during the early years of reformation. Although both sides had valid arguments in these disputes, the fact did not escape public attention that the inner circles of the Kina Ram and Parao Ashrams largely comprised well-educated Rajputs, including the president of the Kshatriya caste association in Banaras. Ranaji, an elderly Brahmin disciple of Baba Rajeshwar Ram, still continued the old custom of refusing to let anyone touch his feet while in the ashram. He echoed the teaching that the Aghori should treat each other as equals before God. I found no postreform disciples who followed this practice. On the contrary, many ashram residents paid close attention to the social standings of the people around them.

Once, while participating in a nine-day festival in Pryadarshi Baba's ashram near a tribal village in Madhya Pradesh, I was surprised to find my fellow guests entering the temple according to social rank. In addition to the usual segregation of women and men within the temple, people appeared to be sitting from front to back according to some combination of age, education, and occupation. They duplicated this sequence when queuing up for meals. In a country where "the queue" is usually a jostling cluster of shoulders and elbows, I was surprised to discover that a hundred and forty people from different parts of India could assemble in such a hierarchy with little or no discussion. I was also uncomfortable with my treatment as a "VIP" throughout the festival. I ate my meals in a separate area with Pryadarshi Baba and slept in separate quarters with a former deputy prime minister of Nepal and a former excise minister of India. The festival was hardly an egalitarian affair.

Hari Baba later provided a relativistic interpretation of these ashram dynamics. "Before coming into contact with Aghor, most of these people would not have even sat down together to eat the same meal," he said. He pointed out that, in these parts of India, even small improvements can be significant. The reform strategy was to encourage incremental changes among the householders when possible and to be tolerant and patient when necessary. If the Aghori babas pushed their ideals too hard, they could alienate the general population and compromise their greater objective of worldly reform. However, if the Aghori did not push hard enough, then they could lose the ideals of nondiscrimination on which the reforms were based. Their argument spoke of the Aristotelian mean and the Middle Way of Buddhism. It reminded me of a parable in the Jataka tales in which the Buddha hears a music teacher tell his students that if the strings of an instrument are too tight, they will break. If they are too loose, the instrument will not play (Strong 2001). Hari Baba's argument was supported by other signs of egalitarianism within the lineage that set the ashram apart from other communities in this region of northern India. The Aghori had achieved some success with their teachings, and I found no signs of broken strings. Then again, two years of fieldwork was not enough for me to ascertain whether the strings could be tighter or if the intended reforms were proceeding at an optimum pace. Such assessments must await future studies.

WESTERNIZATION AND NONDISCRIMINATION

Worldly engagement brought an increasingly Western influence to the Aghor tradition, a trend that accelerated after Hari Baba established an ashram in the United States. Although this development was relatively new, the contact was not without philosophical precedent. The Aghori believe that nondiscrimination is a primordial and universal human condition. Hence, Aghori teachings are not restricted to one sect or cultural tradition. Mr. Asthana often emphasized this fact in his role as the chief public-relations representative of the lineage. He also stated that the Aghori approach is not unusual; one can find it in any spiritual tradition in which people transcend their discriminatory socialization. For these reasons, anyone could become an Aghori: man or woman, renunciate or householder, Indian or Westerner.

Nonetheless, many Indian disciples expressed ambivalence about Western influences in the Aghor tradition. Two signs at the Kina Ram Ashram that bore the same message in Hindi demonstrated this ambivalence: "America is such a country that went from barbarism to richness without passing through civilization." There were 121 written messages posted in the ashram, 119 of which quoted the religious and ethical teachings of Sarkar Baba. This message was the only explicitly political one among them and the only message that appeared on more than one sign. It was also the only message attributed to the current head of the lineage, Baba Siddhartha Gautam Ram. Both signs were prominently displayed in the ashram. One hung above the sign-in book in the reception area. The other sat on a table beside Gautam Baba's picture just outside his apartment door. The message echoed the sentiments of other Kina Rami, who had expressed their concern that Americans have somehow become a world power without the benefit of culture or history. On the surface, the critique fit within the Aghori tradition of resistance to

imperial authority, but it was not directed against imperialism per se.
Rather it was a critique of *unqualified* authority, similar to that of a rit-
ually inferior but economically dominant caste group (see Wiser and
Wiser 2000; Raheja 1988).

Despite these overt signs of criticism, Gautam Baba showed some
interest in Western popular culture. He often wore polo shirts and gym
suits beneath his robes. He was an avid cricket fan and enjoyed watching American action movies on his VCR. He also spent a great deal of
time at the offices and facilities of his Western-style recording studio
across the street from the ashram. Yet he led a simple and quiet life, free
of material clutter and very much in keeping with the lives of the other
renunciates of the lineage. Many of his inner circle had similarly mixed
affinities, being simultaneously fascinated by and distrustful of all things
Western. The resident male disciples of the Kina Ram Ashram often
quizzed me about America in much the same manner that they tested me
to determine my place in their pecking order.

Indian ambivalence about the West posed a special challenge for Hari
Baba, who often found himself introducing American and Indian disciples to one another. Such occasions were usually friendly affairs,
opportunities to put Aghori principles into practice and attempt Swami
Vivekananda's famous (if apocryphal) charge that India and America
adopt the best of each other's cultures. But the best of intentions could
be deflected by differentials of wealth and power, and people had difficulty seeing past the flood of Coca-Cola and *Baywatch* episodes to whatever positive contributions the West might have to offer. Moreover, this
ambivalence extended to distrust of Hari Baba himself. Some referred to
him as "*Mishra* Baba," using his Brahmin name with ironic emphasis.
These same people pronounced "*Sonoma* Ashram" as if the two words
combined to make an oxymoron. They knew that Sonoma was in California, a mythical paradise that they viewed with a mixture of envy and
suspicion. The Sonoma Ashram held the promise of Aghori expansion
into the global village; it also posed the threat of decadence that might
undermine their traditional austerity. For some, Hari Baba represented
the Brahmin priest and the nonresident Indian rolled into one. They
viewed him as if his Brahmin origins were somehow tied to his Western
destination, as if sanskritization and Westernization were two sides of
the same hierarchical coin (cf. Srinivas 1989). These models were both
enticing and understandably threatening.

Ambivalent feelings were often allayed by the Western devotees who
accompanied Hari Baba on his regular sojourns to India, as well as reports

from Indians returning from visits to the Sonoma Ashram. Both were selective encounters, of course. Hari Baba handpicked traveling companions who would serve as good ambassadors. Decadent behavior was unlikely in any case; Western ashrams usually do not attract the Club Med type of tourist. On the Indian side, only those with significant means could afford a trip to the United States, business and professional people educated in English medium schools who had a stake in the global marketplace. Both sides were familiar with the trappings of materialism. They had either moved beyond it, at least to some degree, or learned how to conceal their ongoing attachments. The resulting image was the same either way: that of an international community of Aghori with good intentions, diplomatic skills, and the means to make the world a better place.

Aghori diplomacy was further supported by American service projects in India. Like his Indian counterparts, Hari Baba drew upon professional specialists to accomplish service projects at home and abroad. He brought an engineer to advise some of the Indian ashrams on water and waste management, and he invited educators to help teach and assess the learning needs of schoolchildren. The Sonoma Ashram provided generous support to the Little Stars School for Street and Poor Children; its funding helped expand its average enrollment from thirty to more than four hundred students. The Sonoma ashram provided funds for an ambulance at the Parao Ashram, as well as for construction projects in several other Indian ashrams. Eventually, Hari Baba built his own ashram in Banaras, a relatively small property with a clinic and an orphanage for about eighteen abandoned street children. Much of this support came while the Sonoma Ashram was little more than a trailer and a yurt on rented property. Such commitments did not escape the attention of their Indian disciples.

Sevā notwithstanding, questions remain about the degree to which one can transfer Aghori teachings to Western devotees. Not all Indian Aghori recognize the authenticity of the Vedas, but nearly all have built their faith upon some form of Hindu tradition. Whereas only a few might understand Sanskrit, most Aghori grew up listening to its sounds, chanting its songs, and participating in associated rituals. These symbols are bound to have different valences for monolingual Americans raised in Judeo-Christian environments. Though Americans might be able to achieve the Aghori ideal of nondiscrimination, some Aghori questioned whether they could do so within an Indian religious framework. The question often came up during Hari Baba's Indian visits, to which he usually responded that God is no more Indian than American. Indians and Americans are different in some ways and not others. Both must face their respective challenges for spiritual growth.

In discussing these matters with Hari Baba, Katharine suggested that the main challenge for the American disciple is one of learning, whereas for the Indian disciple, it is one of unlearning. Indeed, one of the major reasons that Hari Baba brought American disciples to India was for them to learn certain habits and customs from their Indian counterparts, especially with respect to guru-disciple relations. Many Sonoma disciples expressed difficulty overcoming their individualist orientations and committing to the teachings of the guru for an entire lifetime. Such are the challenges for members of the "me generation," who are accustomed to changing their religions as often as their spouses; using spiritual teachers as cheap therapists; and obsessively searching for self-realization from within, rather than from the families and communities around them. Spending time in India was one way to learn traditional alternatives to these habits and to see them modeled in the daily actions of their Indian hosts.

On the other side of the exchange, Hari Baba and others noted that American disciples have some advantages over their Indian counterparts in being relatively free of certain prejudices and attachments. Americans may struggle with issues of class and race, but these social categories have yet to achieve the scope and intricacy of India's caste systems. Although an interest in Western cultures may lead to increased materialism, an American interest in Indian cultures often selects for people who are willing to give up a certain level of material comfort and serve as role models for simple living. Finally, most Indian pollution taboos are moot issues for Americans, who are brought up to try just about anything, with personal taste serving as the main criterion for discrimination. As one Indian devotee said, "Americans may have more ego, but they also have [fewer] taboos to overcome."

These differences play out in the ways that Indians and Americans relate to the Aghor babas. Americans often approach Hari Baba for solutions to existential crises, clarifications of purpose, and the palliation of emotional pain. They want a personal audience with the guru, a chance to tell him more about themselves (cf. Vigne 1997). Indians tend to be much quieter. Some simply prefer *darshan,* the blessing that comes from a shared gaze with the divine. Bede Griffiths articulated this distinction in stark terms, saying that Westerners "go to religious people in order to speak. Us, we go there to sit and be silent, to sit down peacefully before them and see God" (Griffiths quoted in Vigne 1997). When Indian visitors speak with the Aghori babas, they usually inquire about practical matters of daily life. Theirs is the pragmatism of poverty, a long list of immediate needs that leave little time for anything else. Under the conditions of day-to-day subsistence, few Indians can afford the luxury of existential reflection. Hari Baba often reflected upon this fact, commenting on the difficulty of getting Indian families to contribute time and resources for *sevā* when many were close to becoming *sevā* recipients themselves.

Despite differences between Indian and American disciples, death continues to be a common domain of learning. Although the rites of cremation partially remove the shroud of death from the view of Hindustani communities, death pollution and taboos continue to reinforce people's aversions to the final sacrifice. And although American disciples might loiter in the *shmashān,* few can identify themselves or their loved ones within the cremation pyre. Without these identifications, the lessons of the *shmashān* could easily remain shrouded in the exoticism of the alien other. Despite the different learning needs of Indian and American disciples, mortality confrontation will remain a common focus of Aghor *sādhanā* for as long as each group retains its fears and prejudices.

THE CULTURAL DYNAMICS OF AGHOR MEDICINE

Aghor philosophy is a medicine for the illness of social discrimination in India. Insofar as anxieties about human mortality drive cultural models of discrimination against human morbidity, the Aghori have sought to transform these models through symbolic confrontations with death. Although the Kina Ram Aghori have shifted their venues from cremation grounds to clinics in recent years, death remains a central feature of their spiritual practice and healing modalities. Yet despite such methods, I found little evidence of change in the discriminatory attitudes of non-Aghori patients as a result of their experiences with Aghor medicine. Most had taken a transportive approach to the healing process—dumping their afflictions on the Aghori and hoping that the latter would wash their problems away like the river Ganga. But a few patients appeared to embrace and internalize the deeper meanings of these healing modalities, especially after resolving their original problems. They constituted a subgroup with the potential to become Aghori themselves someday. As for the patient-disciples, I suggest that their more transformative approach to Aghor as medicine has prompted an important shift in discriminatory attitudes toward other communities in this part of northern India. In this manner, the medicines of Aghor have propagated the transmission of Aghor as medicine.

This field experience has challenged me to confront and discard a number of preconceived images. Because of the Aghori's history of radical asceticism, I initially expected them to be socially marginalized, representing an exception to the pious orthodoxy that pervaded the sacred landscape of Banaras. In contrast, the Kina Rami turned out to be one of the most powerful and well-respected sects within a city that is known for its corruption as much as its reverence. Based on my previous clinical experiences, I expected to develop much closer relations with the patients than with their healers. In contrast, my relationships with Hari Baba and the Mishra family developed into an extensive network of strong connections within the Aghori community. Getting to know patients outside of their clinical contexts was much more difficult, owing to their short durations of treatment, concealment of stigmatized conditions, and overall ambivalence to the Aghori, which often extended to me. Rapport had its trade-offs.

Yet perhaps the greatest disparity between my expectations and field observations was in the outcomes of Aghor treatment regimens for the stigmatization of socially discredited conditions such as leprosy, leukoderma, and infertility. If cultural models of social discrimination against human morbidity are motivated by anxieties about human mortality, then, I thought, confrontation with these anxieties during Aghori healing rituals such as the *dhuni-kund* sequence would bring about a noticeable change of attitude among the patients, at least a change in their self-image. Yet the evidence for this hypothesis was both modest and mixed. The issue was very different for the healers, however: their focus on treatment and *sevā* for the socially discredited had transformed the Aghori from a small sect to a large, powerful, and socially respected organization. One could therefore argue that the patients did more to destigmatize the Aghori than the other way around. This statement is not to say that the Aghori failed to serve their patients adequately. On the contrary, the Aghori used this newfound power to expand their community services, and their greater reputation only served to strengthen the *duwā* of Aghor medicine.

The flowchart in figure 15 illustrates the cultural dynamics of these exchanges. Informed by traditional, and predominantly transportive models of purification, non-Aghori patients approach their healers as metaphysical sinks in which to dump the ritual pollution of sin and dis-

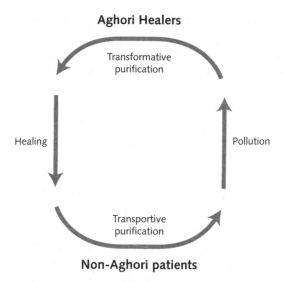

Aghori Healers

Figure 15. Purification and healing between Aghori healers and non-Aghori patients.

ease. For the Aghori, this "dumping" is more of an opportunity than a dilemma. As with the Ganga and *shmashān,* the ritual power of the Aghori—conceived as the feminine and (re)creative heat of *shaktī*—lies in their ability to assimilate the pollution of others. Using this heat within a transformative model of purification, the Aghori internalize and "digest" this pollution, converting it into further power for healing.

This process links the transportive approach of non-Aghori patients to the transformative approach of their Aghori healers through an exchange of ritual pollution and healing. What are the implications of these dynamics for Aghor philosophy as its own form of medicine? The answer comes from expanding this model to include the affective dimensions of death and (non)discrimination and to account for the conversion of non-Aghor patients to Aghor disciples. A transportive approach to Aghor medicine enables non-Aghori patients to avoid their aversions by placing them outside a zone of attribution, thereby reinforcing cultural models of stigmatization and blame. In contrast, a transformative approach to Aghor medicine challenges patients to identify with their mortality in the most intimate way possible—by internalizing its symbols of death and making them part of a healthy body and soul. Whether this latter approach is effective in producing a state of non-discrimination has yet to be tested. In the meantime, the existing social reforms of the Kina Ram Aghori are positive indicators of collective change.

The affective dynamics of death anxiety and nondiscrimination help explain the motivations behind transportive and transformative purification in Aghor medicine. We have seen that these approaches can be complementary. They also appear to provide incentives for attidudinal change among non-Aghori patients. Key to understanding this process is the observation that most of the disciples I knew had initially sought the Aghori for healing of medical conditions or solutions to worldly problems. Only after repeated experiences and testimonies of successful resolution to these problems were they motivated to learn more about Aghor philosophy. Consequently, their healer-patient relationships become guru-disciple relationships.

These conversions were motivated by a conscious, goal-directed cultural model. D'Andrade (1992) introduces the goal-directed model as a bridge between cognitive and affective approaches to cultural anthropology. In contrast to a drives-oriented approach, which emphasizes the motivational influence of innate psychobiological needs or unconscious desires acquired in early childhood, a goal-oriented approach stresses the innate motivational force of cultural models to instigate action through conscious objectives. In Aghor medicine, a cultural model of power as *shaktī* becomes a conscious goal; with every instance of successful healing by the Aghori, patients increasingly recognize the *shaktī* of Aghor and the spiritual authority that this power entails. Just as the desire for healing motivates patients to walk past the skulls at the gate, the desire to acquire further power and truth motivates them to confront deeper aversions and anxieties. From this point, the healer becomes the teacher, presenting the patient-cum-disciple with a drives-oriented approach to overcoming anxiety and discrimination.

D'Andrade contends that "there is no necessary conflict between *drive* and *goal* approaches" (1992: 26). Examples of their integration appear in the works of Shore (1996), who tacks between cultural models within the mind and the external models of culture that have arisen in symbolic anthropology (cf. Geertz 1973). Similarly, Nuckolls (1996) proposes a dialectical model for understanding the complex relationships between the deep motivations elucidated by psychoanalysis and the cultural schemata mapped in cognitive anthropology, positing that culture is a necessarily incomplete synthesis of the two. However incomplete this synthesis might be, a similarly integrated theory helps explain several complex interactions between the patients and healers of Aghor medicine. It explains how most patients are able to access the power of their healers without subscribing to Aghor philosophy. It also explains why some patients go on to become Aghori themselves, resulting in a thousand-fold increase in membership over the past thirty years. Finally, this theory explains how Aghor tradition serves as a medicine for the biosocial illness of discrimination.

In addition to providing these explanations, I hope that this book will contribute more broadly to an interdisciplinary research agenda in human health and healing. For instance, the complexity of medical pluralism in India needs further framing if we are to understand the health practices of more than a billion people. Here, a cultural schema of medicine as a medium helps us relate this pluralism to the pragmatic concerns of Indian societies. It helps avoid the Western preconception that explanatory models of therapy and etiology are necessarily linked. It also builds on the work of previous anthropologists who have suggested the primary importance of the quality of the healer-patient relationship (cf. Nichter and Nordstrom 1989; Kakar 1982; Kleinman 1980). This work presents major health-policy considerations as well as productive avenues for further research.

Finally, I hope that this book will inspire further research in the etiology and prevention of social discrimination. By approaching disease discrimination as an illness, inclusive of its socially marked conditions, I have attempted to move beyond a descriptive analysis of disease stigma and to bring an explanatory framework to this important human issue. I have sought to describe and explain the modest but significant successes of Aghor philosophy and practice, through the media of Aghori ethnomedical practices, as a therapy for the illness of social discrimination. Just as leprosy continues to serve as a major prototype for the stigmatization of other diseases (e.g., HIV/AIDS and schizophrenia), so too might Aghor medicine provide lessons for the prevention or mitigation of this illness within locally organized and culturally relevant traditions of healing. I hope that scholars will find similar ethnographic examples for comparison and make further contributions to a systematic theory of destigmatization. The world needs more of this medicine.

Notes

FOREWORD

1. The earlier phases of my fieldwork in Banaras, largely devoted to other aspects of the city's sacred tradition, coincided with the final years of Baba Rajeshwar Ram's incumbency as the head of the lineage and steward of the Kina Ram Ashram. After his death, the changes in the ashram's ambience and atmosphere, and in the kinds of people who frequented it, were immediate and palpable. I addressed these changes briefly in my account, but—with the hindsight that Barrett provides—I probably failed to fully appreciate their significance. I certainly did not foresee the extraordinary expansion in Aghori popularity that he documents. Had I spent more time at Awadhut Bhagwan Ram's Kushth Seva Ashram on the other side of the river at Parao, and less with Aghori on the cremation ghats and at the Kina Ram Ashram, the balance of my account would likely have been different.—*Jonathan P. Parry*

INTRODUCTION

1. This term entered into usage among the Kina Rami after I introduced it during a follow-up visit to India. Its adoption is a prime example of how the process of ethnography can shape the subject of inquiry.

2. *Emic* is an anthropological term that describes the subjective meanings of cultural phenomena or the perspective from which those meanings are interpreted. It is often contrasted with the *etic,* empirical and objective, aspects of culture. *Emic* and *etic* derive from the linguistic distinction between the phonemic and phonetic elements of speech (see Pike 1954).

3. Vimalananda designated Svoboda to cremate his body, an act traditionally performed by the familial or spiritual successor of the deceased.

4. Smith (1982) traces the "lineage" of this taxonomic approach from debates among eighteenth-century naturalists to those of twentieth-century religious scholars.

5. I had the pleasure of attending Professor Barth's ethnography course at Emory University in 1994. His comments on fieldwork were very insightful, so much so that I took my class notes with me to India. Several other students brought their "Barth notes" with them to the field as well.

CHAPTER 1. THE COSMIC SINK

1. These potential sources are a collection of historical documents at the Calcutta University library; supporting materials from the maharaja's archives at Ramnagar; and, most importantly, original manuscripts of the early Kina Rami held by the descendents of Baba Jainarayan Ram. Happy hunting.

2. This story has variations. However, this version is the most popular among the Kina Ram disciples.

3. Shiva is sometimes depicted on a donkey to emphasize his antinomian aspect. For example, a man dressed as Lord Shiva parades through the city on a donkey during the carnival-like festival of Holi, which Banarsis celebrate in a particularly intense and irreverent manner.

4. The current maharaja of Banaras is the first to have been born into the family since Kina Ram's curse. Supposedly, his birth was possible only after his father made peace with the lineage.

5. *Sanskritization* is the adoption of prescriptive and proscriptive behaviors by caste groups attempting to move up in status over several generations, usually after having acquired a greater degree of temporal power, economic autonomy, and solidarity (see Srinivas 1989).

6. These sacred sites range from Gangotri, near the source of the river, to Rishikesh, Haridwar, and Allahabad, to name just a few major pilgrimage centers upstream from Banaras.

7. The most commonly recited mantra among Hindus, the Gayatri Mantra, is a request for protection from the deity of mantras and songs (see RV III: 36).

8. *Pān* is a mixture of betel nut, lime, spices, and often tobacco that is popular in India. Chewing the betel and lime mixture creates a large amount of bright-red saliva, which the chewer spits in any convenient location. Banaras is famous for its fresh *pān* as well as for the frequency with which the locals chew it.

9. Although adult women do relieve themselves in public places, they tend to be much more discreet about it than men are.

10. This is commonly done on banks just north and south of the city's ghats, and particularly on Prabhu Ghat, typically in the hours just before sunrise. Significantly, Prabhu Ghat is one of the only ghats not to have façades or entrances. It is only a set of steps leading up to a two-tiered walkway before a high wall. Persons defecate facing the wall and away from the river. Many Banarsis disapprove of these practices.

11. Although street sweeping is a government job, the task is considered highly inauspicious and is therefore usually relegated to members of the Dom *jāti*. Certain members of this same historically untouchable caste also perform cremation work.

12. A holdover from the British colonial period, *peon* is an actual term for an office assistant whose job is to run errands.

13. South Asianists debate whether Indians have a concept of individual self (cf. Marriott 1976). For the purpose of this text, I use the word *self* in the broadest possible sense, inclusive of the individual self as well as collective selves.

14. Throughout this book, I distinguish *shaktī* as power from Shakti as deity, although both represent the same underlying mystery.

15. The sign literally says that the guru nurtures the *mana, chitra, buddhi*—three aspects of "mind" described in the classic Yoga Sutras—in addition to the *atma,* or soul.

16. *Darshan* means "to have sight of." The concept of seeing is central to Indian religious traditions, in which sight is a metaphor for direct knowledge of the metaphysical. *Darshan* also works both ways in the interaction between the human and the divine: to see the deity is also to be seen by him or her.

17. This designation is simpler when the guru has already renounced family life, or if his son is the succeeding teacher. It becomes more complicated when the guru is a householder whose successors are other than his living sons.

18. Because the designated cremator tends not to be as adept at the task as a professional attendant, the latter usually ensures that the fire is properly lit and that the body is burned effectively with the available wood. The cremator usually provides a token amount of practical participation, and only then under the guidance of the cremation attendant.

19. My use of the term *digestive transformation* is specific to the cultural context of this study. Readers should not confuse it with a similar term that Isha Schwaller De Lubicz uses in her speculative historical fiction about life in ancient Egypt.

CHAPTER 2. FIRE IN THE WELL

1. *Leukoderma* is a general term for many kinds of skin depigmentation. *Vitiligo* refers to a subset of leukoderma conditions that present with irregular patches of depigmentation. Evidence suggests that the condition can have multiple causes, but an autoimmune mechanism is strongly implicated. Vitiligo does not appear to have adverse health consequences aside from increased exposure to ultraviolet radiation and possible comorbidity with other autoimmune conditions (Grimes 2005).

2. This shared connection among *kushṭh* diseases, infertility, and the sun has had interesting fallout in the treatment of leprosy, with people selling WHO-approved antibiotics on the black market in Banaras, fueled by a popular belief that these drugs can improve fertility.

3. My counts ranged from 37 to 223 bathers between the hours of 7:00 A.M. and 12:00 P.M. I typically found more bathers on Sundays than on Tuesdays.

4. Kamleshwar Baba's endorsement, however, created another methodological challenge. It took time to find the golden mean between his endorsing my role as a researcher and his giving people the impression that talking with me was neither expected nor a part of the healing process. My solution was to talk with the patients in as private a space as possible, away from any authority figures. However, complete privacy is nearly impossible in Banaras. At least one additional friend or family member was usually present during the interviews,

and it was not uncommon to have a few onlookers among the visitor group. Yet with a more subdued endorsement from Kamleshwar Baba, I was able to provide patients with enough space to turn me down in private without my letting anyone else know they had done so. Most patients were not open with me until they had made several visits to the ashram, which I took as a good sign.

5. Sons are also valued in matrilineal societies in which the mother's brother assumes the dominant role for most family decisions. Such inheritance rules can mitigate, but not eliminate, male dominance in most Indian families.

6. The Kina Rami could not confirm this relationship, but the family seemed well-informed about the Kina Ram tradition and lineage.

7. Multi-drug therapy uses a combination of antibiotics to cure leprosy. I elaborate on MDT in chapter 4.

8. As with the interviews along the river, I could not feasibly account for the social and ethnic diversity of Banaras. Moreover, people's opinions were often influenced by friends, family, and curious onlookers who surrounded us whenever we took out the tape recorder. In turn, the ongoing question about whether stated attitudes reflect actual behaviors made efforts toward formal characterizations of these social phenomena highly problematic.

9. Anil's first line of resort, however, was another Aghor ashram clinic across the river in Parao.

10. The popular statement "all the mothers are one"' reflects a predominant nondualist philosophy among Hindu religious traditions that the myriad manifestations of the divine reflect but one underlying reality. Kurtz (1992) uses this phrase as a title to his psychoanalytic study of kinship and goddess worship in India.

11. Parry also relates this schema to the regenerative powers of the Aghori. In this article, however, the connection is not as clear.

12. Of course, this model assumes that all fish in the Ganga are scavengers and bottom feeders.

CHAPTER 3. THE REFORMATION

1. Baba Siddartha Gautama Ram was Burhau Baba's designated successor and is the official head of the lineage today. But Bhagwan Ram was very much in charge until his death in 1991. We will return to Baba Siddartha Gautama Ram later in the book.

2. Cf. *būṛha* (old man) and *buṛhautā* (old age, decrepitude, senility).

3. Ramuji actually used the term *māda chod* (motherfucker) in this story. However, he was likely offering a contemporary interpretation of *bahan chod* (sister fucker), which had been a more popular expletive before the Western media began to have an influence.

4. The Nagas are a warrior-renunciate order that is historically charged with the protection of other Shaivite sects. Their spiritual practices often include trials of self-mortification over the course of several years. The *chimtā* is a scabbardlike metal tool that looks like a spike with a ring on its end. Literally, the word describes a pair of metal fire tongs, but clearly the Nagas have other uses for it. They place a *chimtā* in the ground wherever they establish a *dhuni*.

5. Despite the power of the tongs, I am unlikely to seek further blessings of this sort in the near future.

6. "Pouch" is a low-quality, low-cost wine fortified with ethanol, the name of which derives from the plastic pouch in which it is sold. It smells and tastes like a carcinogenic solvent. Needless to say, pouch can test one's powers of nondiscrimination.

7. *Jūṭhā* are the inauspicious leftovers of someone else's meal or drink. Yet for the Aghori, no leftovers are really *jūṭhā*. The Mishras have made this practice time and again when we've shared food from the same plate.

8. *Awadhut* refers to an enlightened soul living upon earth and is analogous to the Buddhist concept of Bodhisattva. *Sarkar* literally means "government head" or "administrator." That the postreform Kina Rami would commonly address Bhagwan Ram in these terms underscores his status as a saint, rivaled only by Baba Kina Ram, whom many consider to be the same reincarnated soul.

9. A *lungi* is a piece of cloth that men wear wrapped around their waists. The casting aside of old clothes is symbolic of shedding an old skin in personal transformation.

10. The more recent literacy figures from the 2001 census are suspect, given that they report dramatic changes with little improvement in education infrastructure. For a critical analysis of official literacy and poverty measurements in India, see Sainath 1996. The National Family Health Survey 1998–1999, conducted by the International Institute for Population Sciences, defines undernutrition as having a body-mass index of less than 18.5 kilograms per square meter.

11. Such arrangements are especially important because, though most Kina Rami can be categorized within the first three stages of the *ashrama* system, the fourth *sannyasi* stage does not usually occur later in life. Instead, most full-fledged Aghor babas take their vows of renunciation around the age of marriage, when their parents and siblings are still alive.

12. This story not only illustrates the complex relationship that Bhagwan Ram had with his guru and with the lineage as a whole. The miraculous opening of locks without keys could be interpreted as a sign of Sarkar Baba's divine authority to reform the lineage without ever assuming the seat of its official head.

13. When the time came, this designation conflicted with another version of his will, sparking a major controversy within the lineage and an ongoing lawsuit between certain factions of the lineage.

14. In most Indian guru-saint traditions, the teacher does not die in the proper sense but rather remains suspended in *samādhi*, a superconscious state.

15. Parry (1994) describes these business dynamics in detail. However, Sarkar Baba's request may have reflected a broader history of tensions with the Dom community.

CHAPTER 4. THE WRONG SIDE OF THE RIVER

1. A few noteworthy people have defied this warning. The famous poet Kabir, who railed against the hypocrisy of all major religions, insisted on dying across the river from Kashi, making the point that his salvation would depend solely on divine grace and the fruit of his actions.

2. The KSA clinic staff claimed that they could cure most forms of leprosy in three years.

3. The typical monthly prescription for KSA medicines costs between Rs 180 and Rs 220. Although difficult to measure in cash, farm labor in this region is typically about Rs 80 to Rs 100 per day.

4. Although statistics show that Indian women have worse access to health-care resources than men do, one would expect a higher proportion of physical deformities among those women who eventually obtained treatment than among a similar population of men. However, among people who receive treatment, four times as many men have deformities as women. I hypothesize that men's greater participation in certain forms of manual labor subjects them to higher rates of physical trauma, and therefore to a greater frequency of high-titer infections. This phenomenon needs further research.

5. Snakebite and smallpox are the other two afflictions for which cremation is prohibited in most Hindu religious traditions. Babies are not cremated because they have not yet achieved the full status of personhood. Renunciates are buried, for reasons I describe in chapter 3.

6. Kleinman's (1988) case studies illustrate that, though illness and disease are distinguishable from each other, they need not be exclusive categories.

7. The highest bacterial titers are found in nasal secretions, and researchers have hypothesized a number of transmission modes, including respiratory paths (Naafs et al. 2001), water transmission (Matsuoka et al. 1999), and an anaerobic soil intermediary (Chakrabarty and Dastidar 2001). However, the model cannot be validated until scientists can grow the organism under laboratory conditions. To date, the only naturally infected nonhuman host for leprosy is the armadillo, an animal that does not reproduce easily under captive conditions (Bruce et al. 2000).

8. A minority of people who are infected are particularly susceptible to the mycobacteria. Known as lepromatous, or LL cases, these people often require a longer and more involved course of treatment over three to five years (Bryceson and Pfalzgraff 1990).

9. Understandably, activists in the international HD community consider the term *leper* to be highly derogatory (Gussow and Tracy 1977).

10. Dapsone was the leading treatment for *M. leprae* infection until the early 1980s. Unfortunately, the organism began showing resistance to this sulfa drug within a decade of its introduction in 1943. Today, dapsone is considered to be merely bacteriostatic against *M. leprae*.

11. The solution of reintegrating leprosy treatment into primary care services can also be problematic. For a critical perspective, see Justice 1986.

12. See Nichter (2002) for a counterexample in which health providers relabel tuberculosis within a less stigmatizing ethnomedical category in order to improve health seeking and adherence to treatment.

13. Twenty-three out of thirty-one inpatients had previously sought treatment elsewhere: three first sought a homeopathic physician, two sought an Ayurvedic physician, and one was unreported.

14. Chandra Shekhar, who was prime minister from November 1990 to June 1991, was in frequent contact with Sarkar Baba and several senior disciples during his time in office.

CHAPTER 5. *DAWĀ* AND *DUWĀ*

1. I came to believe that the rest were prescribed in the early morning so that nothing worse could happen for the rest of the day. Taste is important in Ayurveda, but this does not mean that Ayurvedic medicines are supposed to taste good.

2. However, Svoboda does not identify with the Kina Ram lineage. See the introduction.

3. *Vipāka* is a primary example of such a transformation, in which the binary opposites of acrid and sweet can be converted into each other. At a broader level, Ayurveda recognizes at least seven successive fires, whereby the greater tissues *(dhatu)* of the body can be generated from the lesser ones (Zimmerman 1987: 159–79).

CHAPTER 6. DEATH AND NONDISCRIMINATION

1. Like many works of classical Greek literature, the Yoga Sutras are most likely the work of multiple authors under the authority of a single name.

2. Vivek Sar is currently in the process of translation and commentary.

3. See Seymour (2004) for a critique of this argument.

4. One could also interpret this role as directly fulfilling a childlike longing for the father (see Freud 1989/1927).

5. Massaging the feet of the guru is a great privilege. It is one of the few physical expressions of love and devotion that a disciple can offer his or her guru.

6. However, the relative auspiciousness of left and right are context dependent in many Hindu rituals (see Das 1997a).

7. An earlier version of this formula is represented in the statement *tat tvam asi*, "thou art that" (Chandogya Upanishad VI: 8.7).

8. Das (1997b) expands on Wittgenstein's thought experiment in which a person points to the hand of another when asked to locate his own. She argues that, like Wittgenstein's hand, pain can in fact be socially communicated as well as socially distributed. The socially distributed nature of leprosy is a prime example of this—especially with regard to the dual loci of the illness (discrimination) and its sign (the mark).

CONCLUSION

1. Lakshmanji's sons claimed their father was around 105 years old. Age is such an auspicious emblem in India that people commonly exaggerate the years of a teacher or relative. Nevertheless, based on the age of Lakshman Mishra's eldest son (seventy) and his beginnings as a homesteader in the 1920s and 1930s, he had to have been at least in his nineties.

2. For further exposition on the elements of a good death in North India, see Justice's (1997) ethnographic study of *mukti bhavans* (traditional hospices) in Banaras. Madan (1987) describes similar elements in a community of Kashmiri pundits.

3. The so-called Sanskritic rules are the behavioral prescriptions and proscriptions of orthodox Brahminical Hinduism regarding issues such as food exchange, ritual observances, and social relationships, including marriage.

Glossary

Āchmani Purification with water, usually performed before a *pūjā*.

Aghor Literally, "not terrible." Among the Kina Rami, a psychospiritual state in which one has no fear or aversion to anyone or anything; also, the spiritual traditions for attaining this state.

Agni Deity of fire.

Agrna Nonaversion. Often translated as "nondiscrimination" by the Kina Rami, who believe that this state is closely related to the state of Aghor.

Akhand Perpetual.

Antyeshṭi saṃskāra The final sacrifice; the rites of cremation.

Ārati Ceremonial worship of deities with a lamp, usually performed at dawn and dusk.

Aughar A carefree person. Used interchangeably with *Aghor* by the Kina Rami (contra Gupta 1993).

Awadhut An enlightened ascetic who has transcended all categories; the highest spiritual epithet among the Kina Ram Aghori.

Ayurveda Traditional system of Indian medicine.

Bhāgya Fate; indicative of karma but more commonly used among people in Banaras.

Bhajan Devotional song.

Bhaktī Devotion; the achievement of salvation or enlightenment through divine grace.

Bhojan Feast; usually for ceremonial purposes.

Bhūt pret Malevolent ghost considered to be the cause of many illnesses and misfortunes.

Chakra Wheel; bodily center in the flow of spiritual energy.

Chakra pūjā Aghori *pūjā* in which participants share the *prasād* in a circle.

Chimṭā Fire tongs, often carried by ascetics of the Naga sect. Also used as a musical instrument.

Daksha Shiva's father-in-law, cursed for not inviting his son-in-law to a sacrifice.

Darshan Divine contact through mutual gazing.

Dattatreya Avatar of Shiva and founding deity of Aghor.

Dawā Medicine.

Dhuni Ritual fire for sacrificial rites.

Duwā Blessing.

Fakīrī medicine Medicines invented and produced through divine inspiration.

Ganga The Ganges River.

Garīb log Poor people.

Ghats Steps.

Havan Ritual fire ceremony modeled after the Vedic sacrifice.

Hinglaj Devi Goddess who directed Baba Kina Ram to Krim Kund.

Japa Repetition of a mantra, usually in silent meditation.

Jaṭharāgni Digestive fire.

Jāti Hereditary groups associated with occupational specialties; one of two
   caste systems (the other is *Varṇa*).

Jivanmukti Spiritual liberation within one's lifetime.

Jūthā Ritually polluted leftovers.

Kāpālika One who carries a skull; ancient predecessor of the Aghori.

Korhi Extremely derogatory term for a person with leprosy.

Krīm Seed mantra of the goddess Kali.

Kund Well; a sacred tank for ritual bathing.

Kushṭh Category of (allegedly) contagious skin conditions that includes leprosy
   and leukoderma.

Leukoderma Benign, noncontagious depigmentation of the skin; often refers to
   vitiligo.

Mahant Chief celebrant of a temple, ashram, or shrine.

Mantra Sequence of words or sounds representing deities or principles that
   people use in spiritual practice.

Muhalla Neighborhood.

Nawab Regional ruler during the Mughal period.

Nazar lagna Evil eye.

Paṇḍā Brahminical ritual specialist.

Parvati Divine consort of Shiva.

Phūl Literally "flower"; also, an area of depigmentation on the skin.

Pīth Seat; both the location and the leadership of a spiritual tradition, school,
   or organization.

Prasād Sacred remnant of a divine offering imbued with the blessing of a deity.

Pūjārī Ritual specialist.

Rajput Warrior *jāti* (Kshatriya *varṇa*) prevalent in northern India.

Sādhanā Spiritual practice.

Saṃsāra Passage; the perpetual cycle of life, death, and rebirth. Sometimes
   referred to as the doctrine of reincarnation.

Saṃskāra Major life-crisis rituals performed in orthodox Hindu traditions.

Sarkar Governmental; term of authority.

Shiva Major deity of the Hindu pantheon, associated with asceticism, antinomianism, and re-creative destruction.

Shmashān Cremation grounds.

Sukhāṇḍī Dryness; dehydration.

Varṇa Four classes (categories) of Hindu society described in classical texts: Brahmins (priests and scholars); Kshatriya (kings and warriors); Vaishya (merchants); and Shudra (peasants). Persons born outside these classes have historically been considered to be untouchable.

Yajña Vedic fire sacrifice.

References

Ablon, J. 1981. Stigmatized Health Conditions. *Social Science & Medicine* 15B: 5–9.

———. 1995. The "Elephant Man" as "Self" and "Other": The Psychosocial Costs of a Misdiagnosis. *Social Science & Medicine* 40 (11): 1481–89.

Adler, S. R. 1994. Ethnomedical Pathogenesis and Hmong Immigrants' Sudden Nocturnal Deaths. *Culture Medicine and Psychiatry* 18 (1): 23–59.

Agar, M. 1996. *The Professional Stranger: An Informal Introduction to Fieldwork*. New York: Academic Press.

Ahmed, S. 1995. Whose Concept of Participation? State-Society Dynamics in the Cleaning of the Ganges at Varanasi. In *Water and the Quest for Sustainable Development in the Ganges Valley*, ed. G. P. Chapman and M. Thompson, 141–60. London: Mansell.

Ainlay, S. C., and F. Crosby. 1986. Stigma, Justice and the Dilemma of Difference. In *The Dilemma of Difference: A Multidisciplinary View of Stigma*, ed. S. C. Ainlay, L. M. Coleman, and G. Becker, 17–37. New York: Plenum.

Alonzo, A. A., and N. R. Reynolds. 1995. Stigma, HIV and AIDS: An Exploration and Elaboration of a Stigma Trajectory. *Social Science & Medicine* 41 (3): 303–15.

Alter, J. S. 1992. *The Wrestler's Body: Identity and Ideology on North India*. Berkeley: University of California Press.

Arole, S., R. Premkumar, R. Arole, M. Maury, and P. Saunderson. 2002. Social Stigma: A Comparative Qualitative Study of Integrated and Vertical Care Approaches to Leprosy. *Leprosy Review* 73 (2): 186–96.

Asthana, V. P. S. 1994a. *Aghor at a Glance*. Varanasi: Sri Sarveshwari Samooh Press.

———. 1994b. *Aghor Mast*. Varanasi: Sri Sarveshwari Samooh Press.

Atre, S. R., A. M. Kudale, S. N. Morankar, S. G. Rangan, and M. G. Weiss. 2004. Cultural Concepts of Tuberculosis and Gender among the General Population without Tuberculosis in Rural Maharashtra, India. *Tropical Medicine & International Health* 9 (11): 1228–38.

Avalon, A. (Woodruff, Sir John). 1960. *The Serpent Power: Being the Shañchakranirâpana and Pàduka-panchakà.* Madras: Ganesh & Company.

Baartmans, F. 2000. *The Holy Waters: A Primordial Symbol in Hindu Myths.* Delhi: B. R. Publishing.

Babb, L. 1975. *The Divine Hierarchy: Popular Hinduism in Central India.* New York: Columbia University Press.

———. 1983. Destiny and Responsibility: Karma in Popular Hinduism. In *Karma: An Anthropological Inquiry,* ed. C. F. Keyes and E. V. Daniel, 163–81. Berkeley: University of California Press.

Banerjee, T., and G. Banerjee. 1995. Determinants of Help-Seeking Behavior in Cases of Epilepsy Attending a Teaching Hospital in India—An Indigenous Explanatory Model. *International Journal of Social Psychiatry* 41 (3): 217–30.

Barrett, R. 1997. Male Health and Leprosy in Northern India: A Biocultural Perspective. Paper presented at the 96th Meeting of the American Anthropological Association, Washington, DC.

———. 2005. Self-Mortification and the Stigma of Leprosy in Northern India. *Medical Anthropology Quarterly* 19 (2): 216–30.

Barth, F. 1994. Personal communication.

Beals, A. R. 1976. Strategies of Resort to Curers in South India. In *Asian Medical Systems: A Comparative Study,* ed. C. Leslie, 184–200. Berkeley: University of California Press.

Becker, E. 1973. *The Denial of Death.* New York: Free Press.

Becker, G. 1981. Coping with Stigma: Lifelong Adaptation of Deaf People. *Social Science & Medicine* 15B: 21–24.

Becker, H. S. 1963. *Outsiders: Studies in the Sociology of Deviance.* New York: Macmillan.

Beidelman, T. O. 1959. *A Comparative Analysis of the Jajmani System.* New York: J. J. Augustin.

Berger, P. L., and T. Luckman. 1966. *The Social Construction of Reality: A Treatise on the Sociology of Knowledge.* New York: Doubleday.

Berkman, L. F., and S. L. Syme. 1979. Social Networks, Host Resistance, and Mortality: A Nine-Year Follow-Up Study of Alameda County Residents. *American Journal of Epidemiology* 109 (2): 186–204.

Bloom, S. S., D. Wypij, and M. das Gupta. 2001. Dimensions of Women's Autonomy and Influence in Maternal Health Care Utilization in a North Indian City. *Demography* 38 (1): 67–78.

Brand, P., and P. Yancey. 1997. *The Gift of Pain.* Grand Rapids, MI: Zondervan.

Brooks, D. R. 1990. *The Secret of the Three Cities: An Introduction to Hindu Shàkta Tantrism.* Chicago: University of Chicago Press.

Brown, M. F. 1988. Shamanism and Its Discontents. *Medical Anthropology Quarterly* 2 (2): 102–120.

Bruce, S., T. L. Schroeder, K. Ellner, M. Rubin, T. Williams, and J. E. Wolf. 2000. Armadillo Exposure and Hansen's Disease: An Epidemiologic Survey in Southern Texas. *Journal of the American Academy of Dermatology* 43 (2 Pt. 1): 223–28.

Bryceson, A., and R. Pfalzgraff. 1990. *Leprosy*. London: Churchill Livingstone.

Buckingham, J. 2002. *Leprosy in Colonial South India: Medicine and Confinement*. New York: Palgrave.

Buckshee, K. 1997. Impact of Roles of Women on Health in India. *International Journal of Gynecology and Obstetrics* 58 (1): 35–42.

Casson, R. W. 1993. Schemata in Cognitive Anthropology. *Annual Review of Anthropology* 12: 429–62.

Chakrabarty, A. N., and S. G. Dastidar. 2001. Is Soil an Alternative Source of Leprosy Infection? *Acta Leprologica* 12 (2): 79–84.

Cohen, L. 1998. *No Aging in India: Alzheimer's, the Bad Family, and Other Modern Things*. Berkeley: University of California Press.

Dalmia, V. 1996. *The Nationalization of Hindu Traditions: Bhataendu Harischandra and Nineteenth-Century Banaras*. Delhi: Oxford University Press.

D'Andrade, R. 1992. Schemas and Motivation. In *Human Motives and Cultural Models*, ed. R. D'Andrade and C. Strauss, 23–44. Cambridge: Cambridge University Press.

———. 1995. *The Development of Cognitive Anthropology*. Cambridge: Cambridge University Press.

Daniel, E. V. 1983. Karma Divined in a Ritual Capsule. In *Karma: An Anthropological Inquiry*, ed. C. F. Keyes and E. V. Daniel, 83–117. Berkeley: University of California Press.

———. 1984. *Fluid Signs: Being a Person the Tamil Way*. Berkeley: University of California Press.

Darian, S. G. 2001. *The Ganges in Myth and History*. Delhi: Motilal Banarsidass.

Das, V. 1997a. Concepts of Space in Ritual. In *Religion in India*, ed. T. N. Madan. Delhi: Oxford University Press.

———. 1997b. Language and Body: Transactions in the Construction of Pain. In *Social Suffering*, ed. A. Kleinman, V. Das, and M. Locke, 67–91. Berkeley: University of California Press.

Dasgupta, M. 1987. Selective Discrimination against Female Children in Rural Punjab. *Population and Development Review* 13 (1): 77–100.

Dharmshaktu, N. S. 1992. A Project Model for Attempting Integration of Leprosy Services with General Health Care Services after the Prevalence of the Disease Is Reduced in the Endemic Districts on Multidrug Therapy for over Five Years. *Indian Journal of Leprosy* 64 (3): 349–57.

Douglas, M. 1966. *Purity and Danger: An Analysis of the Concepts of Pollution and Taboo*. Harmondsworth, U.K.: Penguin.

Dressler, W. W. 1993. Health in the African American Community: Accounting for Health Inequalities. *Medical Anthropology Quarterly* 7 (4): 325–435.

Dube, L. 1996. Caste and Women. In *Caste: Its Twentieth Century Avatar*, ed. M. N. Srinivas, 1–21. Delhi: Viking.

Dumont, L. 1966. *Homo Hierarchicus: The Caste System and Its Implications*. London: Paladin.

Durkheim, E. 1965/1915. *The Elementary Forms of the Religious Life*, trans. J. W. Swain. New York: Free Press.

Eck, D. 1983. *Banaras: City of Light*. London: Routledge & Kegan Paul.

Ell, S. R. 1994. Leprosy in History. In *Leprosy*, ed. R. C. Hasting, 3–10. Edinburgh: Churchill Livingstone.

Enzley, S., and F. Barros. 1997. A Global Review of Diarrhoeal Disease Control. UNICEF Staff Working Papers EVL-97-002.

Farmer, P. 1992. *AIDS and Accusation: Haiti and the Geography of Blame.* Berkeley: University of California Press.

Ferro-Luzzi, G. E. 1989. The Polythetic-Prototype Approach to Hinduism. In *Hinduism Reconsidered*, ed. G. D. Sontheimer and H. Hulke, 187–196. Delhi: Manohar.

Filippi, G. G. 1996. *Mṛtyu: Concept of Death in Indian Traditions.* Delhi: D. K. Printworld.

Flood, G. 1998. *An Introduction to Hinduism.* Delhi: Cambridge University Press.

Frawley, D. 1992. *The Astrology of the Seers: A Comprehensive Guide to Vedic Astrology.* Delhi: Motilal Banarsidass.

Freidson, E. 1979. Illness as Social Deviance. In *Profession of Medicine: A Study of the Sociology of Applied Knowledge*, 205–23. New York: Dodd, Mead, & Co.

Freitag, S. B. 1989. Introduction: The History and Political Economy of Banaras. In *Culture and Power in Banaras: Community, Performance, and Environment, 1800–1980*, ed. S. B. Freitag, 1–23. Berkeley: University of California Press.

Freud, S. 1961. *Civilization and Its Discontents*, trans. J. Strachey. New York: W. W. Norton.

———. 1989/1927. *The Future of an Illusion*, trans. J. Strachey. New York: W. W. Norton.

Frist, T. F. 2000. Stigma and Societal Response to Leprosy: Experience of the Last Half Century. *Indian Journal of Leprosy* 72 (1): 1–3.

Fuller, C. J. 1996. Introduction: Caste Today. In *Caste Today*, ed. C. J. Fuller, 1–31. Oxford: Oxford University Press.

Garro, L. 1993. Chronic Illness and the Construction of Narratives. In *Pain as Human Experience: An Anthropological Perspective*, ed. B. J. Good, 100–37. Berkeley: University of California Press.

Gawkrodger, D. J. 1997. *Dermatology: An Illustrated Colour Text.* New York: Churchill Livingstone.

Geertz, C. 1973. *The Interpretation of Cultures.* New York: Basic Books.

Giddens, Anthony. 1977. *Studies in Social and Political Theory.* New York: Basic Books.

Glucklich, A. 1997. *The End of Magic.* Oxford: Oxford University Press.

Goffman, E. 1963. *Stigma: Notes on the Management of Spoiled Identity.* Englewood Cliffs, NJ: Prentice Hall.

Griffiths, P., Z. Mathews, and A. Hinde. 2000. Understanding the Sex Ratio in India: A Simulation Approach. *Demography* 37 (4): 477–88.

Grimes, P. E. 2005. New Insights and New Therapies for Vitiligo. *Journal of the American Medical Association* 293 (6): 730–35.

Gross, R. L. 1992. *The Sadhus of India: A Study of Hindu Asceticism.* Jaipur: Rawat Publications.

Guenther, H. V. 1971. *The Life and Teaching of Naropa.* New York: Oxford University Press.

Guha, R. 1989. Dominance without Hegemony and Its Historiography. In *Subaltern Studies VI: Writings on South Asian History and Society*, 210–309. Delhi: Oxford University Press.

Gupta, R. P. 1993. The Politics of Heterodoxy and the Kina Rami Ascetics of Banaras. PhD diss., Syracuse University.

———. 1995. The Kina Rami: Aughars and Kings in the Age of Cultural Conflict. In *Bhakti Religion in North India*, ed. D. N. Lorenzen, 133–42. Albany: SUNY Press.

Gussow, Z. 1989. *Leprosy, Racism, and Public Health: Social Policy in Chronic Disease Control*. Boulder, CO: Westview Press.

Gussow, Z., and G. S. Tracy. 1977. Status, Ideology, and Adaptation to Stigmatized Illness: A Study of Leprosy. In *Culture, Disease, and Healing: Studies in Medical Anthropology*, 394–402. New York: Macmillan.

Hertz, R. 1960. *Death and the Right Hand*, trans. R. Needham and C. Needham. Glencoe, IL: Free Press.

Inden, R. 1990. *Imagining India*. Cambridge: Cambridge University Press.

Inhorn, M. 1986. Genital Herpes: An Ethnographic Inquiry into Being Discreditable in American Society. *Medical Anthropology Quarterly* 17: 59–63.

———. 1994. *Quest for Conception: Gender, Infertility, and Egyptian Medical Traditions*. Philadelphia: University of Pennsylvania Press.

Janes, C. R. 1995. The Transformations of Tibetan Medicine. *Medical Anthropology Quarterly* 9 (1): 6–39.

Jayaraman, R. 2005. Personal Identity in a Globalized World: Cultural Roots of Hindu Personal Names and Surnames. *The Journal of Popular Culture* 38 (3): 476–90.

Jeffery, R. 1988. *The Politics of Health in India*. Berkeley: University of California Press.

Jones, E. E., R. A. Scott, and H. Markus. 1984. *Social Stigma: The Psychology of Marked Relationships*. New York: W. H. Freeman and Co.

Jopling, W. 1988. *Handbook of Leprosy*. London: William Heinemann.

Justice, C. 1997. *Dying the Good Death: The Pilgrimage to India's Holy City*. Albany: SUNY Press.

Justice, J. 1986. *Policies, Plans, and People: Culture and Health Development in Nepal*. Berkeley: University of California Press.

Kakar, S. 1981. *The Inner World*. Delhi: Oxford University Press.

———. 1982. *Shamans, Mystics, and Doctors: A Psychological Inquiry into India and Its Healing Traditions*. New York: Alfred A. Knopf.

———. 1999. Clinical Work and Cultural Imagination. In *Vishnu on Freud's Desk: A Reader in Psychoanalysis and Hinduism*, ed. T. G. Vaidyanathan and J. J. Kripal, 216–32. Delhi: Oxford University Press.

Kamat, V. R., and M. Nichter. 1998. Pharmacies, Self Medication, and Pharmaceutical Marketing in Bombay, India. *Social Science & Medicine* 47 (6): 779–94.

Keyes, C. F. 1983. Introduction: The Study of Popular Ideas of Karma. In *Karma: An Anthropological Inquiry*, ed. C. F. Keyes and E. V. Daniel, 1–24. Berkeley: University of California Press.

Kierkegaard, S. 1989 (1849). *The Sickness unto Death*, trans. A. Hannay. New York: Penguin Books.

King, S. B. 1988. Two Epistemological Models for the Interpretation of Mysticism. *Journal of the American Academy of Religion* 56 (2): 257–79.

Kleinman, A. 1978. Concepts and a Model for the Comparison of Medical Systems as Cultural Systems. *Social Science & Medicine* 12: 85–93.

———. 1980. *Patients and Healers in the Context of Culture: An Exploration of the Borderland between Anthropology, Medicine, and Psychiatry.* Berkeley: University of California Press.

———. 1988. *The Illness Narratives: Suffering, Healing, and the Human Condition.* New York: Basic Books.

———. 1992. Pain and Resistance: The Delegitimation and Relegitimation of Local Worlds. In *Pain as Human Experience: An Anthropological Perspective,* ed. B. J. Good, 169–97. Berkeley: University of California Press.

Kopparty, S. N. M., A. P. Karup, and M. Sivarum. 1995. Problems and Coping Strategies of Families Having Patients with and without Deformities. *Indian Journal of Leprosy* 67 (2): 133–51.

Kumar, A., A. Girdhar, V. S. Yadav, and B. K. Girdhar. 2001. Some Epidemiological Observations on Leprosy in India. *International Journal of Leprosy & Other Mycobacterial Diseases* 69 (3): 234–40.

Kumar, N. 2004. Changing Geographic Access to and Locational Efficiency of Health Services in Two Indian Districts between 1981 and 1996. *Social Science & Medicine* 58 (10): 2045–67.

Kumra, V. K. 1995. Water Quality in the River Ganges. In *Water and the Quest for Sustainable Development in the Ganges Valley,* ed. G. P. Chapman and M. Thompson, 131–40. London: Mansell.

Kurtz, S. N. 1992. *All the Mothers Are One: Hindu India and the Cultural Reshaping of Psychoanalysis.* New York: Columbia University Press.

Lamb, S. 2000. *White Saris and Sweet Mangos: Aging, Gender, and Body in North India.* Berkeley: University of California Press.

Larson, G. J. 1993. The Concept of the Body in Ayurveda and Hindu Philosphical Systems. In *Self as Body in Asian Theory and Practice,* ed. T. P. Kasulis, R. T. Ames, and W. Dissanayake, 103–121. Albany: SUNY Press.

Lerner, M. J. 1980. *Belief in a Just World: A Fundamental Delusion.* New York: Plenum.

Leslie, C. 1973. The Professionalization of Indigenous Medicine. In *Entrepreneurship and Modernization of Occupational Cultures in South Asia,* ed. M. Singer, 216–42. Durham, NC: Duke University Press.

———. 1992. Interpretations of Illness: Syncretism in Modern Ayurveda. In *Paths to Asian Medical Knowledge,* ed. C. Leslie and A. Young, 177–208. Berkeley: University of California Press.

Levi-Strauss, C. 1963. The Sorcerer and His Magic. In *Structural Anthropology,* ed. C. Levi-Strauss, 167–85. New York: Basic Books.

Lorenzen, D. N. 1991. *The Kāpālikas and Kalamukhas: Two Lost Shaivite Sects.* Delhi: Motilal Banarsidass.

———. 1995. The Historical Vicissitudes of Bhakti Religion. In *Bhakti Religion in North India: Community Identity and Political Action,* ed. D. N. Lorenzen, 1–32. Albany: SUNY Press.

Lutgendorf, P. 1989. Ram's Story in Shivas City: Public Arenas and Private Patronage. In *Culture and Power in Banaras*, ed. S. Freitag, 34–61. Berkeley: University of California Press.

———. 1995. All in the (Raghu) Family: A Video Epic in Cultural Context. In *Media and the Transformation of Religion in South Asia*, ed. L. A. Babb and S. S. Wadley, 217–25. Philadelphia: University of Pennsylvania Press.

Madan, T. N. 1980. India: Doctors at the All India Institute of Medical Sciences. In *Doctors and Society: Three Asian Case Studies*, ed. T. N. Madan, P. Weibe, and R. Said, 11–112. Delhi: Vikas Publishing House Ltd.

———. 1987. *Non-Renunciation: Themes and Interpretations of Hindu Culture.* Delhi: Oxford University Press.

Malinowski, B. 1984/1922. *Argonauts of the Western Pacific.* Prospect Heights, IL: Waveland Press.

Marriott, M. 1976. Hindu Transactions: Diversity without Dualism. In *Transaction and Meaning: Directions in the Anthropology of Exchange and Symbolic Behavior*, ed. B. Kapferer, 109–42. Philadelphia: Institute for the Study of Human Issues.

Matsuoka, M., S. Izumi, T. Budiawan, N. Nakata, and K. Saeki. 1999. *Mycobacterium Leprae* DNA in Daily Using [*sic*] Water as a Possible Source of Leprosy Infection. *Indian Journal of Leprosy* 71 (1): 61–67.

Mauss, M. 1990/1953. *The Gift: The Form and Reason for Exchange in Archaic Societies*, trans. W. D. Halls. New York: W. W. Norton.

McCall, G. J., and J. L. Simmons. 1969. *Issues in Participant Observation.* Reading, MA: Addison-Wesley.

Minocha, A. A. 1980. Medical Pluralism and Health Services in India. *Social Science & Medicine* 14B: 217–23.

Mira, M. T., A. Alcais, VT Nguyen, M. O. Moraes, C. Di Flumeri, H. T. Vu, C. P. Mai, T. H. Nguyen, et al. 2004. Susceptibility to Leprosy Is Associated with PARK2 and PACRG. *Nature* 427 (6975): 636–40.

Mishra, V. B. 2000. Personal communication.

Mishra, V. 2001. *Bollywood Cinema: Temples of Desire.* New York: Routledge.

Mull, J. D., C. S. Wood, L. P. Gans, and D. S. Mull. 1989. Culture and Compliance among Leprosy Patients in Pakistan. *Social Science & Medicine* 29 (7): 799–811.

Murphy, R. F. 1990. *The Body Silent.* New York: W. W. Norton.

Murphy, R. F., J. Scheer, J. Murphy, and R. Mack. 1988. Physical Disability and Social Liminality: A Study in the Rituals of Adversity. *Social Science & Medicine* 26 (2): 235–42.

Naafs, B., E. Silva, F. Vilani-Moreno, E. C. Marcos, M. E. Nogueira, and D. V. Opromolla. 2001. Factors Influencing the Development of Leprosy: An Overview. *International Journal of Leprosy & Other Mycobacterial Diseases* 69 (1): 26–33.

Natarajan, G. V. 2001. What Happens in a Linguistic Junction? Masala Chai of Ethnicity and Communication in Bastar. *Language in India* 1 (4), www .languageinindia.com/junjulaug2001/bastar.html (accessed 3 June 2007).

Ngubane, H. 1977. *Body and Mind in Zulu Medicine.* London: Academic Press.

Nichter, M. 1992a. Ethnomedicine: Diverse Trends, Common Linkages. In *Anthropological Approaches to the Study of Ethnomedicine*, ed. M. Nichter, 223–47. Philadelphia: Gordon & Breach.

———. 1992b. Introduction. In *Anthropological Approaches to the Study of Ethnomedicine*, ed. M. Nichter, ix–xxi. Philadelphia: Gordon & Breach.

———. 1992c. The Layperson's Perception of Medicine as Perspective into the Utilization of Multiple Therapy Systems in the Indian Context. *Social Science & Medicine* 14B: 225–33.

———. 2002. The Social Relations of Therapy Management. In *New Horizons in Medical Anthropology*, ed. M. Nichter and M. Lock, 81–110. New York: Routledge.

Nichter, M., and C. Nordstrom. 1989. A Question of Medicine Answering: Health Commodification and the Social Relations of Healing in Sri Lanka. *Culture, Medicine, and Psychiatry* 13: 367–90.

Noordeen, S. K. 1995. Elimination of Leprosy as a Public Health Problem: Progress and Prospects. *Bulletin of the World Health Organization* 73 (1): 1–6.

Nuckolls, C. 1996. *The Cultural Dialectics of Knowledge and Desire*. Madison: University of Wisconsin Press.

Obeyesekere, G. 1981. *Medusa's Hair: An Essay on Personal Symbols and Religious Experience*. Chicago: University of Chicago.

———. 1999. Further Steps in Revitilization: The Indian Oedipus Revisited. In *Vishnu on Freud's Desk: A Reader in Psychoanalysis and Hinduism*, ed. T. G. Vaidyanathan and J. J. Kripal, 147–62. Delhi: Oxford University Press.

O'Flaherty, W. D. 1973. *Asceticism and Eroticism in the Mythology of Shiva*. London: Oxford University Press.

———. 1976. *The Origins of Evil in Hindu Mythology*. Berkeley: University of California Press.

Padoux, A. 1986. Tantrism: An Overview. In *Encyclopedia of Religion*, vol. 14, ed. M. Eliade, 272–74. New York: MacMillan.

Pandey, R. 1969. *Hindu Samskaras: Socio-Religious Study of the Hindu Sacraments*. Delhi: Motilal Barnasidass.

Parry, J. 1982. Sacrificial Death and the Necrophagous Ascetic. In *Death and the Regeneration of Life*, ed. M. Block and J. Parry, 74–110. Cambridge: Cambridge University Press.

———. 1986. "The Gift," the Indian Gift and "The Indian Gift." *Man* 21: 453–73.

———. 1994. *Death in Banaras*. Cambridge: Cambridge University Press.

Pasricha, J. S. 1991. *Treatment of Skin Diseases*. Delhi: Oxford University Press.

Pathak, R. K. 1996. Commercial Ventures and Tourbus Scholarship in Banaras. *South Asia Graduate Research Journal* 3 (2): 34–50. Also available at www.infinityfoundation.com/mandala/s_es/s_es_patha_bus_frameset.htm (accessed 3 June 2007).

Pathak, R. K., and C. A. Humes. 1993. Lolark Kund: Sun and Shiva Worship in the City of Light. In *Living Banaras: Hindu Religion in Cultural Context*, ed. B. R. Hertel and C. A. Humes, 205–44. Albany: SUNY Press.

Pfohl, S. 1985. *Images of Deviance and Social Control*. New York: McGraw-Hill.

Pfuhl, E. H., and S. Henry. 1993. *The Deviance Process*. New York: Aldine de Gruyter.

Pike, K. 1954. *Language in Relation to a Unified Theory of the Structure of Human Behavior* (Part 1). Glendale, CA: Summer Institute of Linguistics.

Ponnighaus, J. M. 1995. Leprosy: The Beginning of an End to a Public Health Problem? *Dermatological Clinics* 13 (3): 525–36.

Pool, R. 1987. Hot and Cold as an Explanatory Model—The Example of Bharuch District in Gujarat, India. *Social Science & Medicine* 25 (4): 389–99.

Quinn, N., and D. Holland. 1987. Culture and Cognition. In *Cultural Models in Language and Thought,* ed. N. Quinn and D. Holland, 3–42. Cambridge: Cambridge University Press.

Raheja, G. G. 1988. *The Poison in the Gift: Ritual, Prestation, and the Dominant Caste in a North Indian Village*. Chicago: University of Chicago Press.

Rai, S. 1993. *Kumbha Mela*. Varanasi: Ganga Kaveri.

Rajeshwari, K. N. 1996. Gender Bias in Utilisation of Health Care Facilities in Rural Haryana. *Economic and Political Weekly* 31 (8): 489–501.

Ram, H. 1997. *Oasis of Stillness: Life and Teachings of Aghoreshwar Bhagwan Ramji, a Modern Saint of India*. Sonoma, CA: Aghor Press.

———. 2000. Personal communication.

Rank, O. 1941. *Beyond Psychology*. New York: Dover Publications.

Reissman, R. 2000. Stigma and Everyday Practices: Childless Women in South India. *Gender and Society* 14 (1): 111–35.

Rigopoulos, A. 1998. *Dattatreya: The Immortal Guru, Yogin, and Avatara*. Albany: SUNY Press.

Roland, A. 1990. *In Search of Self in India and Japan*. Princeton, NJ: Princeton University Press.

Rubel, A. J., and L. C. Garro. 1992. Social and Cultural Factors in the Successful Control of Tuberculosis. *Public Health Reports* 107 (6): 626–35.

Russell, B. 1992/1938. *Power*. New York: Routledge.

Sainath, P. 1996. *Everybody Loves a Good Drought: Stories from India's Poorest Districts*. Delhi: Penguin.

Samuels, M. A. 1997. "Voodoo" Death Revisited: The Modern Lessons of Neurocardiology. *Neurologist* 3 (5): 293–304.

Sasaki, S., F. Takeshita, K. Okuda, and N. Ishii. 2001. *Mycobacterium Leprae* and Leprosy: A Compendium. *Microbiology & Immunology* 45 (11): 729–36.

Searle-Chatterjee, M. 1994. Caste, Religion, and Other Identities. In *Contextualizing Caste: Post-Dumontian Approaches,* ed. M. Searle-Chatterjee and U. Sharma, 147–68. Oxford: Blackwell Books.

Seeman, T. E., G. A. Kaplan, L. Knudsen, R. Cohen, and J. Guralnik. 1987. Social Network Ties and Mortality among the Elderly in the Alameda County Study. *American Journal of Epidemiology* 126 (4): 714–23.

Seghal, V. N. 1994. Leprosy. *Contemporary Tropical Dermatology* 12 (4): 629–44.

Seymour, S. 2004. Multiple Caretaking of Infants and Young Children: An Area in Critical Need of the Feminist Psychological Anthropology. *Ethos* 32 (4): 538–56.

Sharma, U. 1973. Theodicy and the Doctrine of Karma. *Man* 8: 347–64.

Shore, B. 1996. *Culture in Mind*. New York: Oxford University Press.

Simon, B. 1993. Language, Choice, Religion, and Identity in the Banarsi Community. In *Living Banaras: Hindu Religion in Cultural Context*, ed. B. R. Hertel and C. A. Humes, 245–68. Albany: SUNY Press.

Singh, R. P. B. 1993. Varanasi: The Pilgrimage Mandala, Geomantic Map and Cosmic Numbers. In *Banaras (Varanasi): Cosmic Order, Sacred City, Hindu Traditions*, ed. R. P. B. Singh, 37–64. Varanasi: Tara Book Agency.

Skinsnes, O. K. 1964. Leprosy in Society. *Leprosy Review* 35 (1): 13–15.

Smith, B. K. 2005. Tantrism: Hindu Tantrism. In *Encyclopedia of Hinduism*, vol. 13, ed. L. Jones, 8987–94. New York: Macmillan.

Smith, J. Z. 1982. *Imagining Religion: From Babylon to Jonestown*. Chicago: University of Chicago Press.

Spradley, J. 1980. *Participant Observation*. New York: Holt, Rinehart, & Winston.

Srinivas, M. N. 1989. *The Cohesive Role of Sanskritization and Other Essays*. Delhi: Oxford University Press.

———. 1996. Introduction. In *Caste: Its Twentieth Century Avatar*, ed. M. N. Srinivas, ix–xxxvii. Delhi: Viking.

Srinivasan, H. 1994. Disability, Deformity, and Rehabilitation. In *Leprosy*, ed. R. C. Hasting, 411–47. Edinburgh: Churchill Livingstone.

Staal, F. 1983. *AGNI: The Vedic Ritual of the Fire Altar*. Berkeley: University of California Press.

———. 1990. *Ritual and Mantras: Rules without Meaning*. New York: Peter Lang Publishing.

Strong, J. S. 2001. *The Buddha: A Short Biography*. Oxford: Oneworld Publications.

Svoboda, R. E. 1986. *Aghora: At the Left Hand of God*. Albuquerque: Brotherhood of Life.

———. 1993a. *Aghora II: Kundalini*. Albuquerque: Brotherhood of Life.

———. 1993b. *Ayurveda: Life, Health and Longevity*. New York: Penguin.

———. 1998. *Aghora III: The Law of Karma*. Albuquerque: Brotherhood of Life.

Thapar, R. 1997. Syndicated Hinduism. In *Hinduism Reconsidered*, ed. G.-D. Sontheimer and H. Kulke, 54–81. Delhi: Manohar.

Thind, A. 2004. Health Service Use by Children in Rural Bihar. *Journal of Tropical Pediatrics* 50 (3): 137–42.

Tirtha, S. V. 1980. *Devatma Shakti*. Rishikesh: Yoga Shri Peeth Trust.

Trawick, M. 1991. An Ayurvedic Theory of Cancer. *Medical Anthropology* 13 (1): 121–36.

Turner, V. 1969. *The Ritual Process: Structure and Anti-Structure*. New York: Aldine de Gruyter.

Urban, H. B. 2003. *Tantra: Sex, Secrecy, Politics, and Power in the Study of Religion*. Berkeley: University of California Press.

Vesci, U. M. 1985. *Heat and Sacrifice in the Vedas*. Delhi: Motilal Banarsidass.

Vigne, Jacques. 1997. *The Indian Teaching Tradition: A Psychological and Spiritual*, trans. K. Zeiss and A. Hall. Delhi: B. R. Publishing Corporation.

von Stietencron, H. 1997. Hinduism: On the Proper Use of a Deceptive Term. In *Hinduism Reconsidered*, ed. G. D. Sontheimer and H. Hulke, 32–53. Delhi: Manohar.

Wade, J. 1984. Role Boundaries and Paying Back: "Switching Hats" in Participant Observation. *Anthropology and Education Quarterly* 15 (3): 211–24.

Ware, N. C. 1992. Suffering and the Social Construction of Illness: The Delegitimation of Illness Experience in Chronic Fatigue Syndrome. *Medical Anthropology Quarterly* 6 (4): 347–61.

Waxler, N. 1981. Learning to Be a Leper: A Case Study in the Social Construction of Illness. In *Social Contexts of Health, Illness, and Patient Care,* ed. E. G. Mishler, 169–94. Cambridge: Cambridge University Press.

Weiss, M. 1980. Caraka Saṃhitā on the Doctrine of Karma. In *Karma and Rebirth in Classical Indian Traditions,* ed. W. O'Flaherty, 90–115. Berkeley: University of California Press.

Weiss, M. G., J. Rama Krishna, and D. Somma. 2006. Health-Related Stigma: Rethinking Concepts and Interventions. *Psychology, Health, & Medicine* 11 (3): 277–87.

White, C. 2002. Sociocultural Considerations in the Treatment of Leprosy in Rio de Janeiro, Brazil. *Leprosy Review* 73: 356–65.

White, D. G. 2003. *Kiss of the Yogini: "Tantric Sex" in Its South Asian Contexts.* Chicago: University of Chicago Press.

Wiser, W., C. Wiser, and S. Wadley. 2000. *Behind Mud Walls: Seventy-Five Years in a North Indian Village* (updated and expanded edition). Berkeley: University of California Press.

Woodroffe, J. 1994/1922. *The Garland of Letters.* Madras: Ganesh and Company.

Wujastyk, D. 1998. *The Roots of Ayurveda.* Delhi: Penguin.

Yoder, L. J. 1998. Personal communication.

Zimmer, H. 1951. *Philosophies of India.* Princeton, NJ: Princeton University Press.

Zimmerman, F. 1987. *The Jungle and the Aroma of Meats: An Ecological Theme in Hindu Medicine.* Berkeley: University of California Press.

Index

Page numbers in italics indicate illustrations.

Text: 10/13 Sabon
Display: Sabon
Cartographer: Bill Nelson
Compositor: BookComp, Inc.
Printer and Binder: Sheridan Book & Journal Services